Certification and Accreditation Law Handbook

Jerald A. Jacobs

Certification and Accreditation Law Handbook

Jerald A. Jacobs

American Society of Association Executives
Washington, DC

Editing, design, indexing, composition:
  EPS Group, Inc.
  Hanover, MD

Copyright © 1992 by the American Society of Association Executives
ISBN 0-88034-054-1

American Society of Association Executives
1575 Eye Street, NW
Washington, DC 20005–1168

Printed in the United States of America

Library of Congress Cataloging-in-Publication Data

Contents

Foreword

Certification and Accreditation Law Handbook is intended to fill a longtime need. The book provides a comprehensive and comprehensible review of the legal principles and rules applicable to private, nonprofit, voluntary organizations that issue credentials in the professions and in academia, usually termed "certification" and "accreditation," respectively. Until now, there has been no single publication covering all legal aspects of the subject of credentialing. Those advising organizations that conduct credentialing programs have relied upon examination of the statutes and cases that affect credentialing, as well as upon the sporadic articles in antitrust law journals and occasional chapters in association law compendia that address credentialing topics. Many legal issues raised in the institution and operation of credentialing programs have not been covered in the legal literature at all. This book, its author hopes, will enhance the ability of credentialing organizations to conduct their programs safely and responsibly in the public interest.

Pervasive throughout the free American society and economy is the concept of credentialing of professionals and institutions. Those who use professional services or follow academic programs seek and expect objective evaluation of the quality of those services or programs. Credentialing is often relied upon intuitively; users come to expect it and may be surprised when they find that it is absent. Traditionally, the quality criteria for certification and accreditation have been established and promulgated by private, nonprofit, voluntary organizations—professional societies or educational associations, independent boards or councils, or other nongovernmental groups—which also conduct evaluations of professionals or institutions to determine if the criteria are met. Credentialing serves an enormously valuable function. Most citizens are not equipped to determine whether minimum competency has been achieved by professionals or institutions. Government resources, which each year seem to be stretched thinner in fulfilling their existing roles, are also clearly not available to replace the extensive credentialing endeavors of private, nonprofit, voluntary organizations if that ever were to become necessary as a societal goal.

The purpose of this book is to help expand and improve professional or institutional credentialing by assisting those responsible for credentialing programs to understand the laws that the programs must follow. The view of the author, and the premise for this book, is that self-regulation of professionals and institutions is virtually always more efficient and more effective than government regulation. The founders of our nation, who believed in the intrinsic goodness and magnanimity of educated citizens, implicitly recognized that fact in their specification of a minimalist federal government, leaving to both the states and to private organizations the regulation of areas that the federal government could not or should not control. Professional credentialing has long been an activity shared by state governments and private credentialing organizations. It is usually called *licensing* when conducted by state governments on a mandatory basis and *certification* when conducted by private, nonprofit, voluntary organizations. Educational accreditation, on the other hand, has largely been the province of private, nonprofit, voluntary organizations, not state governments. This book addresses only certification and accreditation conducted by private organizations.

Certification is already pervasive in the health care, engineering, scientific, technical, research, and other professions. Even where a profession is licensed by the state government, private, nonprofit, voluntary organizations often provide certification for those practicing in specialty fields of the profession. Moreover, professional certification is quickly becoming important in fields beyond health care, engineering, science, technology, and research. Programs now flourish in sales and marketing, management, planning, counseling, law, and other service areas.

Accreditation is also very broadly used throughout the educational system—at primary, secondary, and postsecondary levels, as well as in continuing education of all sorts of professionals. Institutional accreditation is becoming increasingly important beyond the academic area, as well. Programs to accredit business firms or units, departments of larger institutions, and groups of professionals are growing throughout the economy.

The germination of the book was a project performed by the author on behalf of the Certified Association Executive (CAE) program of the American Society of Association Executives (ASAE) in 1988, in which ASAE's entire CAE program was reviewed for its legal ramifications. Members of the CAE Commission, an unincorporated but autonomous board responsible for the program, commented upon the lack of a legal literature in the area and urged the creation of a book such as this. Drawing upon representation of literally scores of private, nonprofit, voluntary certification and accreditation programs over more than 20 years, the author has attempted to address most of the areas in which credentialing programs are at risk legally: antitrust law and common law due process, tort liability, records disclosure, First Amendment considerations, intellectual property, tax exemption, and accommodations for the disabled.

Many other people have contributed their time and talents to this book. If the book succeeds in fulfilling its purposes, those contributors are largely responsible. The book's inevitable failings, however, are the fault of the author alone.

Most chapters benefitted from generously provided research, drafting, or review by others at the Jenner & Block law firm in Washington and Chicago, particularly including those in the firm's Association Practice Group. Chapter 2, "The Legal Framework," is based upon the work of Julie Carpenter, an attorney with the firm; another attorney, Scott Sinder, also contributed to the chapter. Chapter 3, "Liability to Third

Parties," is based upon research and drafting by Deanne Maynard, who served as a summer associate for the firm in both 1990 and 1991. Chapter 4, "Confidentiality of Records," was developed by Frank H. Wu, who served as a summer associate in 1990 and was guided by a partner of the firm, David W. Ogden. Chapter 5, "Use of Credentialing Marks," relates to work by many attorneys of the firm involved in the *Peel* case decided by the United States Supreme Court in 1991 and successfully argued before the Court by partner Bruce J. Ennis. The principal contributor to this chapter is attorney Roger W. Pincus. Chapter 6, "Protecting Credentialing Marks," is based upon the work of firm partner Robert A. Wynbrandt and 1991 summer associate Paul W. Hartzel. Chapter 7, "Tax Exemption," is based on work by an attorney of the firm, Marianne Coulton Kuh, who was guided by tax partner Paula Cozzi Goedert. Chapter 8, "Americans with Disabilities Act," was produced with the assistance of attorney Robert M. Portman.

Four sample documents are included as appendices to the book; they must be used with caution, of course. They are not *model* forms, but *examples* of documents used by other successful credentialing organizations. It is unlikely that any of the documents will fit the needs of a certification or accreditation organization without significant modification under the supervision of experienced legal counsel. The documents are provided as starting points for those considering new credentialing programs or those considering modifications to existing ones. Each of the documents was selected after review of a wide variety of similar ones used by credentialing organizations. Those chosen as the bases for the samples tended to be the clearest and most generic of those reviewed. The sample certification procedures are based upon those used by the National Rural Electric Cooperative (which were informally reviewed and approved by the staff of the Federal Trade Commission in 1985). The sample accreditation procedures are based upon those used by the American Psychological Association (one of the largest association-related accreditation programs in the country). The sample bylaws are based upon those used by the Dental Assisting National Board (a very longstanding and quite extensive private professional certification board).

Four other documents are included in the appendices as important references for credentialing organizations but without comment or analysis (which is best provided by the entities or agencies responsible for those documents). First are the professional certification criteria issued by a private, nonprofit, voluntary entity, the National Commission for Certifying Agencies, and required for professional certification organizations approved by NCCA. Next are academic accreditation provisions issued by another private, nonprofit, voluntary entity, the Council on Postsecondary Accreditation, and required for academic accreditation organizations recognized by COPA. The last are pertinent portions of the regulations of the United States Department of Education that apply to academic accreditation organizations recognized by DOE, and portions of the regulations of the United States Department of Justice that apply to "examinations and course" under the Americans with Disabilities Act.

Invaluable assistance in the editing of the manuscript was provided by Shelly Hedrick, a legislative assistant at the firm. Her consistent ability to make legal writing accessible is a singular talent. Susan Hunt was tireless in her work on the manuscript.

Finally, Elissa Myers, CAE, and her publications staff at the American Society of Association Executives offered encouragement and understanding without which the book simply would not have been published.

Jerald A. Jacobs
Washington, DC
January, 1992

Jerald A. Jacobs is an attorney, a partner in the law firm of Jenner & Block in Washington, DC, and head of the firm's Association Practice Group. The Group represents trade associations, professional societies, and other nonprofit organizations, many of which are involved in professional certification or academic accreditation. Mr. Jacobs founded the Legal Section of the American Society of Association Executives; he has served as a member of the Board of Directors of ASAE; and he is a recipient of the ASAE Academy of Leaders Award. Other books by Mr. Jacobs on association law subjects include *Association Law Handbook*, *Federal Lobbying*, and *Association Issues*.

1

Introduction

This book addresses the law applicable to credentialing—professional certification and academic accreditation by private, nonprofit, voluntary organizations in the public interest. Credentialing is a mode of self-regulation in which interests in professions, businesses, or other fields of endeavor in society band together to control their own numbers for the betterment of society at large.

Self-regulation is one of the highest and best traditions in the American experience. Through self-regulation of professions, businesses, and other fields, organizations directly advance the economic health, social welfare, and moral climate of the entire nation.

Self-regulation is *visible*. Programs of professional certification or academic accreditation provide incalculable public relations value well beyond the immediate constituencies they service.

Self-regulation is *benevolent*. Programs that help assure competence of professionals or quality of institutions are of indisputable worth.

Self-regulation is *aspirational*. Programs for credentialing of professionals or institutions have the capacity to motivate the credentialed toward voluntary achievement.

But self-regulation is also *threatened*. Decades of legal challenges to self-regulatory programs such as credentialing have imposed unacceptable risks for many organizations. Vague, broad, and changing antitrust law, as well as other legal obstacles, have complicated decisions to self-regulate. Programs that should be instituted or expanded are deferred or cut back instead. Most often it is because, on the advice of counsel, the potential legal liability is considered crippling.

This book is an attempt to help balance the clear and present danger to credentialing with some helpful explanations and guidelines on the applicable laws, so that the antitrust and other legal risks can be evaluated, measured, and controlled by those responsible for credentialing programs. Without that knowledge, not only credentialing, but all of self-regulation, risks diminishment or extinction.

Self-Regulation

Regulation is essential to protect society and its members, but regulation need not be accomplished by federal, state, and local governmental agencies alone. Voluntary, private, nonprofit, tax-exempt entities such as credentialing organizations can regulate the conduct of their constituents, often more effectively and more efficiently than the government can.

Self-regulation can establish criteria for fairness, quality, ethics,

1

competence, or safety for professional services or educational endeavors. Professional certification and academic accreditation assure qualifications and competence in individuals and institutions. These collective activities promote competition by facilitating informed choice, responsible conduct, and innovative change. They improve the economy and international competitiveness by building proficiency in services, and they serve society by encouraging honesty and integrity in professions and in academia.

Self-regulatory programs are often superior to governmental regulation. Compared to governmental regulation, these vehicles for self-regulation:

- permit the promulgation and use of higher standards by eliminating mistrust and resistance toward governmental regulation;
- reduce costs by eliminating bureaucratic delay and red tape;
- offer more opportunities for flexibility and responsiveness to changing conditions; and
- draw on volunteers who offer greater expertise than that of government officials.

The Costs of Government Regulation

Polling of public and government attitudes has demonstrated the desire for self-regulation. A Harris poll concluded that public support for government regulation of business in general decreased in the period 1976–1982. In 1976, Harris found that more consumers favored than opposed business regulation by government, but by 1982, consumers opposing governmental regulation outnumbered those favoring regulation by 2 to 1.

This change in attitude reflects a growing public awareness of the enormous and unnecessary costs of government regulation. At the end of 1980, it was estimated that federal regulations cost Americans over one billion dollars a year.[1] A typical family of four paid an extra $1,800 annually for goods and services simply because excessive federal regulations added to the cost of those goods and services.[2] Likewise, American business and industry, particularly small businesses, were spending 1.5 billion hours a year filling out federal forms and coping with Washington's red tape.[3] A significant part of the solution lies in encouraging the shift from expensive bureaucratic government agencies to organizations serving "quasigovernmental" functions.

As *deregulation* has become the watchword, the private sector has gained a unique opportunity to develop effective voluntary methods of dealing with the conditions that otherwise would be subject to governmental regulation. Both major political parties have long been closely scrutinizing government regulatory agencies for waste, inefficiency, and unnecessary duplication of private sector initiatives. An increasing openness to alternatives to traditional government regulatory activities provides a receptive environment for innovative private solutions.

Although the deficiencies of governmental regulation are increasingly perceived by the public, judicial decisions still reflect a skeptical and often even antagonistic view of self-regulation. Courts have tended to focus on the risks associated with self-regulation rather than the benefits; they fear that self-regulatory bodies will adopt rules that limit consumer choice and exclude competitors from the marketplace. Courts tend to identify only those self-regulation features or modes that are *not* legally permissible, rather than those that *are*. Antitrust prescriptions, in particular, are surprisingly vague and have been inconsistently applied. They are enforced only *after* a private, nonprofit, voluntary organization has begun to engage in self-regulation.

The strong perception, if not the reality, is that antitrust and other laws effectively discourage or even prohibit self-regulation of professions and academia. Beneficial activities are often limited or eliminated by the threat of litigation. Legal challenges, even if ultimately unsuccessful, impose substantial financial burdens and other costs on defendants.

Without responsible self-regulation, one of two things happens: either the government regulates in its inevitably limited way, leaving the public unprotected from some unscrupulous practices, or there is no regulation of any sort, leaving the public ignorant of crucial information, and otherwise depriving the economy and society of important benefits.

Frivolous antitrust and other legal challenges, then, are detrimental to self-regulation. But the competitive nature of self-regulation and other practical constraints greatly limit the potential for anticompetitive or other legal abuse through self-regulation. If a self-regulatory body is not fair, effective, and efficient, its activities will command no respect among the beneficiaries of the regulation, causing participants to withdraw their support. An organization that certifies professional competence, for example, retains its influence only as long as its certification is viewed as reliable based upon valid and objective measures. When a voluntary self-regulatory body is viewed as too lax or too strict, unresponsive to new circumstances, lacking adequate procedures, or otherwise out-of-touch, another competing self-regulatory body can and will arise. Unlike governmental regulation, there is usually no natural or governmental monopoly in the self-regulation field.

In addition to this "marketplace" test for criteria and rules developed through self-regulation, the threat of governmental regulation itself serves as an effective safeguard against abuse. If private, nonprofit, voluntary self-regulation efforts fail to achieve their stated goals, the public will demand that the government impose its own regulations directly—a prospect that creates another significant incentive for ensuring the provision of effective, responsible, and fair self-regulation.

Credentialing

A fundamental goal of virtually every individual professional or academic institution is to improve in areas of competence, quality, and effectiveness. Credentialing facilitates the achievement of this goal.

Credentialing encompasses both the certification of individuals who have been found to meet criteria of competence and the accreditation of academic institutions that have been approved as meeting quality standards. Credentialing activities can include: 1) prescribing education and experience qualifications for certification candidates; 2) establishing curriculum, faculty, and facility qualifications for potential accredited institutions; 3) administering competitive examinations; and 4) conducting assessment visits.

For the credentialed individual or institution, the hallmark provides prestige, recognition, and possible increased earning power for the individual or increased enrollment power for the institution. Equally important, credentialing enables the public (as well as government and private third-party payers for professional services) to distinguish between those who have attained some qualifying level of competence from those who have not. In addition, the profession or field retains jurisdiction to revoke credentials from an individual or institution that ceases to meet qualifications.

In short, private, nonprofit, voluntary credentialing programs protect the public by enabling anyone to identify competent people or schools more readily, and, simultaneously, they aid the profession or field, by encouraging and recognizing professional and institutional achievement.[4]

Because of the public need for these services, 120 private organizations were identified as engaging in credentialing in a 1965 survey.[5] Today, over a quarter century later, the number is thought to be five to ten times higher.

Thus, credentialing is the embodiment of self-regulation in place of governmental regulation. It reduces or eliminates the need for occupational or institutional licensing, which state governments may otherwise impose as mandatory conditions for employment of an individual or operation of a facility.

The professions provide an excellent example of the benefits of private, nonprofit, voluntary self-regulation through certification. Professional credentialing protects the public, professionals, and third parties from dishonest, dangerous, incompetent, unnecessary, or otherwise unacceptable services. Because of the highly technical nature of professional services, members of the public are often unable to judge for themselves either the need for the service or its quality. The public would suffer if it could not rely on the credibility and competence of professionals and professional self-regulation.

Notwithstanding the benefits of professional credentialing programs, they have been the subject of scrutiny by both the Federal Trade Commission and the Department of Justice, and the subject of legal challenges by private individuals and institutions that did not attain desired credentials. The only general rule that emerges from the court decisions is that criteria for credentialing may not be arbitrary or unreasonable.[6] Of course, that rule begs the question, and different judges and juries may come to different conclusions about whether a particular standard is reasonable or not.[7] Even when credentialing standards are upheld, vindication may require years of costly litigation.[8]

Judicial Oversight of Self-Regulation

In analyzing self-regulatory activities, the courts historically have applied an open-ended antitrust standard generally known as the *Rule of Reason*. The United States Supreme Court first applied the Rule of Reason in

1918 to the activities of an industry self-regulatory group whose rules and regulations were found to be beneficial and lawful.[9] However, the Supreme Court itself accurately characterized this approach as "an incredibly complicated and prolonged economic investigation into the entire history of the industry involved, as well as related industries, in an effort to determine at large whether a particular restraint has been unreasonable—an inquiry so often wholly fruitless when undertaken."[10] Rather than expose themselves to this trial by ordeal, many groups simply forgo self-regulation. With the bewildering and inconsistent array of antitrust and other legal precedents, the expense of litigating cases can be crippling.

One case highlighting the unpredictability of the current application of antitrust law to self-regulation is the 1982 *Hydrolevel* decision of the Supreme Court.[11] That decision significantly increased the antitrust risks that self-regulatory bodies face. There the Supreme Court held a nonprofit organization liable for treble damages under the antitrust laws for the fraudulent conduct of its volunteer agents acting in direct violation of the organization's own rules. The organization ultimately paid some six million dollars in damages, legal fees, and costs. Regardless of one's attitude as to whether the professional society defendant in this case was responsible for wrongdoing and deserving of the imposition of liability, it is clear that the Court reached its result using an excessively broad test, effectively a new and unique "strict liability" standard for self-regulation. The Court left completely unanswered the question of how any voluntary organization can avoid liability in these circumstances.[12] In a scathing dissent, Justice Powell complained that "the Court is so zealous to impose treble damages liability that it ignores a basic purpose of the Sherman Act, the preservation of private [nonprofit organization] activities contributing to the public welfare."[13] Justice Powell correctly observed that the Court's ruling put "at risk much of the beneficial private activity of the volunteer associations of our country."[14]

Another problem area involves the refusal of antitrust agencies and the courts to permit private entities to pursue through self-regulation important societal values other than promotion of competition. This view inflexibly holds that the promotion of competition is the only valid goal of self-regulatory activities and that any other social or economic goal cannot be considered more important than, or even *as important as*, the promotion of competition.[15]

Another risk, that of abrupt and unanticipated changes in the law, is illustrated by antitrust treatment of whether self-regulatory bodies with substantial commercial power have a special duty to employ disciplinary procedures that incorporate basic due process safeguards, including notice and a hearing. In 1963, the Supreme Court ruled that these organizations have this responsibility;[16] but in 1985 the Court reversed course and held that "the absence of procedural safeguards can in no sense determine the antitrust analysis."[17] In the intervening years, a large number of antitrust cases involving private organization rules and sanctions were decided principally on the basis of the adequacy of the organizations' procedural safeguards.[18] Although the 1985 decision means that an organization will not be held liable automatically for failure to adopt the precise procedural rules that a judge or jury might, in hindsight, prefer, it nonetheless introduces untoward confusion into the law. Courts must now grapple with the basic issue of what standard to apply in reviewing these sorts of activities. Thus, adoption of reasonable procedural rules protecting all those affected by an organization's actions no longer provides insurance against lawsuits, and legal counsel cannot predict with any significant confidence the degree of risk arising from self-regulatory activity.

Conclusion

Democratic society requires regulation for the protection of its citizens. Although governmental regulation is widespread, it is more expensive, more rigid, and less effective than self-regulation, because self-regulation directly involves those who have the best knowledge about the need for action and the most incentive to take action. Self-regulatory activities include professional credentialing and academic accreditation to ensure qualifications and competence in individuals and institutions. Credentialing promotes competition by facilitating informed public choice, responsible professional or institutional conduct, and excellence in professional services and education.

The primary obstacle to successful self-regulation is the risk of antitrust and other legal challenges. Because the judicial system is naturally concerned with correcting impermissible behavior, courts generally focus on the risks attendant to self-regulation rather than on the benefits. Numerous certification and accreditation programs have been successfully challenged with attendant publicity. The result is a "chilling effect" even on potential programs that have no anticompetitive or illegal purposes or effects. The laws are designed to encourage challenge. Plaintiffs' cases are often taken by attorneys on a contingent fee basis, with virtually no risk that an unsuccessful plaintiff will be held responsible for the fees and costs of a prevailing defendant. Plaintiffs are deemed "private attorneys general" and are offered the prospect of winning significant damages or, in antitrust cases, even three times the actual damages. The standards used to evaluate self-regulatory activities tend to be vague, inconsistently applied, and enforced only *after* an organization has engaged in self-regulation. The result can be a flood of frivolous challenges.

Many reported decisions exist in which courts have declared particular credentialing activities to be in violation of the law. Those decisions create the *perception* that self-regulation is legally dangerous— that the risks exceed the benefits.

As a consequence of this awesome legal exposure, many groups are reluctant to engage in self-regulation such as credentialing at all. To the extent that the *perception* of legal liability reduces responsible self-regulation, either the government is forced to regulate or there is no regulation. Society is left without the important information, protection, or advantage provided by regulation.

Although it will not specifically *reduce* legal risks, an effort to educate the professional and academic communities more fully regarding the legal aspects of credentialing may help to facilitate measurement of the risks. In many cases, an informed review of the legal ramifications of a proposed new or expanded credentialing or other self-regulatory program might lead to the conclusion that the risks are acceptable.

Notwithstanding that some court decisions, based as they must be on the particular facts of each case, are difficult to mold into a coherent legal policy on credentialing, there certainly are some general themes that emerge from any review of the pertinent decisions. For example, programs that affect prices or fees for goods or services are clearly more at risk under the antitrust laws than other kinds of programs.

The aim and approach of this book is to help with an understanding of antitrust and other legal limits on self-regulation so that those risks can be better controlled. No one can completely "de-mystify" the law or completely correct the perception that credentialing is singularly at risk. Nevertheless, it is hoped that this book is the beginning of an approach to those goals.

Endnotes

1. Carol E. Dinkins, U.S. Deputy Attorney General, "The Role of Self-Regulation in Regulatory Reform," in *The White House Conference on Association Self-Regulation* 1984, 68.
2. *Id.*
3. *Id.*
4. *See* the extensive discussion of this subject in Wallace, "Occupational Licensing and Certification: Remedies for Denial," *William and Mary Law Review* 14 (1972): 46.
5. J. Bradley, *The Role of Trade Associations and Professional Business Societies in America* 1965, 95–96.
6. *E.g., United States v. College of American Pathologists*, 1969 Trade Cas. (CCH) par 72,825 (N.D. Ill. 1969) (consent decree).
7. *Compare Salter v. New York Psychological Association*, 14 N.Y.2d 100, 248 N.Y.S.2d 867, 198 N.E.2d 250 (1964) (upholding denial of membership in professional society because the educational requirements for membership were not "abitrary" or "unreasonable" and there was no proof of "economic necessity" for membership), *with Falcone v. Middlesex County Medical Society*, 170 A.2d 791, 34 N.J. 582 (1961) (overturning denial of membership in medical society because membership conferred significant "economic benefit" on members by enabling them to join the staff of local hospitals).
8. *See Levin v. Doctors Hospital, Inc.*, 233 F. Supp 953 (D.D.C. 1964) (granted summary judgment to a not-for-profit hospital accreditation organization because it could not be sued in the District of Columbia and because its accreditation criteria were reasonable), *rev'd sub. nom. Levin v. Joint Commission on Accreditation of Hospitals*, 354 F.2d 515, 518 (D.C. Cir. 1965) (reversing the decision of the trial court because the plaintiff "might eventually" establish a basis for the antitrust claim).
9. *Chicago Board of Trade v. United States*, 246 U.S. 231 (1918).
10. *Northern Pacific Railway Co. v. United States*, 356 U.S. 1, 5 (1958).
11. *American Society of Mechanical Engineers v. Hydrolevel Corp.*, 456 U.S. 556 (1982).
12. *See id.* at 593 (Powell, J., dissenting).
13. *Id.*
14. *Id.* at 594.
15. *National Society of Professional Engineers v. United States*, 435 U.S. 679, 695–96 (1978). *See also* the AMA case cited in footnote 9.
16. *Silver v. New York Stock Exchange*, 373 U.S. 341 (1963).

17. *Northwest Wholesale Stationer's, Inc. v. Pacific Stationery and Printing Co.*, 472 U.S. 284, 293 (1985).
18. *See Denver Rockets v. All-Pro Management, Inc.*, 325 F. Supp 1049 (C.D. Cal. 1971), *Pinsker v. Pacific Coast Society of Orthodontics*, 12 Cal. 3d 541, 116. Rptr. 245, 526 P.2d 253 (1974); *Deesen v. PGA*, 358 F.2d 165 (9th Cir.), *cert. denied*, 385 U.S. 846 (1966).

2

The Legal Framework

Despite the ubiquitous benefits provided by credentialing, certain aspects of credentialing programs have at times come under legal attack. The Federal Trade Commission and the Department of Justice have frequently pursued alleged illegal practices by private, nonprofit, voluntary organizations; some of those challenges have involved credentialing. In addition, private suits have occasionally arisen against credentialing programs, usually brought by those who have been excluded by the programs from qualification.

This summary of the law of credentialing focuses on decided cases in which credentialing has been challenged. From a review of these decisions, one can begin to perceive themes in the law and to fashion guidelines to help assure that credentialing organizations either are not challenged legally or are at least well prepared to defend against legal challenges successfully.

Legal Background

Courts and government agencies generally have recognized that a private, nonprofit association, board, or other similar organization serves the public interest by establishing and measuring against quality standards. The self-regulation of a profession or field of endeavor by an organization typically is assumed to benefit the public by promulgating information that particular individuals or institutions have achieved and maintained accepted criteria of quality, such as in professional practice or in programs of education. However, a private organization could certainly operate a credentialing program that would disserve the public. Especially when the motive behind the program is anything other than dissemination of information to the public, the organization risks a challenge to, and liability for, credentialing. Measures that are anticompetitive, discriminatory, not rationally related to objective standards, or implemented without procedures to ensure fairness are likely to attract challenges and risk liability.

Through the credentialing processes, organizations may become self-policing and thus, self-regulating. The ways of accomplishing credentialing are myriad: organizations may adopt educational qualifications necessary for membership; they may impose ethical obligations that all members must adhere to; they may require particular professional experience and successful completion of competitive exams as conditions to the holding of professional certification titles; they may require certain program attributes as conditions to attaining accredited status; and they may inspect or "audit" organizations to ensure that criteria are maintained. Professional certification and academic accreditation are the major conventional mechanisms for credentialing used by associations, boards, or other similar private organizations; however, a wide variety of other mechanisms have been used.

An inevitable and necessary aspect of credentialing by private, nonprofit, voluntary organizations is the resulting exclusion of those who do not meet the standards established by the credentialing organization. Any such exclusionary activity is likely to result in disgruntled applicants or candidates; thus, private, civil litigation challenging the program is almost predictable. Furthermore, the organizations that initiate, sponsor, or conduct credentialing are often composed of groups of competitors. Any activity by a group of competitors that significantly affects the business or economic prospects of those competitors is likely to be carefully scrutinized by the U.S. Department of Justice Antitrust Division, by state antitrust departments, or by the Federal Trade Commission. The most common private and governmental challenges to credentialing are based on antitrust laws.

Vulnerability of Credentialing Bodies

The credentialing process is subject to challenge particularly by those individuals or institutions who have been denied the credential offered by the credentialing organization either because they do not meet the criteria to apply for the credential or because, having applied, they fail to pass some necessary examination, inspection, or other requirement. The complaints from those denied a desired credential tend to be based on alleged anticompetitive behavior or the violation of some perceived duty of fair procedures. Thus, any organization engaged in a credentialing program or considering one should analyze whether the program is vulnerable to antitrust or procedural attacks.

Antitrust Challenges

When a credentialing program is initiated, sponsored, or conducted by an organization that includes competitors, it is usually subject, almost by definition, to scrutiny under the Sherman Act. This federal law prohibits agreements or understandings that unreasonably restrain trade that is transacted across the borders of the states. A number of court decisions regarding private credentialing programs have been based on Sherman Act violations. However, in a few situations, courts have held that a particular credentialing program was not subject to the Sherman Act at all, thus precluding any consideration of whether the program was pro- or anticompetitive.

Noncommercial Purpose

There is some authority for the proposition that the antitrust laws do not apply to the certifying or accrediting activities of a private, nonprofit, voluntary organization when the objectives of those activities are not commercial. For example, noting that the Sherman Act was designed for the business world rather than for the noncommercial aspects of education, the United States Court of Appeals for the District of Columbia Circuit once held, in the *Marjorie Webster* case, that the denial of accreditation to a junior college due to its status as a for-profit institution was "an activity distinct from the sphere of commerce; it goes rather to the heart of the concept of education."[1] The court further noted that in the context of the liberal arts and the learned professions, an incidental restraint of trade, without an intent to affect the commercial aspects of a field or profession, would not be subject to the antitrust laws.

In 1975, however, the United States Supreme Court decided a case that cast some doubt on the viability of holdings in *Marjorie Webster*. In *Goldfarb v. Virginia State Bar*,[2] the Court rejected the notion that, because the "learned professions" provide services that are not "commercial" in the same sense that business products or services are, they should not be subject to the antitrust laws. It held that an agreement among lawyers in a bar association to establish minimum charges for title searches in real estate transactions was sufficiently commercial to warrant applying the antitrust laws. The Supreme Court cautioned, however, that courts could not automatically apply the antitrust concepts developed in the business context to every professional practice, because professions involve aspects of public service that might distinguish particular practices from the same activities in a business.[3]

In sum, the "learned profession" exemption is not the barrier to application of the antitrust laws it once was. The distinction between profession/education and business, or noncommercial and commercial, still may have some relevance, however. The more an organization's credentialing program advances public service, the less likely it is to raise antitrust concerns.

State Action

Courts may also refuse to apply the Sherman Act to credentialing activities of private, nonprofit, voluntary organizations when the activities are regarded as, effectively, the result of action by a state. State action is exempt from the antitrust laws. In *Parker v. Brown*,[4] the Supreme Court held that a state-mandated marketing program for raisins that restricted competition was exempt from the antitrust laws because the Sherman Act prohibits actions of individuals, not of states. Similarly, in *Bates v. Arizona State Bar*,[5] the court held that ethical rules restricting advertising by members of the Arizona State Bar were restrictions imposed by the state and were, thus, exempt from the antitrust laws.

The reach of the state action defense is limited; it is likely that the state must have *compelled* the organization to engage in the activity before the defense will protect actions.[6] Unless the state or an agency of the state specifically requests or requires an organization to provide a credentialing program and indicates that it intends the organization to be exempt from the antitrust laws, the state action defense is not likely to protect an organization from antitrust liability.[7]

Congressional Intent to Exempt

Congressional intent to immunize particular entities from antitrust liability may also protect a credentialing program of a private association, board, or other similar organization. In what is probably a unique case, a federal appellate court in *Berhagen v. American Basketball Association of the USA*[8] found that, although the ABA/USA was a private association, Congress evidenced intent in the Amateur Sports Act that the association would exert "monolithic control" over the sport and that it, thus, intended the association to be exempt from the antitrust laws. Weighing heavily in the court's analysis was the articulated reason for enacting the Amateur Sports Act—"to correct disorganization and factional disputes that seemed to plague amateur sports in the United States."[9]

First Amendment

As early as 1925, the U.S. Supreme Court declared that the dissemination of information to consumers has a presumptively procompetitive effect on the market, and an organization engaged in that activity was doing just what associations ought to do.[10] More recently, the Seventh Circuit Court of Appeals has declared, "An organization's towering reputation does not reduce its freedom to speak out."[11] Thus, if the credentialing program of an organization truly serves the essential purpose of dissemination of information, its effect is procompetitive. The program may, therefore, be considered outside the scope of the antitrust laws.

Beyond a general tolerance for dissemination of information, the courts have provided particular protection for private organizations engaged in political speech. Under the *Noerr-Pennington* doctrine, concerted efforts to influence government decision making are protected, as long as they are made in good faith.[12]

However, if the actions of the organization are intended to restrain trade and, in fact, do restrain trade, an incidental influence on the government will not immunize those actions. Thus, in *Allied Tube & Conduit Corp. v. Indian Head, Inc.*,[13] the defendants argued that their action of excluding the listing of a plastic conduit from the new edition of the National Electric Code promulgated by a trade association was incident to a valid effort to influence governmental action, because the anticompetitive effect of excluding the conduit stemmed from the fact that the Code was routinely adopted by a number of state and local governments as their standards. Noting that the meeting of the association at which the new code was voted upon was "packed" with those sympathetic to the steel competitors whose business the plastic conduits would harm, the Supreme Court held that the restraint resulted from private action. The court stated, "where, as here, an economically interested party exercises decision-making authority in formulating a product standard for a private association that comprises market participants, that party enjoys no *Noerr* immunity from any antitrust liability flowing from the effect the standard has of its own force in the marketplace."[14]

Impact on Interstate Commerce

The federal courts do not have jurisdiction under the Sherman Act unless the alleged illegal activity has an impact on interstate commerce. Indeed, the Supreme Court has held that congressional power to regulate trade exists only when the conduct exerts a "substantial economic effect" on interstate commerce.[15] Thus, to establish an antitrust violation, the challenger must show an impact on interstate commerce from the activities complained of. In *Veizaga v. National Board for Respiratory Therapy*,[16] the court held that allegations that the defendant, a private certification board established by a professional association, advertised nationally for candidates, administered its certification examination on a nation-wide level, and caused the price of respiratory services to be higher than it would otherwise have been, sufficiently demonstrated an impact on interstate commerce so as to withstand a motion to dismiss.[17]

In reality, courts can find an impact on interstate commerce in almost any situation, particularly where the defendant is an association, board, or other similar organization made up of competitors. Nevertheless, the impact is jurisdictional; if there is insufficient impact on interstate commerce, the court has no power to review the credentialing process under the antitrust laws.

Fairness Challenges

Organizations that engage in credentialing, such as through certification or accreditation, are particularly subject to challenge by an unsuccessful candidate for the credential. A common challenge in this situation is a challenge to the "fairness" of the denial of the credential.

Although private, nonprofit, voluntary organizations are not required by the Constitution to provide "due process" when engaging in credentialing, a judicially evolved parallel to the constitutional due process requirement, the *fairness doctrine*, may vest candidates for a credential with judicially recognized "rights," violation of which may cause a court to intervene in the credentialing process. Persuading a court to intervene is the threshold of a challenge to the fairness of a credentialing program.

Constitutional Due Process

Although some plaintiffs in challenges to credentialing by private, nonprofit organizations have alleged a right to due process under the Fifth or Fourteenth Amendments to the U.S. Constitution, courts have not found a constitutional due process right where the state or the federal government is not involved in the credentialing program. Schools, for example, that attempted to argue that the lack of accreditation will deny them the right to obtain federal or state monies for financial aid have found the argument to be unsuccessful.[18] Similarly, the certification of physicians that does not affect the state licensing procedure necessary to practice does not implicate state action.[19]

The lack of constitutional protection, however, has not barred courts from reviewing, and sometimes regulating, the credentialing procedures of private organizations. The *Marjorie Webster* court noted that the "increasing importance of private associations in the affairs of individuals and organizations has led to substantial expansion of judicial control over [the internal affairs of the associations]."[20] That court concluded that varying deference would be due the professional judgment of the organization depending on the subject matter at issue, and noted in a footnote that less deference may be due when the question is one of procedural fairness.[21]

Public Policy Intervention

The justification for judicial intervention was most cogently expressed in *Falcone v. Middlesex County Medical Society.*[22] Upon finding that membership in the local medical society was an economic necessity because the local hospitals required staff physicians to be members of the society, the court stated, "[p]ublic policy strongly dictates that this power [to exclude members] should not be unbridled, but should be viewed judicially as a fiduciary power to be exercised in a reasonable and lawful manner for the advancement of the interests of the medical profession and public generally."[23]

Courts following *Falcone* have hinged their decisions on the "economic necessity" argument. Thus, in *Salter v. New York State Psychological Association,*[24] where a psychologist excluded from a state professional association could show only that he experienced a "down-grading" of his reputation, the court responded, "exclusion from any selective group of high-standard professional leaves the rejected ones without desired kudos and prestige—but no court has ever taken it on itself to review such selections." Other courts have agreed.[25]

Judicial Review of a Credentialing Program

If the credentialing program of an association, board, or other similar private, nonprofit, voluntary organization is challenged and if the court determines that no exemption applies and the program is subject to legal review, how will the court review that program? What factors will be important? Will the courts review the substantive criteria for awarding the credential, or simply the procedures for granting or denying it? What safeguards can be built into the program to reduce vulnerability? An examination of decided cases in which credentialing and similar programs were at issue suggests some possible answers.

Antitrust Judicial Review

The judicial review of any practice alleged to be in violation of the antitrust laws follows a two-step analysis. First, the court determines whether the practice is so clearly anticompetitive as to justify a summary determination of illegality without wasting time on reviewing the purpose, rationale, or effect of the alleged restraints. If the practice is so clearly anticompetitive, the court holds the practice to be *per se* violation of the antitrust laws. To date, *per se* violations of the antitrust laws in cases involving private organizations have usually been price-fixing or fee-setting violations (see, *Goldfarb*). If the challenged practice does not obviously stifle competition, but it may have an anticompetitive purpose or effect, the court will review it under a "reasonableness" test. This does not mean that if the practice is reasonable, it will be allowed, but rather, that if it does not reasonably restrain interstate commerce, it will be upheld. Thus, if the challenged practice promotes competition, it will be found reasonable and not in violation of the law.

Per se Analysis

Although credentialing activities of private, nonprofit, voluntary boards and other similar organizations have consistently been reviewed by the courts under the rule of reason, some other activities of those organizations have been subjected to review under the *per se* standard. In *Goldfarb*, the court held that a bar association rule setting minimum charges for title searches was *per se* unreasonable. The court refused to consider evidence concerning the reasonableness of the rule. Similarly, in *Arizona v. Maricopa County Medical Society*,[26] a maximum fee understanding among physicians was found to be price-fixing, a *per se* violation of the antitrust laws. Regardless of the laudable and reasonable purpose of providing lower cost medical benefits to some patients, the practice was held illegal because all agreements or understandings to raise, lower, or stabilize prices or fees are clear violations of the Sherman Act. Finally, in *National Society of Professional Engineers v. United States*,[27] the court held that an engineering association's ethical ban on competitive bidding was a *per se* violation, regardless of the ban's reasonable objective of maintaining the quality of engineering services.[28]

It is worth noting that each of these activities was closely tied to the commercial or business interests of the organizations and of their members. Because a credentialing program is likely to be more removed from commercial interests and closer to public interest goals, the review of a credentialing program is likely to be under the rule of reason analysis.[29] Even if the plaintiff alleges what might be a *per se* violation in a purely business context, the courts have noted that the action must have a predominately anticompetitive effect before the court will hold that it is a *per se* violation.[30]

Rule of Reason Analysis

The usual standard for reviewing credentialing activities of private, non-profit, voluntary organizations is the rule of reason standard. This analysis imposes upon the plaintiff the burden of showing that the purported anticompetitive effects of a challenged activity are unreasonable. The defendant has the opportunity to justify the conduct in light of other factors. The Supreme Court has framed the test in this way: "The true test of legality is whether the restraint imposed is such as merely regulates and perhaps thereby promotes competition, or whether it is such as may suppress or even destroy competition."[31]

Recognizing that professions and organizations of professionals have public service objectives, courts have held that properly motivated standard making is a legitimate function of those organizations.[32] "With respect to professions, as opposed to commercial businesses, the *per se* standard has been particularly restricted."[33]

In reviewing particular activities under the rule of reason analysis, courts must determine whether the practice is anticompetitive in light of surrounding circumstances. Factors important to this determination are whether the activity is justified in light of the market, the nature of the profession or field of endeavor, the nature and effect of the restraint, the reasons for adopting the practice, and the condition of the profession or field before and after the restraint.

Economic Effect

Whether a private, nonprofit, voluntary organization's credentialing program has an economic effect is likely to be the first issue of concern for a reviewing court because, without economic effect, the program is not likely to be anticompetitive. Indeed, the scope of the economic effect may be determinative in a challenge to credentialing. Credentialing programs are always likely to have some economic effect; indeed, that effect is one incentive for professionals or institutions to seek the credential offered by private organizations. The benefits to the individual who receives professional certification include prestige, recognition, and contact with other professionals. These benefits will translate into economic advantage by way of being able to command higher salaries or fees, to obtain better assignments or referrals, and otherwise to be more successful. Third-party payors may use certification to determine whose services they will cover. The benefits to the educational program that receives academic accreditation also include prestige and recognition, which may enhance the ability to attract better teachers, better students, contributions, and research grants. Courts will evaluate these kinds of economic ramifications to determine the reasonableness of the credentialing measures.

Credential Essential to Practice

Most privately issued credentials provide advantages but are not required. But where possession of such a credential is, in all practicality, a requirement to practice a profession or operate an academic program, courts are likely to find an overwhelming economic effect. If the credential is absolutely required, this may be because the credential has been adopted and specified by a state government. If it is essentially a government licensing program, it may be entitled to antitrust immunity under the state action defense.

Even where the effect of a credentialing program may be to preclude an individual or institution from obtaining a professional license or other government approval, an indirect preclusion does not establish an antitrust violation. In *Zavaletta v. American Bar Ass'n*,[34] the court held that the refusal of the ABA to accredit a law school was not a violation of the Sherman Act, although students attending a nonaccredited law school were precluded in many states from sitting for the bar examination required to practice law. The court held, "in accrediting a law school the ABA merely expresses its education opinion—at the school's own request—about the quality of a school's program." The court noted that the ABA had no power to license practitioners and instructed the plaintiffs to take their grievance to the state licensing body that had adopted the ABA's accreditation list as its own.[35]

However, a plaintiff need not allege that a credential is an obsolete necessity to maintain a challenge that the credentialing program violates the antitrust laws. The allegation that a "legitimate professional interest" was denied has been held sufficient to allege an antitrust injury.[36]

Third-Party Payment Conditioned on Credential

A number of plaintiffs have argued that, if the effect of the credentialing program is to make third-party payment conditioned upon the possession of that credential, the denial of a credential could be an antitrust injury. In *Schachar v. American Academy of Ophthalmology, Inc.*[37] the plaintiff alleged that, because insurance companies based procedure reimbursement decisions on the defendant's recommendation regarding surgical procedures, the labeling of a surgical procedure as "experimental," which allegedly restricted the availability of insurance funding for the performance of that procedure, was an antitrust violation. The Seventh Circuit, however, found no evidence of injury.[38] Similarly, in *MacHovec v. Council for National Register of Health*,[39] the plaintiffs alleged that, because insurance companies used the National Register to determine which psychologists would be covered providers, the denial of their applications to be listed in the National Register was an antitrust violation. That court also held, however, that plaintiffs adduced no evidence that the third parties used the Register in such a way as to exclude nonlisted psychologists or to hamper their ability to practice; and so there was no injury.[40]

The Credential as a Source of Referrals

Some plaintiffs have alleged that the denial of referral opportunities that come with credentialing is an antitrust injury. The plaintiffs in *MacHovec* argued such a loss based on the denial of their applications to be listed in the National Register; but, because they could adduce no evidence to support the loss, the court did not address whether such a loss could be an antitrust injury. Had they been able to demonstrate their claim, however, they may well have shown the necessary economic effect.

Benefit of Credential in Advertising

The listing of one's name or service in publicly available materials can be an important benefit of organizational membership; such a listing may constitute an economic effect. A plaintiff whose product was denied listing in an electrical code that was widely adopted by state and local governments challenged the failure to list. Finding that the standard making in that case had an unreasonably anticompetitive effect, the court found a violation of the antitrust laws.[41]

Motive

The Supreme Court has recognized that factors relevant to a determination of whether a restraint is anticompetitive or procompetitive include "the purpose or end sought to be obtained. . . . This is not because a good intention will save an otherwise objectionable regulation or the reverse, but because knowledge of intent may help the court to interpret facts and to predict consequences."[42] Thus, the motive behind the measure is relevant to the review. The stated objective of most credentialing programs is to provide a standard to which the public can look to determine levels of professional or academic competency. This motive clearly serves the public interest and is procompetitive in effect. However, if, in a challenge to credentialing, the plaintiff can show evidence of an anticompetitive motive, the reviewing court may disregard the public service motive as sham.[43]

Patient Care Motive

Many organizations of health care professionals or institutions are motivated in their credentialing programs by a concern for better patient care. Whether a patient care motive will be sufficient to repel an antitrust challenge to health care credentialing will depend upon the facts of each case. In *Wilk v. American Medical Ass'n,*[44] the plaintiff charged the defendants with refusing to deal with chiropractors and causing antitrust injury by establishing an ethical rule that prohibited AMA members from associating with chiropractors. Although this was not a credentialing case, an analysis was used by the court that is similar to that used in credentialing cases. The defendants' affirmative defense was that the refusal to deal was in the interest of the welfare of the public, because the defendants believed that chiropractic was "dangerous quackery."[45] The court held that once the plaintiffs had established an anticompetitive effect from the defendants' actions, the burden was on the defendants to show that they were genuinely concerned for what they perceived as the scientific method in the care of each person with whom they have entered into the doctor-patient relationship; that the concern was objectively reasonable; that the concern was the dominant motivating factor in promulgating the rule of the organization to refuse to deal with chiropractors; and that the concern for the scientific method could not have been adequately satisfied in a manner less restrictive of competition.[46]

Other Motives

In areas other than the health care field, motive or purpose has also been a factor in determining whether the credentialing program violates the antitrust laws.[47]

Nature of the Restraint

Once a plaintiff demonstrates some anticompetitive effect from a challenged credentialing program, courts may examine the substantive criteria for reasonableness. However, in light of the specialized knowledge of the organizations that engage in credentialing, courts may be reluctant to inquire too closely. A federal court decision illustrates the relative latitude courts have given to credentialing organizations when evaluating the criteria. In *Bishara v. American Board of Orthopedic Surgery*,[48] the court rejected the antitrust claim of a physician who was barred from taking the defendant's certification examination because he had served only 33 instead of 36 months in an accredited residency program. The court found no violation by the private certification body, noted that "the line must be drawn somewhere," and stated that, "it is entirely reasonable for a voluntary organization which certifies the qualifications of medical specialists to insist that applicants possess a minimum amount of training before taking the certification examination."[49] Similarly, in *Sherman College*, the court refused to presume any anticompetitive effect from increased educational requirements in the absence of any evidence as to that effect.[50]

Public Information Factor

Finally, there is an emerging line of authority holding that, when a private organization provides information, such as on the certification of a professional or the accreditation of an educational program, but does not constrain others to follow its recommendations, the organization does not violate the antitrust laws.[51]

Special Features

Credentialing programs of private, nonprofit, voluntary organizations often share some kinds of criteria or procedures that courts have evaluated. Grandfather clauses, educational requirements, limited practice requirements, and tying arrangements are features that have been addressed.

Grandfathering Provisions

Especially when first introduced, many professional certification programs include some provision for awarding the credential to those persons who have achieved the required level of competence by experience, while exempting them, at least temporarily, from other newly established requirements of the program, such as examinations. In part, this is a recognition of the fact that the program simply must start somewhere. This kind of provision is subject to challenge, however, by those who believe that they too should be exempted or granted a temporary credential while fulfilling the requirements.

Although courts have clearly held that legislative grandfathering provisions are not illegal,[52] few courts have addressed the legality of grandfather provisions in private organization credentialing. Only two cases have even briefly discussed grandfather provisions. In *Kreuzer v. American Academy of Periodontology*,[53] the court upheld a grandfather provision on the grounds that it was not "manifestly anticompetitive." Similarly, the court in *Dietz v. American Dental Ass'n*,[54] upheld a provision that allowed some dentists to be certified as "diplomates" without examination and others to be certified without requiring advanced schooling. Neither court explained its views on either the substance or the procedure of grandfathering at any length.

In light of these cases, the most that can be said is that if the grandfather provision is reasonable, it is probably not anticompetitive. Thus, if a program balances the need for a nationally recognized level of competence with the practical restraints on practitioners who may have provided service for some time in a jurisdiction that did not require adherence to the criteria set up to obtain the credential, it is likely to be reasonable and, thus, not in violation of the antitrust laws.

Educational Criteria

Courts are particularly reluctant to review educational criteria substantively. In *Bishara v. American Board of Orthopedic Surgery*,[55] the court refused to hold that the requirement of 36 months experience was excessive or an unreasonable restraint on trade. Myriad courts have ruled similarly.[56] Although courts may be reluctant to enter the minefield of determining whether a particular test actually measures competence, a credentialing organization that can show that objective experts believe that its test is reasonably effective in testing competence can use this fact to demonstrate the reasonableness of its credentialing program. In at least one case, the plaintiffs have alleged that the credential was not a valid measure of competence. *Veizaga v. National Board for Respiratory Therapy*,[57] Although the court never reached the merits of the complaint, the fact that the challenge was brought may suggest an area of vulnerability.

Limited Practice Requirements

In an organization in which membership itself is a credential, the organization may require that members limit their practices to the specialty that the organization represents. In *Kreuzer v. American Academy of Peridonotology*,[58] a periodontist alleged that the requirement that members limit their practices exclusively to periodontics in order to maintain active membership in the Academy constituted a group refusal to deal. The court reviewed the requirement under the rule of reason analysis and remanded the case to the district court for a determination of whether the limited practice requirement was the least restrictive alternative and whether the patient care motive was legitimate.

Tying Arrangements

Where a requirement for a particular credential is membership in another organization, the requirement must be reasonable. In *Boddicker v. Arizona State Dental Ass'n*,[59] dentists who wanted to be members of their state and local dental associations were dropped from the rolls of those groups when they failed to pay their dues to the American Dental Association. Membership in the national association was a prerequisite for membership in the state and local associations. The dentists alleged that the associations had set up a tying agreement in violation of the antitrust laws. The court held that the requirement was not "so obviously designed to improve dental services to the public" as to justify dismissing the complaint; the case, was, therefore, remanded for further proceedings.[60]

Judicial Review of Fairness Doctrine Challenges

The decision to grant or deny a credential is also subject to challenge under the notion of common law fairness. Although this doctrine is nebulous, it has vitality; a credentialing program that violates this doctrine is subject to judicial censure. The fairness doctrine is two-pronged: *substantive fairness* (whether the decision was rationally related to a legitimate association purpose) and *procedural fairness* (whether the decision was arbitrary and unreasonable). Courts may feel more comfortable, however, giving a closer review to the procedural aspect of credentialing because that aspect requires no specialized knowledge of the substance of the credential. Furthermore, fair process is familiar to courts because they deal with procedure every day. Thus, the process involved in obtaining a credential may be more closely examined than the substantive requirements when a credentialing program is challenged.

Procedural Fairness

The need for fair procedures in the credentialing process is roughly equivalent to the requirement of "due process" in the constitutional sense. Thus, courts have found that the process that is due depends upon "the nature of the alleged right involved, the nature of the proceeding, and the possible burden on that proceeding."[61] Because courts have generally limited judicial intervention in credentialing decisions to those cases where the credential is an economic necessity, the nature of the alleged right is fairly compelling. Although courts have held that a trial-type hearing is not required, they have often required notice, a statement of the credentialing organization's reasons for denying the credential, and some meaningful opportunity for the applicant to be heard. The courts have not developed specific requirements, however, and if the procedure is fair and reasonable in light of the facts of the case, the procedure is likely to survive a challenge.

For example, in *Kronen v. Pacific Coast Society of Orthodontists*,[62] an applicant to the society failed the required examination. He was then given the opportunity to withdraw his application, improve his skills, and re-apply. Although he subsequently passed the examination, he could not get the necessary recommendations. The court concluded that the process afforded the applicant was fair and not arbitrary and that the reason for his exclusion from the society was a professional one. Thus, the challenge failed.

A number of accrediting cases also address the process that is due when an institution's accreditation is revoked or denied. In *Medical Institute of Minnesota v. Nat'l Ass'n of Trade and Technical Schools*,[63] the court considered whether the decision to deny re-accreditation was arbitrary or unreasonable, and whether it was supported by substantial evidence. The court held that the accrediting organization was obliged "to conform its actions to fundamental principles of fairness" and held that the organization's procedure of notice and a hearing before a three-person panel was sufficient to protect the plaintiff's interest.[64]

Disciplinary Procedure versus Evaluative Procedure

Some courts have distinguished between disciplinary procedure and evaluative procedure for procedural review purposes. In those cases when a credential or membership is revoked for disciplinary violations, the individual may be entitled to "more" process than when a credential is originally denied. This divergence may stem from the sense that once a credential has been earned, the holder has some continued right to it, assuming that actions are consistent with the rules of the issuing credentialing organization. The decision of whether to grant the credential at all, however, is entitled to more deference from the court because the applicant has no "right" to obtain the credential and because that decision relies in large part on the substantive criteria. Thus, in *Higgins v. American Society of Clinical Pathologists*,[65] the court engaged in a more detailed judicial review of an expulsion decision than it would have allowed a certification decision on the theory that a member of an organization has a valuable personal relationship to the organization and a status that, once conferred, may not be arbitrarily revoked.[66]

Substantive Fairness

Review of the substantive fairness of a credentialing program is probably limited to a determination of whether the decision is arbitrary or capricious, and whether the decision was supported by substantial evidence.[67] As long as the standards are sufficient to guide professionals or institutions in their own fields, a court is not likely to find them vague.[68] Criteria for accrediting paralegal schools by the American Bar Association (ABA) were found to be reasonable in light of evidence that the program was a response to inquiries and that the ABA had worked with paralegal schools to establish standards.[69] In general, courts will review the substantive fairness with deference to the credentialing organization. Barring any evidence that the criteria are applied in a discriminatory or uneven way, courts are likely to find substantive fairness.[70]

Guidelines

In view of the decisions of courts and federal agencies when private, nonprofit voluntary credentialing programs were challenged, some general guidelines for conducting those programs can be fashioned.

Criteria

The fundamental bases of any credentialing program are requirements, conditions, prerequisites, standards, or qualifications that are established as criteria for certification or accreditation. In determining if the criteria are reasonable, the following guidelines should be considered.

- The criteria should be no more stringent than necessary to assure that minimum competency or quality levels have been attained by applicants for credentialing. This is particularly true when credentialing is of significant economic value, for example as a prerequisite for employment or third-party reimbursement.
- Any combination of reasonable education, experience, examination, or other requirements can be used as criteria for professional certification; likewise, any combination of reasonable self-evaluation, site visit, or other requirements can be used as criteria for academic accreditation. However, it may be advisable to establish alternative criteria where the requirements for credentialing are difficult or expensive for many potential candidates.
- Criteria for credentialing must not have the purpose or effect of unreasonably restricting or boycotting competitors.
- Criteria for credentialing may include continuing requirements and periodic reassessment of those previously certified or accredited.
- Criteria should be established only after treasonable notice to all those who may be affected by credentialing requirements, including potential candidates and users of their services. Notice should include an opportunity to participate in the establishment of credentialing criteria, such as the opportunity to comment on proposed criteria.

Procedures

In addition to reasonable criteria, any credentialing program should include policies and procedures assuring that the criteria are applied to all candidates for certification or accreditation. The following guidelines should be considered:

- Participation in a private organization's credentialing program must ordinarily be voluntary (except when government agencies authorize organizations to administer licensing or other mandatory programs).
- Participation in a credentialing program should not be denied because a candidate is not a member of an organization that initiates, sponsors, or conducts the program. However, fees charged to nonmembers for credentialing may be higher than those charged to members to reflect any members' dues or assessments that contribute to funding the program.
- It is not clear whether it is legal to "grandfather" particular individuals or entities summarily into a new credentialing program— that is, provide automatic certification or accreditation—without determining if the grandfathered individuals or entities meet reasonable requirements; the legality will depend upon the facts and circumstances in each case.
- Organizations may promote their credentialing programs to potential participants or to the public as good measures for determining the qualifications of professionals or institutions. However, care should be used in promoting credentialed individuals or schools by name, and there should be no disparagement of the noncredentialed.
- Denial of credentialing should not be used to "blackball" individuals or institutions, to limit the number of competitors, or otherwise arbitrarily to deny potential applicants access to credentialing or receipt of certification or accreditation.
- Denial of certification or accreditation should be made by written notice to the applicant giving the reasons for denial and an opportunity for appeal—either in writing or at a hearing held for that purpose—with the ultimate decision on appeal made by a body other that making the original denial.
- Assessment of the qualifications of applicants for certification or accreditation may be made best by an objective body or organization not composed exclusively of those who have received their credentials.
- All qualifying candidates should receive the same certification or accreditation title or denomination for which they qualify, with no discrimination or differentiation.
- All policy-making functions of a credentialing organization should be kept as independent as is feasible from influence or domination by a parent or related organization whose functions include promoting the economic well-being of the profession or field of endeavor. In short, the credentialing organization should be autonomous with respect to all credentialing functions. Indications are that federal antitrust enforcers would also prefer autonomy

with respect to administration of credentialing organizations—that is, funding, staffing, and so forth—but there is as yet no clear legal compulsion for administrative autonomy in addition to the more clearly required functional autonomy.

Conclusion

Credentialing by private, nonprofit, voluntary organizations is perhaps the best method of "self-regulation" to avoid excessive government regulation. To the extent that credentialing programs are conducted with fairness and impartiality, they are likely to withstand increased government scrutiny and controls. Therefore, organizations involved in credentialing programs should take care to assure that they are aware of (or even ahead of) the rapid legal developments that could affect these activities.

Endnotes

1. *Marjorie Webster Jr. College v. Middle States Association of Colleges and Secondary Schools, Inc.*, 432 F.2d 650, 655 (D.C. Cir. 1970), *cert. denied*, 400 U.S. 965.
2. 421 U.S. 733 (1975).
3. *Id.* at 788–89, n.17.
4. 317 U.S. 341 (1943)
5. 433 U.S. 350 (1977).
6. *See, Goldfard, supra* (because state did not require the bar association to fix fees, no state action); *Cantor v. Detroit Edison Co.*, 428 U.S. 579 (1976) (the state's mere acquiescence in private utility's practice did not support the state action defense).
7. *See California Retail Liquor Dealers Association v. Midcal Aluminum, Inc.*, 445 U.S. 97, 105 (1980) (for *Parker* immunity to apply, restraint must be "clearly articulated and affirmatively expressed as state policy" and be "actively supervised" by the state itself).
8. 884 F.2d 524 (10th Cir. 1989).
9. *Id.* at 528 (citations omitted).
10. *Maple Flooring Mfrs. v. United States*, 268 U.S. 563 (1925).
11. *Schachar v. American Academy of Ophthalmology, Inc.*, 870 F.2d 397 (7th Cir. 1989).
12. *See, e.g., Federal Prescription Service v. American Pharmaceutical Association*, 663 F.2d 253 (D.C. Cir. 1981), *cert. denied*, 102 S.Ct. 1293 (1982) (Pharmacists' associations' attempts to have state pharmacy board restrict mail-order pharmacy services was protected); *Sherman College of Straight Chiropractic v. American Chiropractic Association*, 654 F. Supp. 716 (N.D. Ga. 1986) (defendant association's activities in persuading state licensing bodies to permit only graduates of pro-diagnostic schools to be licensed were protected under *Noerr-Pennington* doctrine).
13. 108 S.Ct. 1981 (1988).
14. *Id.* at 1942. *See also Va. Academy of Clinical Psychologists v. Blue Shield of Virginia*, 624 F.2d 476 (4th Cir. 1980) (agreement to restrict commercial activity in defiance of state did not come under *Noerr-Pennington* protection).
15. *Wickard v. Filborn*, 317 U.S. 111, 125 (1942).
16. 1977-1 CCH Trade Cases 61, 274 (N.D. Ill. 1977).
17. *See also Boddicker v. Arizona State Dental Association*, 549 F.2d 626, 629 (1977) (multi-state scope of ADA membership, programs, and dues demonstrates substantial impact).

18. *See Parsons College v. North Central Association of Colleges and Secondary Schools*, 271 F. Supp. 65, 75 (N.D. Ill. 1967); *Medical Institute of Minnesota v. National Association of Trade and Technical Schools*, 817 F.2d 1310 (8th Cir. 1987).

19. *See Salter v. New York State Psychological Ass'n*, 14 N.Y.2d 100, 248 N.Y.S. 2d 867 (1964); *Falcone v. Middlesex County Medical Society*, 34 N.J. 582, 170 A.2d 791 (1961).

20. 432 F.2d at 655.

21. *Id.* at 656 n. 28.

22. 34 N.J. 582, 170 A.2d 791 (1961).

23. *Id.* at 799.

24. 248 N.Y.2d 867, 872 (Ct. App. 1964).

25. *See Treister v. Academy of Orthopedic Surgeons*, 78 Ill. App. 3d 746, 396 N.E.2d 1225 (N.D. Ill. 1979) (court would review procedures if membership was an economic necessity, but where membership was only a "practical necessity [needed] to realize maximum potential achievement and recognition in [a] specialty," procedure was not reviewable); *Hawkins v. North Carolina Dental Society*, 230 F. Supp. 805 (W.D.N.C. 1964), *rev'd on other grounds*, 355 F.2d 718 (4th Cir. 1966) (membership in a voluntary private association is a privilege, not a right). *But see Pinsker v. Pacific Coast Society of Orthodontists*, 12 Cal. 3d 541, 526 P.2d 253 (1974) (although membership in societies was not economic necessity, societies wielded sufficient monopoly power to affect significant economic and professional concerns so as to justify review of procedures and of substantive rule for arbitrariness). *See also Northwest Wholesale Stationers v. Pacific Stationery and Printing Co.*, 472 U.S. 284 (1985) (lack of procedural protection does not establish an antitrust violation).

26. 102 S. Ct. 2466 (1982).

27. 435 U.S. 679 (1978).

28. *See also Blalock v. Ladies PGA.* 1973-1 CCH Trade Cases par. 74,597 (N.D.Ga. 1973) (suspension of golfer from LPGA play was illegal group boycott since golfer's direct competitors voted to suspend).

29. The Fifth and Seventh Circuits, the only circuits to address the issue, have both conclusively held that a private organization's self-regulation program may not *per se* violate Section 1 under any circumstances. *See Consolidated Metal Products*, 846 F.2d at 292; *Schachar*, 870 F.2d at 399. *See also Allied Tube & Conduit Corp. v. Indian Head, Inc.*, 486 U.S. 492, 501 (1988) ("the potential for procompetitive benefits . . . has led most lower courts to apply rule of reason analysis to product standard setting by private associations."); *U.S. Trotting Ass'n v. Chicago Downs Ass'n Inc.*, 665 F.2d 781, 789 (7th Cir. 1981) (holding that a rule banning association members from racing at non-association affiliated tracks was not subject to a *per se* analysis); 2 Von Kalinowski *Antitrust Laws & Trade Regulation* § 6I.02 at 6I-14 (1991) (collecting cases in which the rule of reason analysis has been applied to association membership restrictions).

30. *See MacHovec*, 616 F. Supp. at 269 ("The mere allegation of a concerted refusal to deal does not suffice because not all concerted refusals to deal are predominately anticompetitive.") quoting *Northwest Wholesale Stationers v. Pacific Stationery and Printing Co.*, 472 U.S. 284, 298 (1986).

31. *Chicago Board of Trade v. United States*, 246 U.S. 231, 238 (1918).

32. *See, e.g., Eliason Corp. v. National Sanitation Foundation*, 614 F.2d 126, 128-28 (6th Cir. 1980), *cert. denied*, 449 U.S. 826 (1980).

> [T]o survive a Sherman Act challenge a particular practice, rule, or regulation of a profession, whether rooted in tradition or the pronouncements of its organizations, must serve the purpose for which the profession exists, *viz.* to serve the public. That is, it must contribute directly to improving service to the public. Those which only suppress competition between practitioners will fail to survive the challenge. This interpretation permits a harmonization of the ends that both the professions and the Sherman Act serve.

> *Boddicker v. Arizona State Dental Ass'n*, 549 F.2d 626, 632 (9th Cir. 1977).

33. *Paralegal Inst., Inc. v. American Bar Ass'n*, 475 F. Supp. 1123, 1128 (E.D.N.Y.

1979), *aff'd*, 662 F.2d 575 (2d Cir. 1980). *See also U.S. Trotting Association v. Chicago Downs Ass'n, Inc.*, 665 F.2d 781, 790 (1981) ("sporting associations and organizations are entitled to a fuller form of antitrust analysis in recognition of their need for self-regulation").

34. No. 89-326-N, slip op. (E.D. Va. May 10, 1989).

35. *See also Sherman College of Straight Chiropractic v. American Chiropractic Association, Inc.*, 654 F. Supp. 116 (N.D. Ga. 1986) (although effect of association's activities was to preclude graduates of plaintiff college from becoming licensed in most states, no antitrust violation where plaintiffs could not show unreasonable anticompetitive effect).

36. *Bogus v. American Speech & Hearing Ass'n*, 582 F.2d 277, 286 (3rd Cir. 1978).

37. 870 F.2d 397 (7th Cir. 1989).

38. *Id.* at 398.

39. 616 F. Supp. 258 (E.D.Va. 1985).

40. *See also Virginia Academy of Clinical Psychologists v. Blue Shield of Virginia*, 624 F.2d 476, 483 (4th Cir. 1980) (association of neuropsychiatrists' efforts to persuade Blue Shield to use the services of its members, absent any coercion, was not illegal).

41. *Allied Tube & Conduit Corp. v. Indian Head, Inc.*, 108 S.Ct. 1931 (1988). *See also Hester v. Martindale-Hubbell, Inc.*, 659 F.2d 433 (4th Cir. 1981) (refusal to publish plaintiff's "professional card" in nationwide listing of attorneys because card had not been rated by ABA or North Carolina Bar was alleged as an antitrust violation); *MacHovec, supra.*

42. *Board of Trade of the City of Chicago v. United States*, 246 U.S. 231, 238-38 (1918).

43. There is a general requirement that the standard-setting activity be "legitimate." *See, e.g., Clamp-All Corp. v. Cast Iron Soil Pipe Institute*, 851 F.2d 478, 487 (1st Cir. 1988). The activity is not "illegitimate" if the standard setting procedure served no legitimate interest or if a market participant improperly influences the standard-setting or certification process. *See Id.* (citing *George R. Whitten, Jr., Inc. v. Paddock Pool Builders, Inc.*, 508 F.2d, 547, 558 n. 19 (1st Cir. 1974). *See also Allied Tube & Conduit Corp. v. Indian Head, Inc.*, 108 S. Ct. 1931 (1988) (The court, addressing a case in which a market participant had perverted a safety certification process for plastic wiring, did not reach this issue but affirmed the lower courts' denial of *Noerr-Pennington* immunity to the market participant defendant.).

44. 719 F.2d 207 (7th Cir. 1983).

45. *Id.* at 217.

46. *Id.* at 277. *See also Kreuzer v. Am. Academy of Periodontology*, 735 F.2d 1479 (D.C. Cir. 1984).

47. *See U.S. Trotting Ass'n v. Chicago Downs Ass'n Inc.*, 665 F.2d 781, 789 (1981) (no showing of a purpose to exclude competitors, but rather to insure honest harness racing); *Eliason Corp. v. National Sanitation Foundation*, 614 F.2d 126 (1980) (standards which determined whether products would be listed by association were developed to promote uniformity in requirements of different jurisdictions and did not constitute a group boycott); *Hatley v. American Quarter Horse Ass'n*, 552 F.2d 646, 653 (5th Cir. 1977); *E.A. McQuade Tours, Inc. v. Consolidated Air Tour Manual Committee*, 467 F.2d 178 (5th Cir. 1970), *cert. denied*, 409 U.S. 1109 (1973).

48. No. 85 C 3400, slip op. (N.D. Ill. Dec. 30, 1986) 1986 WL 15265.

49. *Id.*

50. 654 F. Supp. 716, 722 (N.D. Ga. 1986). *See Northwest Wholesale Stationery, Inc. v. Pacific Stationery and Printing Co.*, 472 U.S. 284 (1986) (absence of procedural safeguards in expelling association member did not establish a *per se* antitrust violation).

51. *See, e.g., Schachar v. American Academy of Ophthalmology, Inc.*, 870 F.2d 397, 399 (7th Cir. 1989) (holding that the labeling of a surgical procedure as "experimental" was not a restraint on trade at all and therefore did not constitute an antitrust violation, because the organization did not constrain others to adopt its recommendation); *Consolidated Metal Products, Inc. v. American Petroleum Institute*, 846 F.2d 284, 295 (holding same in dismissing

a claim based upon the denial of an oil well rod certification); *Clamp-All Corp. v. Cast Iron Soil Pipe Institute*, 851 F.2d 478, 487 (1st Cir. 1988) (The court, in the course of dismissing a challenge to a pipe standard certification program, stated that "If such an activity [credentialing], in and of itself, were to hurt [plaintiff] by making it more difficult for [plaintiff] to compete, [plaintiff] would suffer injury only as a result of the defendants' joint efforts having lowered information costs or created a better product. And, that kind of harm is not "unreasonably anticompetitive." It brings about the very benefits that the antitrust laws seek to promote. That is to say, activity that harms competitors because it lowers production or distribution costs or provides a better product carries with it an overriding justification.")

52. *Watson v. Maryland*, 218 U.S. 173 (1910).
53. 558 F. Supp. 683, 685 (D.D.C. 1983), *aff'd in part, rev'd in part on other grounds*, 735 F.2d 1479 (D.C. Cir. 1984).
54. 479 F. Supp. 554, 560-61 (E.D. Mich. 1979).
55. No. 85-C-3400, *slip op.* (N.D. Ill. Dec. 30, 1986) 1986 WL 15265.
56. *See Sherman College*, 654 F. Supp. 716, 721 (N.D. Ga. 1986) (regulation of curriculum is inherently appropriate for accrediting body).
57. 19771-1 CCH Trade Cases par 61274 (N.D. Ill. 1977).
58. 735 F.2d 1479 (D.C. Cir. 1984).
59. 549 F.2d 626 (9th Cir. 1977).
60. *See also Bogus v. American Speech & Hearing Ass'n*, 582 F.2d 277 (1978) (requirement of membership in professional association in order to be awarded certification that was a "professional necessity" in some submarkets was conceivably a violation of the antitrust laws; court remanded for further development of the facts).
61. *Hannah v. Larche*, 363 U.S. 420, 422 (1960).
62. 237 Cal. 2d 289, 572 P.2d 32 (1977).
63. 817 F.2d 1310 (8th Cir. 1987).
64. *See also Transport Careers, Inc. v. Nat'l Home Study Council*, 646 F. Supp. 1474 (N.D. Ind. 1986) (common law due process satisfied with notice, receipt of detailed written report, opportunity to respond to report, opportunity for oral hearing, and opportunity to be represented by counsel).
65. 51 N.J. 191, 238 A.2d 665 (1968).
66. *See also Duby v. American College of Surgeons*, 468 F.2d 364, (7th Cir. 1972) (assuming some due process was required in a disciplinary expulsion, notice and hearing at which plaintiff was given opportunity to defend satisified requirement).
67. *Medical Inst. of Minn. v. Nat'l Ass'n of Trade and Technical Schools*, 817 F.2d 1310, 1314 (8th Cir. 1987) (decision to not reaccredit school was not arbitrary or unreasonable in light of standards of accreditation).
68. *Transport Careers, Inc. v. Nat'l Home Study Council*, 646 F. Supp. 1474, 1481 (N.D. Ind. 1986) (standards regarding advertising, promotion, business standards, recruiting, and control of field staff, though flexible, were sufficiently definite to guide professionals in field of education).
69. *Paralegal Inst., Inc. v. American Bar Ass'n*, 475 F. Supp. 1123, 1130 (S.D.N.Y.) *aff'd* 662 F.2d 575 (1979).
70. *Marjorie Webster*, 432 F.2d at 655, 656. *See also Deesen v. Professional Golfers Ass'n of America*, 358 F.2d 165 (4th Cir. 1966), *cert. denied*, 385 U.S. 846 (1966) (where purpose of requiring certain level of competence was to insure competition in tournaments, and there was no evidence of blackballing, program was even-handed).

3

Liability to Third Parties

Certification requirements establish objective criteria for judging professionals based on their education, experience, and performance on examinations. In some fields, certification has become a de facto requirement of employment.[1]

The use of certification by consumers and employers of professionals as an indicator of competence, however, may cause a certification organization to be held liable when a patient, client, or customer suffers harm at the hands of a certified professional.[2] Although there has not been much case law directly on point, inferences can be made from similar fact situations as to the approaches courts are likely to take if faced with a claim against a certifier. Liability to third parties could theoretically be asserted in the academic accreditation context as well as in the professional certification context. So far that has happened only rarely, so this chapter focuses upon liability to third parties from professional certification.[3]

The case law on negligence involves strict liability, negligence, and negligent misrepresentation claims. Strict liability is ordinarily limited to products liability claims and, therefore, may not apply to the certification of professionals.[4] This chapter addresses only claims of negligence and negligent misrepresentation. The courts usually evaluate these claims under common law or § 324A of the Restatement (Second) of Torts, or both.[5]

The first question courts ask is whether or not the certifier owed a duty to the third party.[6] Often, the courts will consider the amount of control or enforcement procedures a certifier has over its certifees in determining the existence of a duty. Alternatively, if the certifier has assumed a duty that would otherwise be owed by its certifees to their patients, clients, or customers, then the certifier may be held liable if its negligent performance has caused injury to the ultimate user of the certified professional. In addition, for the certifier to be held liable, the user must have relied on the certification. Even if the court finds both duty and reliance, no liability is likely to be found unless the certification process itself was inherently negligent.[7] Additionally, the negligent certification must have proximately caused the plaintiff's injury.

Duty of Certifier to User of Certification

At least two cases have upheld causes of action against certifiers or testers of products. In *Hempstead v. General Fire Extinguisher Corp.*,[8] the plaintiff was injured when a fire extinguisher exploded while being operated by a co-worker. The fire extinguisher had been approved by a nonprofit product testing service, Underwriters' Laboratories, and carried its seal of approval when purchased by the apartment complex that employed the plaintiff. The court held that Underwriters', as well as the manufacturer, could be held liable for injury to a third party user if the plaintiff could show that: 1) the testing service was negligent in approving the product; 2) the purchaser relied on the approval; and 3) the injured plaintiff was within a class of persons who could be expected to be harmed if the product were poorly constructed.[9] The court noted that the injury would also have to be a result of the testing service's negligent approval.[10]

Applied to certification organizations, *Hempstead* could provide precedent for holding a certifier liable. Certifiers expect patients, clients, or customers to rely upon the certification; indeed, that is one of their primary purposes. Thus, the plaintiff would likely fall within a class of those who could be expected to rely on the certification. The issue, then, would focus on whether there was actual reliance, a negligent certification process, and causation.

In the second leading case holding that a certifier could be liable to an end user, *Hanberry v. Hearst Corp.*,[11] the plaintiff had purchased shoes endorsed with "Good Housekeeping's Consumers' Guaranty Seal." The shoes had a slick sole that created little friction on vinyl floors. While wearing the shoes, the plaintiff slipped on her vinyl kitchen floor and injured herself. The court held that the Hearst Corporation's *Good Housekeeping Magazine*, as the certifier of the product, owed a duty to the ultimate consumer on a theory of negligent misrepresentation because the certifier could have expected, and indeed intended, consumers to rely on its certification. For the plaintiff to prevail, however, the court noted that she must show that: 1) the certifier did not test the product or, if so, negligently tested it; 2) she relied on the certification; and 3) she was injured because of her reliance.

Both *Good Housekeeping Magazine* and the certification organizations present themselves as possessing specialized knowledge with which to judge products or professionals, respectively. Hence, as in *Hanberry*, certification organizations may be held liable for negligent misrepresentation of fact or opinion.[12] One possible distinction between the *Hanberry* case and professional certification organizations is that, as the court specifically noted, the Hearst Corporation was endorsing products for its own economic gain—to increase the value of its magazine to both advertisers and consumers.[13] That is not usually the case with private, nonprofit, voluntary certification organizations.

In *Benco Plastics, Inc. v. Westinghouse Electric Corp.*,[14] the court distinguished *Hanberry* and *Hempstead* to find a product testing service not liable to a third party consumer. Underwriters' Laboratories had tested a lampholder for a lampholder manufacturer and had approved it for outdoor use. The plaintiff, a producer and seller of outdoor signs, incorporated the lampholder into its signs. Underwriters' also certified the plaintiff's finished signs. The court found Underwriters' not liable based on "practical policy considerations" of tort liability rather than on "whether such a claim against an endorser conveniently fit[] within a legal nitch[*sic*]."[15] The policy considerations were:

(1) the degree of closeness between the injured party and the endorser; (2) the nature of plaintiff's injury; (3) the causal connection between plaintiff's injury and the endorser's representation; (4) the evidence of reliance on the endorser's representations; (5) the moral culpability attached to the endorser's conduct; (6) the policy of preventing future harm; and (7) the nature of the endorser's business.[16]

The court specifically noted that in *Benco*, unlike in *Hempstead* and *Hanberry*, no "physical injury to an ultimate consumer" had occurred, indicating that liability may be more readily found in physical injury cases.

Although a court's weighing of policy considerations makes the outcome less predictable, such a formulation may be beneficial to certifiers given the social benefits of a profession voluntarily evaluating itself and providing information with which the public may evaluate specialized professionals.

Assumption by Certifier of Certifees' Duty

In one leading case, a nonprofit organization was found to have a duty to third parties because it had assumed duties its members owed to ultimate consumers. In *Hall v. E.I. DuPont DeNemours & Co.*,[17] the plaintiffs, all children, had been injured by blasting caps. On a theory of "enterprise liability," plaintiffs sued all blasting cap manufacturers and their trade association, the Institute of Makers of Explosives (IME), for failure to place warnings on individual blasting caps.

The *Hall* court held that a claim against all manufacturers of an industry and its trade association stated a cause of action on the theories of both negligence and strict liability. This holding turned on the fact that the specific manufacturer of the injuring blasting caps was not known and the allegation that the industry had delegated safety investigation to the association.[18] The court noted, however, that to succeed on the merits, plaintiffs would have to show that the defendants' failure to warn caused their injuries.[19]

In a different fact situation, courts may be reluctant to find a delegation of duty to a trade association. In *Beasock v. Dioguardi Enterprises, Inc.*,[20] Beasock died after injuries that resulted from trying to inflate a 16-inch tire on a 16.5-inch rim. His wife sued the Tire and Rim Association (TRA) on grounds of strict liability, breach of warranty, and negligence. TRA had no part in manufacturing the tire but had promulgated and published standards for tires and rims and their recommended pressures and weight loads.

The court held that the manufacturer's association owed no duty to the general public for injuries caused by the products of a member/manufacturer. Although the tire and rim standards suggested by TRA were, in effect, the industry standards, TRA "had neither the duty nor the authority to control what the manufacturers produced."[21] The *Beasock* court distinguished *Hall v. E.I. DuPont DeNemours & Co., Inc.* on the grounds that the tire and rim manufacturer was known and that no authority had been delegated to the TRA.

Similarly, in *Meyers v. Donnatacci*,[22] the court held that the National

Spa and Pool Institute (NSPI) owed no duty to ultimate consumers of its member/manufacturers' pools and that it had assumed none of their duties. The plaintiff was rendered paraplegic after diving headfirst into the shallow end of a private swimming pool. The plaintiff alleged that the NSPI, along with the homeowners and the manufacturer and distributor of the pool, were negligent in failing to warn against the dangers of diving into shallow water.

The trade association had performed research on pool safety and disseminated it to its members and the public, and had also suggested minimum standards to its members. The plaintiff made no claim that the information was incorrect.[23] In dismissing the claims, the court based its decision on both the lack of control by NSPI over its members and also on policy considerations, noting that nonprofit trade associations "serve many laudable purposes in our society."[24]

The court also refused to hold the association liable under § 324A of *Restatement (Second) of Torts*, noting that no New Jersey court had held an association liable under this provision.[25] In holding that NSPI did not increase the risks to the plaintiff as defined in § 324A(a), the court stated that "[i]n reality, the risk to Plaintiff was an attempt to execute a shallow dive. There was nothing NSPI did or failed to do which increased the risk to Plaintiff."[26] The court also noted that the manufacturers had not relied on NSPI and that the association had done nothing "which induced its members to forego [*sic*] their responsibilities to the consumer."[27]

The *Meyers* court's statement that the risk to the plaintiff was the attempt to dive in shallow water may be helpful in a professional certification case on the causation element. One would argue that the direct risk to third parties is the negligent actions of the professionals, not the actions of the certification organization, which merely promulgates criteria and evaluates candidates' qualifications under these criteria; the certifier cannot influence the professional actions of the certifee.

Reliance on Certifier

In a factually similar case to *Meyers*, *Howard v. Poseidon Pools, Inc.*,[28] the court held that the NSPI owed no duty or authority to control the pool manufacturers and hence no duty to the injured plaintiff. In *Howard*, the judge interpreted the plaintiff's complaint to be allegations of negligent misrepresentation, strict product liability, breach of warranty, and negligence. The plaintiff's main assertion was that NSPI had failed to warn the general public about the dangers of diving into above-ground pools. On the negligent misrepresentation claim, the court noted that to succeed the plaintiff must not only rely on the information but must be within a group that the association could reasonably have expected would rely on any representation made.[29]

As discussed above, given the purposes of certification organizations, courts would probably hold that certifiers expect patients, clients, and customers to rely on their certification. Still, the certification would have to be negligently granted for the organization to be liable.[30]

Although in many certification cases reliance may likely be found, if not presumed, in at least one case, *Collins v. American Optometric Ass'n*,[31] lack of actual reliance relieved an association of liability.[32] In *Collins*, the plaintiff charged the American Optometric Association with negligently misrepresenting the abilities of optometrists. Plaintiff suffered irreversible eye damage following the failure of three optometrists to diagnose his glaucoma. The plaintiff could not, however, identify any publication by the association upon which he had relied or which even contained the alleged misleading information.

The court held that the association could not be liable to a patient of one of its members in the absence of reliance by that patient on information disseminated by the association. Also, the court stated that in an action for fraudulent misrepresentation, the plaintiff would have to show that the information materially misrepresented a past or present fact and that reliance upon the misrepresentation is what proximately caused the injury.[33]

Was the Certification Negligent?

Even if the court finds that the certifier had a duty to the ultimate patient, client, or customer who in fact relied upon the certification, the plaintiff would also have to prove that the certification was granted negligently. Both *Hempstead* and *Hanberry*, the two leading cases in which a cause of action against a certifier has been upheld, involved allegations that the product had been negligently tested, or not tested at all.

Neither *Hempstead* nor *Hanberry* analyzed the reasonableness of the respective certification processes involved. Therefore, there is little case law on how a court would analyze a professional certification process. But some guidance may be found in employment discrimination cases where the validity of employment criteria are in question. One such case, *Veizaga v. The National Board For Respiratory Therapy*,[34] involved a class action by black and hispanic plaintiffs who had failed the National Board For Respiratory Therapy's (NBRT) professional certification examinations. The plaintiffs claimed that the tests were not predictive of ability to perform as a respiratory therapist and that the tests disproportionately excluded blacks and hispanics from the profession.[35]

The NBRT's certification process involved two stages. First, to become a "Certified Respiratory Therapy Technician," the applicant had to pass a written examination. Then to become a "Registered Respiratory Therapist," the applicant had to complete a test successfully with both written and oral elements. The tests had never been fully validated as predictive of job performance. Although the court did not rule on the validity or reasonableness of the tests because the parties agreed to a settlement, it did comment on the tests in its approval of the class action settlement. The court noted that the agreement required NBRT to validate that all its examinations were predictive of job performance. In response to objections of certified respiratory therapists who feared that the settlement would lower the standards of the profession, the court stated that any modifications made in the testing procedure would make it more predictive of job performance and would, therefore, "enhance rather than diminish the standards of the profession."[36]

Another employment discrimination case, *Davis v. City of Dallas*,[37] discusses the standard a court may use in evaluating whether the criteria of a certifier are indicia of future performance in a professional position. In *Davis*, black plaintiffs brought a class action suit under Title VII of the Civil Rights Act of 1964, claiming that the criteria used to judge applicants to be police officers were not job related and were discriminatory. In upholding the criteria, the court noted that less validation is required of criteria used in measuring applicants for professional positions, as opposed to criteria for less skilled jobs, because the skills and abilities necessary for professional positions are more difficult to define and measure.[38] This may indicate that courts would be willing to give some deference to the criteria defined by a certifier of professionals.

Although employment discrimination cases usually concern whether the criteria were too stringent, and negligence claims most likely question whether the criteria were too lax, the key to both inquiries is whether the examinations were valid and appropriate measures of ability to perform successfully in the profession. If the examinations are valid measurements, and if the examinations are administered with reasonable care, it seems courts would be less likely to find a certifier liable for the acts of its certifees.

Issues Courts Will Consider

On the basis of the cases discussed above, several questions can be posited that courts will probably address if confronted with a case involving the alleged liability of a private, nonprofit, voluntary certification organization to a third party user of the services of professionals certified by the organization.

Control Over Certifees

The more ability that the certifier has to control the actions of the professionals it has certified, the more likely it is that a court may find that the certifier has a duty to third parties and is, therefore, liable. Employer-employee situations are the most typical examples of control over a professional. A certifier is unlikely to have such direct control over its certifees. However, control could be found in a certifier's ability to revoke certification. Revocation power could be seen as an enforcement mechanism over the actions of the certified professionals, creating a duty on the part of the certifier to the professional's patients, clients, or customers.

A certification organization that does not have revocation or reviewing powers is probably less likely to be found to have control over its certifees. Both the NSPI, in *Howard* and *Meyers*, and the TRA, in *Beasock*, set standards but held no enforcement power. Both had no means as certifiers to ensure that its certifees maintained the minimum requirements of certification.

Assumption of Responsibilities of Certifees

Unlike products liability cases, where the associations may assume or be delegated responsibilities of the manufacturer, as in the *Hall* blasting cap case, it is hard to imagine a case in which the certification organization would be deemed to have assumed the duties of the professionals it certifies. It is not hard, however, to imagine a case in which the organization could be found to have assumed some of the responsibilities of the employer of the professional. If, for example, the employer hires only professionals who have been certified, then it is possible that a court could find that the certifying organization has assumed some of the duties that an employer owes to the professional's patients, clients, or customers. Such reliance by the employer would be similar to the apartment association's reliance in *Hempstead* on Underwriters' testing and certification of the fire extinguisher.

A certification organization may want to emphasize in its pronouncements and promotions that its certification merely supplements an employer's evaluation of a potential professional employee but does not supplant it.[39] Also, one distinction between certifying products and certifying professionals is that with products a tester can certify the design, which, if manufactured accordingly, should perform consistently as tested. A professional, however, is much less likely to perform in the workplace exactly as he or she performed on examinations. Therefore, an employer of a professional should reasonably expect to have to judge the professional's abilities for himself and not merely rely on the certification organization.

Certification Negligently Granted

If the criteria used to grant professional certification have been empirically validated as predictive of job performance, then a court is not likely to find the substance of the certification to be negligent. The certifying organization may be able to avoid liability even without empirically validated evidence if it can show that there are subjective elements involved in judging competence that cannot be empirically validated. The organization probably would also need to show that the minimum examination performance required for certification was sufficiently high to ensure that only competent professionals were certified.

Additionally, if the organization has established a reasonable procedure for granting certification from which it has not deviated, it is less likely to be found negligent. If, for example, the organization made an exception from its established procedures when it granted the tortious professional his or her certification, the court may be more likely to hold the organization liable to the patient, client, or customer.

Reliance by Injured Party on Certification

Reliance by the patient, client, or customer can be presumed in some kinds of cases. As shown by the *Collins* case, however, a professional certification organization may avoid liability by showing that there was no actual reliance on its certification. Conversely, as with *Hanberry*, if the plaintiff can prove actual reliance on the certification, then the organization may be liable. Also, reliance by the employer of a professional on the certifier may create liability for the certifier. Because reliance by both the public and the employers on the certification is one of the primary purposes of professional certification, the liability of certification organizations will most likely turn on considerations of duty, causation, and policy.

Reliance as Cause of Injury

As with the diver in *Meyers*, the real risk to a patient, client, or customer is a tortious professional, not the information supplied by the certifier. Nevertheless, a court could hold that if the certifying organization had not granted the certification upon which the injured plaintiff relied, the injury would not have occurred. The issue of causation is not discussed in the pertinent cases because most have dealt with dispositive motions— whether or not a cause of action had been stated. The question of causation, however, would likely be collapsed into a consideration of whether or not there was a duty. If a duty is found, causation will probably be found as well.

Nature of Injury

If the injury to the plaintiff is a physical one, as in *Hempstead* or *Hanberry*, the court is more likely to find the certifier liable than if the injury is purely monetary, as in *Benco*. However, even with a physical injury, as in *Beasock* when the plaintiff died as a result of his injury, the court may not hold a certifier liable.

Nonprofit Organization Certifier

There is some suggestion in *Hanberry* that a profit-seeking certifier is more likely to be held liable than a nonprofit one. The cases that discuss policy considerations also support this theory. These courts consider certification organizations to be quality control entities performing the quasigovernmental function of voluntarily testing the members of a profession.

Implications of Certifier Liability

Although courts may not decide a tort suit on policy grounds as forth-rightly as the *Benco* court, courts are likely to consider the policy implications of their decisions. Certification organizations provide the public with evaluations of professionals by their colleagues who, presumably, are in a better position to make such judgments than the general public.

Holding certification organizations liable for the actions of certified professionals will deter this socially beneficial activity.

However, if certification is negligently granted and subsequently relied on by a patient, client, or customer to his or her detriment, then the social benefit derived from certifiers is diminished. Therefore, in such a situation, the certification organization may be found liable.

Conclusion

The potential liability of private, nonprofit, voluntary professional certification organizations to third-party patients, clients, and customers is not clear. Policy considerations weigh against imposing liability in a wide range of circumstances. The limited case law relating to certifiers, however, could be applied to hold a certifier liable in some situations. If the court finds that 1) the certifier owed a duty to the plaintiff, 2) the certifier negligently granted the certification, 3) the injured plaintiff relied on the organization's certification of the professional, and 4) the reliance proximately caused the injury, then the certifier is likely to be liable.

Endnotes

1. *See generally* Jerald A. Jacobs, *Association Law Handbook* 2nd ed. (Washington, D.C.: Bureau of National Affairs, 1986) 331–32.
2. There have been cases brought by third parties against certifiers in other contexts. In *I.D. Rogers v. R.J. Reynolds Tobacco Co.*, 761 S.W.2d 788 (Tex. Ct. App. 1988), a deceased smoker's family and estate sued the Tobacco Institute, a trade organization, for conspiracy to conceal the negative health effects of smoking.
3. In *Zavaletta v. American Bar Association*, 721 F. Supp. 96 (E.D. Va. 1989), third year law students brought an antitrust action against the American Bar Association (ABA) asking the court to order the ABA to accredit their law school.
4. *See Kohr v. Johns-Manville Corp.* 534 F. Supp. 256, 260 (E.D. Pa. 1982) (holding that persons who provide a service cannot be held liable under theories of strict liability); *Hanberry v. Hearst Corp.*, 276 Cal. App. 2d 680, 81 Cal. Rptr. 519, 524 (1969) (stating that "one not directly involved in manufacturing products for, or supplying products to, the consuming public" could not be held liable under a theory of strict liability).
5. Section 324A of *Restatement (Second) of Torts* provides:
   One who undertakes, gratuitously or for consideration, to render services to another which he should recognize as necessary for the protection of a third person or his things, is subject to liability to the third person for physical harm resulting from his failure to exercise reasonable care to [perform] his undertaking, if
   (a) his failure to exercise reasonable care increases the risk of such harm, or
   (b) he has undertaken to perform a duty towed by the other to the third person, or
   (c) the harm is suffered because of reliance of the other or the third person upon the undertaking.
   Restatement (Second) of Torts § 324A (1965).
   Many states have adopted § 324A as a rule of law. *See* Wellington and Camisa, *The Trade Association and Product Safety Standards: Of Good Samaritans*

and Liability, 35 *Wayne Law Review* 37, 45 (1988) (citing cases in eleven different states adopting § 324A).

6. "'[D]uty' is a question of whether the defendant is under any obligation for the benefit of the particular plaintiff; and in negligence cases, the duty is always the same—to conform to the legal standard of reasonable conduct in the light of the apparent risk." Keeton, Dobbs, Keeton & Owen, *Prosser and Keeton on the Law of Torts*, 5th ed (,1984), 356.

7. Vicarious liability, meaning non-negligent *A* being held liable for the tort of negligent *B*, is currently justified on the policy grounds of shifting the risk to one better able to allocate its cost and prevent the occurrence of harm. *See* Keeton, Dobbs, Keeton & Owen, *Prosser & Keeton on The Law of Torts*, 5th ed., 1984), 499–501. In addition, joint enterprise liability—each participant in a joint undertaking being vicariously liable for the acts of others in the enterprise—turns on, among other factors, "equal right of control." *Prosser & Keeton* at 517–18.

8. 269 F. Supp. 109 (D. Del. 1967).

9. See 260 F. Supp. at 117.

10. The *Hempstead* court seemed to suggest that in Virginia there could only be liability without privity if the product were "imminently dangerous." *See* 260 F. Supp. at 117–18.

11. 276 Cal. App. 2d 680, 81 Cal. Rptr. 519 (1969).

12. *See* 81 Cal. Rptr. at 523.

13. *See* 81 Cal. Rptr. at 521–22.

14. 387 F. Supp. 772 (E.D. Tenn. 1974).

15. 387 F. Supp. at 786.

16. 387 F. Supp. at 786.

17. 345 F. Supp. 353 (E.D.N.Y. 1972).

18. *See* 345 F. Supp. 374–75.

19. *See* 345 F. Supp. 367.

20. 130 Misc.2d 25, 494 N.Y.S.2d 974 (1985).

21. *Beasock*, 494 N.Y.S.2d at 979.

22. 220 N.J. Super. 73, 531 A.2d 398 (1987).

23. *See* 531 A.2d at 401.

24. 531 A.2d at 404–05.

25. *See* 531 A.2d at 405.

26. 531 A.2d at 406.

27. 531 A.2d at 407.

28. 133 Misc.2d 50, 506 N.Y.S.2d 523 (1986), *aff'd*, 134 A.D.2d 926, 522 N.Y.S.2d 388 (1987).

29. 506 N.Y.S.2d at 525.

30. *Cf.* 506 N.Y.S.2d 523 (1986).

31. 693 F.2d 636 (7th Cir. 1982).

32. In another case, *Harmon v. National Automotive Parts Ass'n*, 720 F. Supp. 79 (N.D. Miss. 1989), the court held that proof of reliance would have to be shown before any theory of liability could prevail. In *Harmon*, the plaintiff had been injured when his truck battery, which bore the National Automotive Parts Association (NAPA) label, exploded in his face. The court held that NAPA could not be liable on strict liability or negligence claims because it "was not so involved in the placing of this battery in the stream of commerce that it should be treated as a manufacturer." 720 F. Supp. 81.

    The court did not answer the question as to whether one who "allows the use of its name on certain products" should be held liable. 720 F. Supp. at 81. The court did note, however, that policy considerations weighed against extending liability to a nonprofit corporation which did not charge for the licensing of its name, did not control the pricing of the products bearing its name, and therefore could not effectively spread the cost of liability among all consumers. 720 F. Supp. at 82.

33. *See* 693 F.2d at 639–640.

34. No. 75 C 3430 (E.D. Ill. July 14, 1980) (LEXIS, Genfed library, Newer file).

35. Additionally, the plaintiffs claimed that several hospitals along with the NBRT and the American Association for Respiratory Therapy (AART) had violated

the Sherman Act by attempting to monopolize the profession and by refusing to deal with non-certified applicants for respiratory therapists' positions.

36. *Veizaga*, No. 75 C 3430, at 5 (LEXIS, Genfed library, Newer file).

37. 777 F.2d 205 (5th Cir. 1985).

38. 777 F.2d at 215–16.

39. In cases involving safety inspections of workplaces, some courts have distinguished between "supplementing" another's legal duty and actually "supplanting" the duty, finding liability only in the latter case. *See Blessing v. United States*, 447 F. Supp. 1160, 1194 (E.D. Pa. 1978) (holding that the defendant would be liable to third parties for a negligent inspection only if it had undertaken the inspection "*in lieu* of" the one who actually owed the duty) (emphasis in original). *But see Santillo v. Chambersburg Engineering Co.*, 603 F. Supp. 211, 215 (E.D. Pa. 1985), *appeal dismissed*, 802 F.2d 447 (3d Cir.), *aff'd*, 802 F.2d 448 (3d Cir. 1986) (holding that "one does not have to assume the entire responsibility of another party" to be liable to third parties for safety inspections).

4

Confidentiality of Records

In the course of both research and credentialing activities, credentialing organizations gather and analyze information on a confidential basis. Frequently, third parties seek access to the files of credentialing organizations through discovery procedures for the purposes of their own litigation. To fulfill their previous guarantees of confidentiality and ensure future participation in their fact-finding efforts, credentialing organizations consider it essential that the integrity of their files be maintained.

This chapter provides a general overview of the pertinent case law and suggests strategies for protecting the confidentiality of credentialing, investigation, and research files.

Summary

When a credentialing organization is not a party to litigation but is confronted with a discovery request for material from confidential files, it might consider the following:

(I). Do not divulge any information whatsoever, because a court might later find that it had breached a confidence or waived any privilege that otherwise would have been respected.

(II). Refer the parties to other sources for the same information, because courts generally will consider whether the information sought is available with less burden from another source.

(III). Seek to quash the subpoena and seek a protective order, both on the basis of an absolute or qualified privilege and under the court's general supervisory powers over discovery and a balancing test of the relative burdens and needs involved, using arguments from among the following, if applicable.

    A. The credentialing organization is not a party to the underlying lawsuit and, therefore, is especially entitled to protection against overdiscovery.

    B. The information was gathered under a pledge and reasonable expectation of confidentiality and it could not have been gathered without such confidentiality.

    C. The discovery request is speculative or a "fishing expedition."

    D. The information that is sought is irrelevant to the underlying claim or at least does not go to the "heart" of it.

    E. Even if the information sought is relevant, the parties have

not demonstrated a sufficient need for it, which would out-
weigh the burdens imposed upon the organization by disclosure.

F. The organization only has information about the general subject and not about the specific facts of the underlying lawsuit.

G. Not only the data, but also the sources of information are
confidential.

H. The discovery request is similar to past discovery requests or
potential future ones, so compliance would require vast expenditures of time and money, all the more so with redaction
of the materials.

I. The credentialing organization must appear through its individual volunteers, whose expert opinions are a valuable com-
modity, and compelling their testimony represents a form of
involuntary servitude.

J. The information constitutes part of academic and scientific
research, and disclosure would create a chilling effect that
would deter individuals from participating in the future with
the same candor.

K. Courts have recognized that credentialing organizations further important societal interests through academic, scientific,
and peer review work.

L. The particular research or investigation is on-going and premature disclosure of the information would cut off a necessary
in-flow of information as well as undermine the credibility of
the results.

M. The organization provides the public with information through
its credentialing pronouncements and, therefore, is entitled to
a journalist's privilege.

N. First Amendment associational rights protect the organization's relationships, which are threatened by prying into confidential relationships.

O. The organization engages in critical examination of its constituent field, which cannot take place without guarantees of
confidentiality and which, therefore, should be protected by
the privilege extended to critical self-examination processes
in other contexts.

P. The organization's investigatory functions are similar to a government agency's and, therefore, it should be protected, as are
the agencies.

(IV). In the alternative, the credentialing organization might seek to distinguish between the raw data and statistics it has gathered, and
its analyses and opinions, seeking protection for the latter.

(V). In the alternative, the organization might seek an *in camera* inspection for particularly sensitive items.

A professional certification or academic accreditation organization
will probably not be able to establish an absolute privilege, but it might
be able to establish a qualified one. Even if it is unable to establish a
qualified privilege, courts most likely will perform a balancing of the
burdens and needs of discovery. The case law shows an almost even
mix of cases favoring and limiting discovery and no clear trend.

Background

Few cases have directly addressed the question of whether a non-party, nonprofit private organization's investigation files are protected by a privilege. In two of the cases, the privilege was rejected; in one case, it was accepted in part; and in the last, it was accepted in whole.

Discovery of Non-Party Files

The leading state case in this area is *Berst v. Chipman*.[1] There, a newspaper defending a libel action sought to discover documents and information gained by the National Collegiate Athletic Association (NCAA), a non-party, in the course of its investigation of the same controversy that gave rise to the libel suit. The Kansas Supreme Court held that the newspaper could "discover only specified statements made to [the NCAA investigator] by the litigants, their fellow employees and other individuals, which were *specifically relevant to the libel action*."[2]

The court repeatedly mentioned that the NCAA had a policy of keeping all of its investigation materials confidential.[3] In the NCAA files, "there may be allegations and speculation about an individual's sexual preferences, mental capacity, drug and alcohol use, and financial condition; academic records," and "anonymous letter and memoranda of telephone calls, and internal memoranda of interviews which contain the investigator's mental impressions, speculations and conclusions."[4] The NCAA also kept a member institution's formal response to an investigation confidential.

The NCAA's policy of confidentiality created the interests that weighed against discovery, which were: 1) the privacy of persons "to whom information in the files relates;" 2) the privacy of persons "who have passed on information to the NCAA under a pledge of confidentiality;" and 3) the NCAA's ability to conduct "one of its primary functions," policing its membership.[5]

On the other hand, the interests that weighed in favor of discovery included the general policy of a public "right to every man's evidence."[6] Moreover, the information sought went to "the 'heart of the plaintiff's claim,'" which alone might have been sufficient to outbalance all countervailing considerations.[7] The last considerations were the possibility that, *without* the information, the newspaper defendant would have to "go on a 'fishing expedition'" and that the defendant had a "limited amount of time" to prepare its defense.[8]

Despite holding that the newspaper would be able to conduct discovery of the confidential files, the court wrote that "a key limitation on a litigant's right to discover material held in the hands of another" is relevancy.[9] The defendant had admitted that not all of the information within the NCAA files was "*connected with [the plaintiff's] or the newspaper's defense*." (emphasis in original).[10] Thus, the court ordered an *in camera* inspection as "an appropriate and useful proceeding."[11]

The aspect of this case most threatening to confidentiality is the court's willingness to accept the defendant's claim that the information goes to the "heart" of a claim, especially as the court's scrutiny of that claim was no more than cursory and it made that claim dispositive. Furthermore, the reversal of the usual "fishing expedition" concern gives parties seeking discovery a method of avoiding any requirement that they exhaust other sources for the requested information. To some extent, it allows courts and parties seeking discovery to ignore other sources of the same information. The court acknowledged that "it may have been possible for the [newspaper] to gather on its own the same information."[12]

Berst is distinguishable on three factual grounds. First, the NCAA is described as a voluntary organization of 750 colleges and universities. One of its "primary duties" is enforcing standards for "recruiting, admissions, financial aid and academic standards."[13] The Supreme Court, however, has recognized that sports leagues are different from other organizations, as the existence of organized sports requires cooperation among the teams and a structure for rulemaking.[14] So, in a significant sense, the NCAA is a party to the events. The underlying libel action in *Berst* is not described, but the NCAA's investigations are more likely to be conducted with press and public attention.

Next, as the Kansas Supreme Court itself recognized, the claim that information goes to the "heart" of a claim is especially relevant "in a libel action."[15] Although the claim may not be entirely irrelevant in other contexts, it at least is not as "crucial."[16] Finally, the court also found it important that the newspaper only had "a limited amount of time in which to conduct an investigation."[17] Again, while time pressures always exist in litigation, other courts will not necessarily find them as critical in other cases.

The leading federal case in this area is *Wright v. Patrolmen's Benevolent Association*.[18] There, the plaintiff judge sought to discover information obtained by the New York bar association, a non-party, in its investigation of the plaintiff's transfer from one division of the bench to another. The court denied the bar's motion for a protective order.

The bar asserted that any First Amendment journalist's privilege should be extended to it, because "it provided information to the public in the same manner . . ."[19] The court rejected this argument in part based on the Supreme Court's concerns about the definition of a *journalist*.[20] Additionally, it distinguished cases that did extend the privilege, based on the fact that in such cases, the sources were unknown. In the instant case, the plaintiff had been able to identify all of the sources and only wished to know what they had said.[21]

The bar also argued that its files should be protected under a privilege for critical self-examination. The court assumed that such a privilege existed, but held that it was a qualified one. It applied to protect only opinions and conclusions, and not to shield factual and statistical information.[22] Finally, the court rejected any limitation of discovery based on "the possible existence of other avenues of inquiry."[23]

The language in *Berst* and *Wright* that suggests a disregard of other sources for the desired information is limited by Fed. R. Civ. Pro. 26(b)(1)(i)(as amended 1983), which expressly refers to the possibility that discovery "is obtainable from some other source that is more convenient, less burdensome, or less expensive . . . ." If the Rule itself is ambiguous at all, the Comment makes it clear that it is meant "to deal with the problem of over-discovery."[24] The Rule specifies that when the discovery is obtainable from another source, it "*shall* be limited by the court . . ." (emphasis added).[25] Thus, a court may have considerable latitude in determining whether the discovery actually is obtainable from another source, but once it has decided that it is, then it may not have discretion over whether to limit discovery.

Cases that cite *Berst* and *Wright* do not involve non-party organizations. The two opinions represent the extreme in favor of discovery. *Berst* at least requires relevancy and an *in camera* inspection, and *Wright* protects opinions and conclusions. No court will allow discovery of irrelevant material, but parties from whom discovery is sought bear the preliminary burden of demonstrating why it should be limited. Most courts will perform an *in camera* inspection or at least consider arguments regarding specific materials that are sought.

Factual versus Analytical Data

Like *Berst*, the other federal case in this area also divided the information sought to be discovered into two categories: 1) "factual or statistical data," and 2) "analyses or opinions drawn from such materials."[26]

In *Ross*, the underlying suit alleged illegal trading in securities. The plaintiff and defendant both sought information from the investigative files of the non-party National Associational of Securities Dealers (NASD).

NASD had prevailed in two similar cases.[27] It already had agreed to furnish the defendant's monthly trading blotters and confirmation slips, but it refused to produce anything else.

The court specifically allowed NASD to withhold "twenty-odd unsworn depositions" on the grounds that "the witnesses deposed as well as the questions asked reveal the nature and direction of [the] investigation."[28] Although the court rejected NASD's argument that it was entitled to a quasi-governmental privilege, it accepted the same reasoning as showing that NASD had an interest similar to the government's in "encouraging witness cooperation" and "maintaining the integrity of its investigative techniques."[29]

Moreover, the court found it significant that NASD's investigation had focused on nationwide trading patterns and not the instant parties.[30] The fact that NASD was not a party to the underlying litigation served to distinguish the case from a later case in which the Mercantile Exchange made the same privilege claims, but in which it also was a party.[31]

Admittedly, *Ross* permits the discovery of factual and statistical information. But the factual and statistical information available from NASD probably differs significantly from the "facts" available from most other nonprofit organizations. That is, NASD's monthly trading blotters and the like are much closer to raw empirical data. Most private organization credentialing information, even the most factually oriented of it, is likely to be more impressionistic and contain an evaluative element. Any of this purely factual information likely can be found through other sources.

Given that *Ross* permits the discovery of factual and statistical information, it remains a useful case. As NASD, other credentialing organizations have a stake in preserving the integrity of their investigatory work. Under the *Ross* court's standards, a legally significant difference exists between a credentialing organization's work when it has studied only a general phenomenon, for example, in peer review of research, as distinct from the occasions when it has examined a particular case, for example, in investigating claims of an individual's ethical transgressions. If it has only general knowledge and no particular contact with the facts of the underlying litigation, then its case is strengthened. Its link to the case is even more tenuous than that of a non-party.

Protection by Privilege

The only case recognizing a privilege for nonprofit organizations' confidential investigations was *Petition of Illinois Judicial Inquiry Board.*[32] There, the Illinois Judicial Inquiry Board sought records relating to the Chicago Bar Association (CBA) evaluation of Cook County judges. Since its founding in 1874, the CBA had conducted confidential evaluations of judges and released recommendations. The court held that the Judicial Inquiry Board had not shown a particularized need for the information and, therefore, could not obtain it.

The court used Professor Wigmore's four-part test for privileges.[33] It "stress[ed]" that both the Judicial Inquiry Board and the CBA were "keenly concerned with the betterment of the judiciary."[34] Both parties served the public interest; the question was "how that public interest is best served."[35]

The court analogized the discovery of the bar's judicial review process to discovery of a journalist's confidential sources and discovery of confidential peer review processes.[36] The court distinguished *Wright* as involving a party seeking discovery with knowledge of the sources of the statements. Unfortunately, the court also distinguished *Wright* as involving a voluntary release of some information to the party seeking discovery, which "eroded" the later "claim of confidentiality."[37] Although parties from whom discovery is sought rightly attempt to cooperate by directing inquiries elsewhere and even by furnishing non-confidential information, often without negative consequences imposed by courts, this decision and a handful of others may leave a credentialing organization with no option but an absolute position, if it is to preserve any confidentiality.[38] Thus, however repugnant complete "stone-walling" might be, it is the prudent course in this situation.

Arguments Against Discovery

In conclusion, this small group of cases suggests seven different arguments that a credentialing organization may advance when faced with discovery requests. To maximize the protection against discovery, the organization can: 1) characterize the information sought as irrelevant or at least not going to the "heart" of the underlying claim; 2) characterize the discovery request as speculative or a "fishing expedition;" 3) emphasize that it is not a party to the suit; 4) when possible, refer the parties to other sources for the same information and point out to the court that discovery from the other sources would be less burdensome; 5) when possible, point out that it has only information about the general subject and not about the specific facts involved in the suit; 6) when possible, point out that the sources themselves and not just the data are confidential; and 7) in the alternative, distinguish between its analyses and opinions it has developed and the facts and statistics given to it. Again, a credentialing organization should not release any information without determining that it is not even arguably confidential, lest its cooperation be used against it.

In some instances, credentialing organizations in scientific and medical fields can also rely directly on two other lines of cases, involving: 1) non-parties' academic and scientific research; and 2) medical peer review statutes. In addition, five related lines of cases are frequently used to draw analogies in analyzing discovery requests directed at private organizations: 1) the First Amendment's journalists' privilege; 2) the First Amendment's associational rights; 3) the critical self-examination privilege; 4) academic peer review privileges; and 5) the government's various privileges.[39]

Protection for Academic and Scientific Research

The federal courts have yet to recognize the often-proposed absolute privilege for academic and scientific research. Nonetheless, they have usually extended limited protection from discovery to research files. A handful of cases have recognized a qualified privilege.

In the most common line of cases, although the courts decline to recognize an academic privilege, they then consistently use their general discretionary powers over discovery to limit its scope, often substantially.[40]

Indeed, the courts often unequivocally reject the existence of any academic privilege, despite a holding protecting the confidentiality of research. One federal district court, for example, agreed with the holding in a case refusing to quash a subpoena, that, "there is no general academic privilege," and "assertions of confidentiality of sources do not confer absolute immunity."[41] But the court immediately turned to its discretionary authority to control the discovery process.

The research in question was part of the same study of jeep-type vehicles that was involved in *Wright*,[42] which also had been sought in a third reported case as well as an unreported one, and which potentially would be sought in 88 more suits pending in the federal courts.[43] The court concluded that a balancing of the burdens, needs, and circumstances required that it quash the subpoena.[44] Professors Wright and Graham have criticized this opinion as "frankly using [a] protective order to supply protection not available under applicable state law."[45]

Qualified Privilege in Seventh Circuit

The three cases that come closest to creating an absolute privilege stop just short of doing so. The Seventh Circuit has written the most opinions in this area, and it has gone as far as establishing a qualified privilege. The circuit began in a case involving research on the toxic effects of herbicides on monkeys, by discussing a First Amendment interest of academic freedom as "properly figur[ing] into the legal calculation of whether forced disclosure would be reasonable," but it did not expressly decide that a privilege existed, in *Dow Chemical Co. v. Allen*.[46] It reserved the question of privilege.[47] In *Dow*, the research had not yet been completed.

The Seventh Circuit later considered the confidentiality interest of research conducted by the Registry for Hormonal Transplacental Carcinogenesis at the University of Chicago, the only repository of information about that particular disease. It relied on its earlier opinion to state, "We agree *arguendo* that the [research] files may enjoy a qualified privilege and are not to be pried into unnecessarily; however, such privileges are not absolute," in *Deitchman v. E.R. Squibb & Sons, Inc.*[48] Again, the research was on-going, and presumably would be on-going in perpetuity.

The New York state courts, in a product liability suit against tobacco companies, have come almost as close to recognizing a privilege.[49] The tobacco companies sought the production of "data, tapes, documentation relating to interviews, questionnaires, medical records, death certificates, x-rays, autopsies and computer tapes as well as previous or follow-up studies using a subset or superset of data" and material from "present, on-going medical research."[50] All of the requested materials related to studies of the relationship between cigarette smoking, asbestos exposures, and cancer. With as much of a discussion of the practical difficulties of gathering the 324 linear feet of materials, contained in 97 file cabinet drawers in 19 separate file cabinets and 250 bound volumes, as of academic freedom, the court used language and reasoning very similar to that of the Seventh Circuit. It referred to the doctors' "opportunity of first publication of their work," and a possible chilling effect of discovery on "future scientific endeavors" to conclude that an "interest in academic freedom may properly figure in the legal calculation of whether forced disclosures would be reasonable."[51] It held that "compliance with the subpoenae would place an unreasonable burden upon the medical and scientific institutions involved and would unduly disrupt the ongoing research. . . ."[52]

Second Circuit Rejection of Privilege

Only a few courts, but notably including the Second Circuit, have both refused to recognize an academic privilege as well as refused to give any protection to files.[53]

In an opinion likely to become the most important decision favoring discovery, the Second Circuit discussed a request by tobacco companies for data, similar to the one made in *R.J. Reynolds*.[54] The Second Circuit acknowledged that the Seventh Circuit had recognized a qualified privilege, but characterized it as "principally to protect scholars from the premature disclosure of their research."[55] But the Second Circuit described the New York state court opinion in *R.J. Reynolds*[56] as "discursive" and not necessarily "based on the existence of a privilege."[57] The Second Circuit upheld the federal district court's protective order, which allowed researchers to redact identifying information, such as names and social security numbers, but not counties of residence, union locals, and birth and death dates.[58] The court also reduced the burden imposed by discovery to the risk of plagiarism, dismissing any burden of time and effort as "most gainfully employed discovery targets could contend that compliance would take time away from their regular work," and because "publication" of studies invites their use.[59] Notwithstanding its lack of concern for the time burden placed on the researchers, the court then found that the "inordinate amount of time" that the tobacco companies would need to duplicate the requested study established a sufficient need for the information.

The court stated that, in the federal proceedings, the tobacco companies altered their requests significantly. They sought only computer tapes, rather than raw data in their original form, and they restricted the request to material pertaining to events prior to publication of the studies.[60] Taken as a whole, though, the holding was a victory for the tobacco companies seeking discovery. The victory is especially significant because the Second Circuit ruled as a matter of law rather than based solely on the facts of the instant case. Factors that other courts were willing to consider in a balancing process, such as a chilling effect on research, are simply irrelevant in the Second Circuit's approach— or, to the extent that they are weighed, it is not to protect research data from discovery but only from "needlessly repetitive disclosures."[61]

Compulsion of Testimony from Experts

Finally, a handful of cases have addressed the subject of compelling individual experts to present their opinions, either in depositions or at trial.[62] The early cases in this area involved professionals who collectively decided not to appear as witnesses in malpractice suits.[63]

Later cases have not involved the same mass refusal to cooperate, but instead have focused on individuals who do not wish to be retained as experts. In a Massachusetts criminal prosecution, for example, the defendants sought to compel an expert on voice identification, who planned to vacation overseas, to appear at trial.[64] The court held "that a party may not by summons compel the involuntary testimony of an expert witness solely for the expertise he may bring to trial, and in the absence of any personal knowledge on his part related to the issues before the judge and the jury."[65]

Rhode Island has established an apparently absolute privilege against compelled expert testimony, on the grounds that it "would in essence involve a form of involuntary servitude that should not normally be inflicted upon a person merely because of his professional expertise."[66] There, the plaintiffs in a personal injury accident sought to compel a physician to appear at trial as an expert witness.[67]

Most of these cases turn heavily on the fact that the individual expert witness is unwilling to testify as to his opinion about the facts in litigation. They do not directly address the question of an organization or an individual attempting to protect the confidentiality of research already completed or in progress, with the exception of an Iowa case that tangentially involves such research.[68]

There, the plaintiff learned that the defendant physician in her medical malpractice suit had provided factual information to the National Bariatric Surgery Registry at the University of Iowa. She sought to depose the director of that registry for both the factual information he had acquired and his expert opinion on the medical treatment underlying the suit.[69] "The case does not make it clear why the defendant had provided information to the director of the registry, but it does make it clear that the defendant did so confidentially and to the expert in [the expert's] capacity as director of the registry."[70]

The director of the registry did appear at his deposition and "he answered all questions involving the factual information but repeatedly refused to answer any questions based on his expertise."[71] The expert's willingness to answer factual questions, notwithstanding the confidentiality in which he had received the information, makes the case difficult to rely on for the protection of confidences. As in *Ondis*,[72] the expert presented economic arguments. His testimony would be "a form of intellectual property with considerable economic value."[73] The court accepted the argument, to the extent that compelled testimony would represent "the abrogation of an expert's right to freely contract for his services."[74] It ultimately held that the trial courts would have "wide discretion" in quashing subpoenas or issuing protective orders, and in compelling testimony "whenever a litigant establishes a compelling need for the testimony."[75]

States that have adopted a rule prohibiting compelled testimony from experts for reasons unrelated to confidentiality, such as Rhode Island and possibly New York, should have an even greater reason to prohibit the disclosure of confidential research materials. The expert who for her own reasons, economic or otherwise, wishes not to testify does not present as compelling a case as the expert who wishes not to testify in the interest of research that serves the public and because of promises of confidentiality.

This area of the law is still developing. The trend has been favorable to the experts, but wide variations exist among the states.

Decisions in the Absence of a Privilege

Aside from the specific discussions of a privilege for academic and scientific research, the Supreme Court has made it clear that "evidentiary privileges are not favored, and even those rooted in the Constitution must give way in proper circumstances."[76] They are not favored because "they are in derogation of the search for truth."[77]

But "it is well-settled that disclosure of subpoenaed information may be restricted where compliance would force an unreasonable burden on the party from whom production is sought."[78] Furthermore, the "liberal discovery provisions" of the federal rules are the "very reason that the application of the rules of discovery [are] subject to the supervisory discretion of the trial judge . . ."[79]

It is not unprecedented, in other contexts, for a federal district court to provide detailed rules regulating discovery, including specific provisions for claimed privileges.[80]

Accordingly, attempts to shield confidential files should begin with an argument for privilege, but should then devote a substantial amount of energy to the more successful argument that the discovery request is simply unreasonable. The case law is well-developed, but no single test of reasonableness has emerged. Instead, a multitude of different factors figure in the balancing, none of them alone dispositive.

Actions of Federal District Courts in Diversity

When addressing a federal question, "federal common law is the source of any privilege."[81] When sitting in diversity, however, the federal district court should apply the law of the place of the deposition with regard to privileges.[82] When the federal district court is ruling on the discovery motion only, with the case itself pending elsewhere, "because such 'ancillary' courts will find it more difficult to have a complete understanding of the case and what is relevant," they "therefore, should err on the side of permitting discovery."[83] The procedural rules governing privilege questions suggest tactical considerations in scheduling depositions for states in which favorable case law exists, and filing any motions to limit discovery in the same district court in which the action itself is pending, to avoid any bias toward permitting discovery.

It is well established that Federal Rule of Civil Procedure 26(b)(4), which governs discovery regarding experts, does not apply unless the expert's facts and opinions have been acquired or developed in anticipation of litigation. Thus, it almost certainly will not apply when discovery is sought from a non-party.[84]

Rather, either Rule 26(b)(1) governing the scope and limits of discovery in general,[85] or Rule 26(c) governing protective orders, will be used to analyze the burden of producing the information and the need for it.[86,87] Under these Rules, generally, "[t]he person resisting discovery on the basis of confidentiality must first demonstrate that disclosure might be harmful. . . . The burden then shifts to the party seeking discovery to establish that the disclosure is both relevant and necessary to the action."[88] The fact that it is a non-party from whom information is sought is "far from decisive" but is "entitled to some measure of consideration."[89] The federal district court is given wide discretion in ruling on quashing subpoenas and an appellate court will reverse a decision only with a showing of "a clear abuse of discretion."[90]

Several courts have expanded upon the list of factors presented in the Federal Rules. In *Anker*, the court gave the following list of considerations, which essentially parallel the Federal Rules: 1) whether the discovery is cumulative and available elsewhere; 2) whether the party seeking it has had an opportunity to obtain it elsewhere; 3) whether it would be unduly burdensome and expensive, taking into account, a) the needs of the case; b) the amount in controversy; c) the parties' resources; d) the importance of the issue in litigation; and e) the societal interests in full and complete litigation, along with f) the values "deserv[ing] of confidentiality or protection even though not formally privileged."[91]

An early Second Circuit opinion added the following considerations: 1) whether the expert is called because of his knowledge of the facts of the case as opposed to general knowledge; 2) whether the expert is asked for a previously formed opinion or a new one; 3) whether the expert is unique and whether a comparable witness can be found; 4) whether the expert "has been oppressed by having continually to testify."[92] As in the cases directly addressing the question of the confidentiality of an association's files, Professor Wigmore's test has also been cited in the academic and scientific privilege context.[93]

The Burdens of Discovery

If discovery were allowed, a credentialing organization would suffer two distinct types of burdens: a) the immediate burden of the economic and practical difficulties of gathering files, litigating the confidentiality issues, and then possibly preparing for depositions, which is not related to and which indirectly hinders the organization's important credentialing functions; and b) the long-term burden of eroding confidence and, thus, participation in the evaluative and research processes, which directly hinders the organization's credentialing functions. The courts have recognized both types of burdens. The case law is mixed on the importance of the immediate practical burden, but generally sympathetic to claims of the long-term burden.

The burden of showing the existence of a privilege is on the party from whom discovery is sought.[94] Moreover, a credentialing organization faces the same task as Sisyphus; it can momentarily lift its burden, but it can never free itself. Neither *res judicata* nor collateral estoppel "can be raised in a subsequent discovery attempt."[95] "Nor does the relevance of [research] to lawsuits . . . come within a statutory limitations period."[96] Ironically, an expert must litigate to persuade the court to take into account the burden of repeatedly litigating. And even if in every instance the expert prevails in protecting the confidentiality of its files, it has incurred the expense, time, and trouble of going through the process of doing so.

Even though the *Snyder* court ultimately quashed the subpoena, which was directed toward an expert who had retired and moved from Michigan to Arizona, and sought the same research on jeep-type vehicles as in three previous cases and potentially in 88 pending suits, it still noted that each subpoena "calls for a fresh weighing" of the issues.[97] But it made "the series of legal skirmishes . . . imposed on the researcher who is a stranger to each of [the] lawsuits" almost dispositive. Such legal skirmishes "might suffice to establish the excessively burdensome nature" of the discovery request.[98] As another court dealing with the research on jeep-type vehicles wrote, "Compliance with the subpoena would require the expert who has no direct connection with the litigation to spend many days testifying and disclosing all of the raw data . . . accumulated over the course of a long and detailed study."[99]

Other courts, themselves not faced with the repeated requests of the jeep-type vehicle research cases, have accorded less weight to the immediate practical burdens of complying with a subpoena. In one case in which market analysts were subpoenaed by the government for an antitrust action against IBM and sought to invoke privileges, although not on the basis of confidentiality concerns, the court wrote that it "would indeed have cause for concern if, for example, a world-renowned surgeon were forced to spend a considerable share of his time in the courtroom rather than the operating room; the interest in saving lives outweighs a party's interests in obtaining testimony from an expert having no previous connection to the case."[100] Still, the immediate case did not present the same concern, presumably because the experts had been called upon on only one occasion. Also, the government claimed that the experts "had initially agreed to testify but later declined at the direction of their firms."[101]

Another court has virtually rejected the immediate practical burden as relevant: the fact that an expert "may well be subject to multiple subpoenas from many plaintiffs as may occur in DES litigation, auto-mobile crash litigation or IUD litigation" only "rarely" justifies quashing a subpoena.[102] Again, the *Anker* court was considering only "the first subpoena which [the expert] has received."[103] It suggested that the party seeking the deposition and records on IUD research should "keep such records and make them available to subsequent requesters." Worse, in *American Tobacco*,[104] the court altered the purpose of balancing, so that a balance favoring the party from whom discovery is sought "does not warrant a bar against disclosure but only protection against needlessly repetitive disclosure." Unlike almost all other courts, the *American Tobacco* court reduced the "legitimate chilling effect" to plagiarism by other researchers.[105]

The *Snyder* court's concerns and the *Anker* court's solution can be harmonized, but with the inequitable result of requiring that experts and credentialing organizations which are successful in protecting their con-fidential files, by virtue of their success, incur the greatest expense of repeated litigation. Conversely, experts and credentialing organizations that fail in their efforts to protect their confidential files will not have to continue litigating the issue, but will see their work collected and disseminated by third parties. In other words, *res judicata* and collateral estoppel in this area do not operate to protect the party from whom information is sought, but rather to ensure that once a single party has breached the confidence, all other parties also will be able to do the same.

The second and more important burden imposed by the discovery of academic and scientific research files is the long-term impact on the guarantees of confidence necessary to conduct much of the work. Most courts have recognized that discovery can exert a chilling effect.[106] The individuals deterred from participation in research include not only scholars considering an area of research or participation as a peer re-viewer, but also lay persons who contribute vital data to studies.[107]

Indeed, several courts have termed repeated discovery the equiv-alent of harassment, especially when it is conducted by corporations or individuals whose products or services are negatively evaluated in the research.[108] One court went so far as to write, "It is not unduly speculative to imagine that a large private corporation, through repeated securing broad-based subpoenas ... could make research in a particular field so undesirable as to chill or inhibit whole areas of scientific inquiry."[109]

The fear of a chilling effect forms a large part of the motivation for restricting discovery attempts. "[T]he courts, in order to prevent a chilling of the uninhibited conduct of academic and scientific research, have recognized an interest in protecting from discovery the analyses, opinions and conclusions drawn from researchers from their data."[110] In *Plough*, the National Academy of Sciences (NAS), a non-party, had been retained not to conduct research itself but to review the results of a pilot study of the relationship between aspirin use and Reye's Syndrome, conducted by the United States Department of Health and Human Services in conjunction with a private contractor. The NAS did not perform the actual experiments, but its participation in the research process was vital. The *Plough* court emphasized that the party seeking discovery already had access to the raw data from the pilot study and was pursuing the NAS evaluation.[111]

The same policy considerations were articulated in *Solarex*.[112] In that case, the defendant in a patent infringement case sought the identity of a peer reviewer who had evaluated a manuscript submitted to the American Physical Society, a nonprofit scholarly organization.[113]

The court referred to Professor Wigmore's four-part test and rejected part of the Society's argument under that test, in part because "[t]he Wigmore model seems calculated to advance a societal interest in a close personal relationship, such as attorney-client or husband-wife." In the peer review process, however, "we have neither a close personal relationship nor an individual who is benefitted by the disclosure of personal information within the confines of such a relationship."[114] Regardless, the Society has an interest in protecting the confidentiality of the peer reviewer. The party seeking discovery "has adduced no facts to dispute the Society's showing that confidentiality of reviewers is necessary to preserve the integrity of its peer review process."[115] The court concluded that "the Society ha[d] demonstrated a strong interest in preserving the confidentiality of the reviewer's identity" and that "the values it seeks to foster in resisting this disclosure have traditionally been accorded substantial weight in assessing the competing needs and hardships involved in pre-trial discovery."[116]

The concern about a chilling effect becomes stronger when the subject of research is more controversial or of greater public interest. Questions of public policy are, as one court tautologically stated, "the very subjects in which the public interest is greatest."[117]

The long-term burden on the party from whom discovery is sought increases when the research is continuing and when the sources of the data are confidential. When the research is ongoing, the chilling effect is greater. In *Deitchman*,[118] the researcher's "real and deepest objection is that he must be allowed to divulge to the public the results of his studies only in his own time and way." The party seeking the discovery "not surprisingly, makes absolutely no counter-showing" that "the loss of confidentiality will adversely affect the research and that, as the district judge stated, 'all society will be the poorer.' "[119]

Similarly in *Plough*,[120] the court wrote that "[e]ven limited dis-closure of the preliminary conclusions, hypotheses, thoughts and ideas . . . prior to their being test[ed] and criticized" would "discourage" free deliberation and possibly cause some individuals to "refrain from participating in [the research] altogether."[121]

When an expert has completed the information-gathering for a study, but has not yet delivered the study to the sponsor, then "unlike the [*Deitchman*] public health project, there is simply no factual basis . . . for concluding that [the] 'study' is any way dependent on a continuing 'in-flow' of information."[122] Consequently, there also is no reason to protect the facts gathered in the research—although the court did allow the expert "at her own expense, [to] redact from the documents which she produces the names of individuals who communicated with her under a promise of confidentiality."[123]

In *Kennedy*, the parties seeking the discovery were plaintiffs in a sex-discrimination action brought against the state police and the study was a sociology Ph.D. thesis on gender integration in that very police force.[124] The case does not make clear whether the Ph.D. thesis would have been subject to peer review or exactly what else remained unfinished.[125]

Several cases mention the fact that corporations, in particular, may purposefully chill research that negatively evaluates its products.[126] They may be distinguishable on that basis from cases in which individuals, particularly plaintiffs, seek discovery from the same sources and under the same conditions. The identity of the party seeking discovery in and of itself should not be legally relevant, and no case has turned on that fact.[127]

Irrespective of the identity of the party seeking discovery, the mere fact that confidential information could be revealed to other sources—in violation of not only the promise of confidentiality but also the ethical standards of academic and scientific research—can chill research in sensitive areas. While an individual plaintiff seeking discovery is unlikely to do so repeatedly, he or she may be joined by many other plaintiffs who wish to obtain the same information. The only difference between the individual plaintiff's and the corporate defendant's request is that the former party is unlikely to *intend* any harassment. The chilling effect remains the same.

When a credentialing organization faces subpoenas of its confiden-tial files relating to academic or scientific research, it can point out the two different burdens that are imposed. The immediate practical burden, which affects the organization regardless of its success in opposing subpoenas, and which arguably increases with success, becomes more persuasive when the organization has previously faced similar discovery requests or anticipates further litigation on the subject. Although the court cannot alleviate the burden entirely, by ruling against discovery it can deter future requests. The long-term erosion of confidence pre-sents the more important burden. It has been successfully invoked by academic and scientific researchers, including the NAS, but it may be limited to use against discovery requests by corporations.

Arguments Used by Parties Seeking Discovery

To avoid a showing of need for the requested information, parties seeking discovery of confidential research files have frequently argued that the party from whom discovery is sought was not an expert in the context of the litigation, but an ordinary eyewitness, an observer, or a participant.[128]

The most persuasive case for characterizing an expert as an actor or viewer of the events in litigation is *Quarantillo v. Consolidated Rail Corp.*[129] There, the expert had been the plaintiff's personal physician for 14 years. He had treated the plaintiff's back condition for 12 years prior to the injury in question, so he had not been pursuing research of any sort and he also had not developed his opinion in anticipation of litigation. The court wrote that the physician was not an expert, and even if he were an expert with regard to his opinion after the injury in question, he was an actor with regard to the other matters on which the defendant sought his testimony. Therefore, the court held that he could be deposed.

A credentialing organization will itself very rarely be an actor or viewer and still a non-party. Unless an individual official of the organization has participated in the events giving rise to the litigation or has directly observed them, a party seeking information from the organization will be unable to present a credible argument based on the actor-viewer approach.[130] However, two cases have expanded the scope of the actor-viewer approach in a way that might lead to its acceptance in unusual cases.[131]

In *Kennedy*, the Ph.D. candidate had "conducted on-site research as a 'participant-observer.' "[132] The court wrote that it could not "blind itself to [the expert's] status as an eyewitness. The purpose of her presence aside, she had a unique opportunity to observe *facts* and *events* on whose occurrence the outcome of this lawsuit may well depend." (emphasis in original).[133] The court's reasoning comports with neither common sense nor logic. The expert's research and her own observations are virtually the same; the court's reasoning transforms every expert into an eyewitness. That the expert's research and observations concerned gender integration and the lawsuit arose over the same subject is hardly a coincidence, as even the most aggressive litigants do not attempt to obtain confidential research that has no bearing whatsoever on their case.

In *Doe*, the government called a Harvard University professor before a grand jury to answer questions about who had possession of copies of the Pentagon Papers or knowledge of the participants in that study. But the government did not limit its questions to the professor's knowledge of who had the Pentagon Papers. It also wished to know who, in the professor's opinion, might have copies of the Pentagon Papers.[134] The professor claimed an academic research privilege, which the court rejected with regard to his knowledge of facts but accepted with regard to his opinions.

The court wrote, that "to the extent that a scholar *qua* scholar is asked about statements made to him by other scholars we do not conceive of him as in any different position from that of a doctor asked about his conversations with other doctors, or a lawyer about his talks with other lawyers."[135] Coupled with *Kennedy*, an extension of the *Doe* court's reasoning could be used to attack the confidentiality of a credentialing organization's files, at least so far as the files are not records of research but documentation of conversations—or where the records of research consist of records of conversations. In *Doe*, however, the court did not directly address research. Moreover, the professor's casual conversations with his peers, albeit on a subject of mutual professional interests, do not rise to the same level of formality and confidentiality as the peer review process, investigations or research.

Parties seeking discovery have also attempted to bolster their showing of a need for the information by arguing that the party from whom discovery is sought relied on hearsay. Due to the reliance on hearsay, the parties argue that they must be allowed to obtain the original data or personally contact the subjects of research. The courts have not accepted this argument as an additional factor, much less given it any weight.[136]

Demonstration of Need

The showing of need by the parties seeking discovery is necessarily case specific. Generally, the parties have not made especially detailed showings, and courts have analyzed issue of need in a superficial and conclusory manner. In a few instances, the parties have made remarkably poor showings of need. In *R.J. Reynolds*,[137] the tobacco companies mysteriously stated that "the mass of material accumulated by [the researchers] is *not needed by [us] to evaluate the studies' conclusions*." (emphasis supplied by the court). Perhaps defendants meant that they did not need the raw data but only the computer records, but whatever the material to which the statement referred, the court unsurprisingly wrote that the party's "actual need for the material appears to be seriously diminished" by the admission.[138] In *Solarex*,[139] the court pointed out that the party sought material which "would disprove [its] defenses."

Solarex also contained the standard response to any need argument: the party seeking discovery is going on a "fishing expedition."[140] If further developments in the proceedings show that an expert's opinion is relevant, then the party may still be able to shift the balance to favor discovery.[141] Even if the party is not going on a "fishing expedition," some files will only be tangentially related to the issues in litigation. When that is the case, then the discovery request seeks only "supplementary" information and is properly denied.[143]

If all else fails, a credentialing organization might at least be able to limit the disclosure of the discovery materials to the attorneys and expert witnesses involved in the litigation, preventing full exposure of the information to the public.[143]

Conclusion

In conclusion, there remains very little precedent on the question of confidentiality of credentialing records or information in the possession of a private, nonprofit, voluntary credentialing organization, a question that arises most typically when the records or information are sought by third parties in litigation involving the organizations. There are, however, numerous theories or rationales for arguing that the credentialing organization should not be compelled by a court as a non-party to disclose what it maintains as confidential, particularly in the areas of academic and scientific research.

Endnotes

1. 653 P.2d 107 (Kan. 1982).
2. *Id.* at 111.
3. *E.g., id.*, at 110, 111, 112.
4. *Id.* at 111.
5. *Id.* at 111.
6. *Id.* at 114.
7. *Id.* at 116.
8. *Id.*
9. *Id.* at 112.
10. *Id.*
11. *Id.* at 113.
12. *Id.* at 116.
13. *Id.* at 111.
14. *See National Collegiate Athletic Association v. Board of Regents of the University of Oklahoma*, 104 S.Ct. 2948, 2960 (1984), *citing* R. Bork, *The Antitrust Paradox* 1978), 278.
15. *Id.* at 116.
16. *Id.*
17. *Id.*
18. 72 F.R.D. 161 (S.D. N.Y. 1976).
19. *Id.* at 163.
20. *Id., relying on, Branzburg v. Hayes*, 92 S. Ct. 2646 (1972).
21. *Wright*, 72 F.R.D. at 163–64.
22. *Id.* at 164.
23. *Id.*
24. Fed. R. Civ. Pro. 26(b), Comment to 1983 Amendments (1990).
25. Fed. R. Civ. Pro. 26(b)(1).
26. *Ross v. Bolton*, 106 F.R.D. 22, 24 (S.D.N.Y. 1985). *See also Moll v. U.S. Life Title Insurance Company of New York*, 113 F.R.D. 625, 631 (S.D. N.Y. 1987) (discovery regarding kickbacks sought from non-party attorneys who claimed the Fifth Amendment privilege), *relying on Ross*, 106 F.R.D. 22.
27. *Ross*, 106 F.R.D. at 24, *citing, Garnatz v. Stiel, Nicolaus & Co.*, No. 75–934 C(2) (E.D. Mo. June 21, 1976) *and Sumrall v. Hackert/Modesitt Investments Ltd.*, No. 84–4717 (Denver Dist. Ct., Col., Dec. 3, 1984).
28. *Id.* at 24.
29. *Id.* at 23.
30. *Id.* at 24–25.
31. *Apex Oil Co. v. DiMauro*, 110 F.R.D. (S.D.N.Y. 1985).
32. 471 N.E.2d 601 (Ill.App. 1st Dist. 1984).
33. Professor Wigmore's four-part test is as follows: "[F]our fundamental conditions are recognized as necessary to the establishment of a privilege against the disclosure of communications: (1) The communications must originate in a *confidence* that they will not be disclosed. (2) This element of *confi-*

dentiality must be essential to the full and satisfactory maintenance of the relation between the parties. (3) The *relation* must be one which in the opinion of the community ought to be sedulously *fostered*. (4) The *injury* that would inure to the relation by the disclosure of the communications must be *greater than the benefit* thereby gained for the correct disposal of litigation." J. Wigmore, *Evidence* 1961, (J. McNaughton, ed., § 2285 at 527 (emphasis in original).

34. *Id.* at 603.
35. *Id.*
36. *Id.* at 604.
37. *Illinois Judicial Inquiry*, 471 N.E.2d at 605, *discussing Wright*, 72 F.R.D. at 164.
38. *See Bergman v. Kemp*, 97 F.R. 413, 417 (W.D.Mich. 1983)(voluntary disclosure "destroyed" confidentiality and critical self-examination privilege); *Davidson v. Light*, 79 F.R.D. 137, 140 (D. Col. 1978)(discussing "breach of confidentiality" by hospital seeking privilege).
39. *See Solarex Corp. v. Arco Solar, Inc.*, 121 F.R.D. 163 (E.D.N.Y. 1988), *aff'd* 870 F.2d 642 (Fed. Cir. 1989) (discussing First Amendment editorial, critical self-examination and academic peer review privileges).
40. *See Anker v. G.D. Searle & Co.*, 126 F.R.D. 515, 519 (M.D. N.C. 1989)(protective order preferred over quashing deposition altogether). *See, e.g., Buchanan v. American Motors Corp.*, 697 F.2d 151, 152 (6th Cir. 1983) (assuming no privilege but affirming quashing of subpoena); *Solarex Corp. v. Arco Solar, Inc.*, 121 F.R.D. 163 (privilege would not be created but discovery request denied); *Farnsworth v. Proctor & Gamble Co.*, 101 F.R.D. 355, 357 (N.D. Geo. 1984) (not reaching privilege issue but issuing protective order), *aff'd* 758 F.2d 1545 (11th Cir. 1985); *Richards of Rockford v. Pacific Gas & Electric*, 71 F.R.D. 388, 389 n.2 (N.D. Cal. 1976)(holding not based on privilege but on court's supervisory powers). *Accord United States v. Doe*, 460 F.2d 328, 355 (1st Cir. 1972)(discussing grand jury witnesses and conversations rather than research) ("even apart from constitutional claims, we should exercise our supervisory power").
41. *In Re Snyder*, 115 F.R.D. 211, 213 (D. Ariz. 1987) *citing Wright v. Jeep Corp.*, 547 F.Supp. 871 (E.d. Mich. 1982).
42. 547 F. Supp. 871.
43. *Id.* at 213–14.
44. *Id.* at 214.
45. C. Wright and J. Graham, *Federal Practice and Procedure Evidence*, (1990) Supp. § 5341 at 228. *See also Buchanan*, 697 F.2d 151 (third reported case seeking jeep-type vehicle research).
46. 672 F.2d 1262, 1276–77 (7th Cir. 1982).
47. *Id.* at 1276.
48. 740 F.2d 556, 560–61 (7th Cir. 1984).
49. *In the Matter of the Application of R.J. Reynolds Tobacco Co.*, 518 N.Y.S.2d 729 (Sup. 1987).
50. *Id.* at 731.
51. *Id.* at 733.
52. *Id.* at 734.
53. *Application of American Tobacco Co.*, 880 F.2d 1521 (2nd Cir. 1989). *See, e.g., Wright*, 547 F. Supp. at 875 (refusing to quash subpoena except with regard to location of deposition). *See also Kaufman v. Edelstein*, 539 F.2d 811, 820 (2nd Cir. 1976) (mandamus denied because order not appealable without contempt).
54. 518 N.Y.S.2d 729. *American Tobacco Co.*, 880 F.2d 1521.
55. *Id.* at 1528.
56. 518 N.Y.S.2d 729.
57. *Id.*
58. *Id.* at 1530.
59. *Id.* at 1529.
60. *Id.* at 1527.
61. *Id.* at 1530.

62. *See, generally,* Annotation, *Right of Independent Expert to Refuse to Testify as to Expert Opinion,* 50 A.L.R.4th 680 (1986), *and cases cited therein.*

63. *See, e.g., Agnew v. Parks,* 343 P.2d 118 (Cal.App. 2nd Dist. 1959) (holding that medical association's members concerted refusal to testify in malpractice actions was not actionable).

64. *Commonwealth v. Vitello,* 327 N.E.2d 819, 827 (Mass. App. Ct. 1975).

65. *Id.*

66. *Ondis v. Pion,* 497 A.2d 13, 18 (R.I. 1985).

67. *See also Sousa v. Chaset,* 519 A.2d 1132 (R.I. 1987)(medical malpractice claim), *relying on Ondis,* 497 A.2d 13. *See also R.J. Reynolds,* 518 N.Y.S.2d at 732 ("Policy in New York, unlike most other jurisdictions, has accorded privilege to experts" against compelled testimony), *citing People ex rel. Kraushaar Bros. v. Thorpe,* 72 N.E.2d 165 (1947).

68. *Mason v. Robinson,* 340 N.W.2d 236 (Iowa 1983).

69. *Id.* at 238.

70. *Id.*

71. *Id.*

72. 497 A.2d 13.

73. *Mason,* 340 N.W.2d at 241.

74. *Id.* at 242.

75. *Id.* at 243.

76. *Herbert v. Lando,* 99 S. Ct. 1635, 1648 (1979).

77. *United States v. Nixon,* 94 S. Ct. 3090, 3108 (1974).

78. *Dow,* 672 F.2d at 1269.

79. *Richards of Rockford,* 71 F.R.D. at 391.

80. *See, e.g., United States v. American Telephone & Telegraph Co.,* 86 F.R.D. 603 (D.D.C. 1979)(issuing fifty-four pages of procedures regulating discovery in AT&T antitrust case). *See also, generally, Truswal Systems Corp. v. Hydro-Air Engineering, Inc.,* 813 F.2d 1207 (Fed. Cir. 1987)(discussing protective order in a patent infringement action where party sought sales records of non-party competitor); *Heat & Control, Inc. v. Hester Industries, Inc.,* 785 F.2d 1017 (Fed. Cir. 1986).

81. *Socialist Workers Party v. Grubisic,* 619 F.2d 641, 643 (7th Cir. 1980).

82. *Anker,* 126 F.R.D. at 519 n.2.; *Wright,* 547 F. Supp. at 875. *But see American Tobacco,* 880 F.2d 1520 (strictly construing possible state law privilege). See also Wei v. Bodner, 127 F.R.D. 91 (D.N.J. 1989 (When both federal and state claims are made, federal privileges apply to all claims.)

83. *Anker,* 126 F.R.D. at 515.

84. *See, e.g., Wright,* 547 F. Supp. at 874; *In Re Snyder,* 115 F.R.D. at 214–15; *Tahoe Insurance Co. v. Morrison Knudsen Co.,* 84 F.R.D. 362, 364 (D. Idaho 1979).

85. The Rule reads in relevant part: "The frequency or extent of use of the discovery methods . . . shall be limited by the court if it determines that: (i) the discovery sought is unreasonably cumulative or duplicative, or is obtainable from some other source that is more convenient, less burdensome, or less expensive; (ii) the party seeking discovery has had ample opportunity by discovery in the action to obtain the information sought; or (iii) the discovery is unduly burdensome or expensive, taking into account the needs of the case, the amount in controversy, limitations on the parties' resources, and the importance of the issues at stake in litigation." Fed. R. Civ. Pro. 26(b)(1)(1990).

    The Comment explains that the Rule was amended in 1983 "to deal with the problem of over-discovery" and "to encourage judges to be more aggressive in identifying and discouraging discovery overuse." Fed. R. Civ. Pro. 26(b), Comment to 1983 Amendments (1990).

86. The Rule reads in relevant part: "Upon motion by a party or by the person from whom discovery is sought, and for good cause shown, the court in which the action is pending or alternatively, on matters relating to a deposition, the court in the district where the deposition is to be taken may make any order which justice requires to protect a party or person from annoyance,

embarrassment, oppression, or undue burden or expense..." Fed. R. Civ. Pro. 26(c).

87. *See e.g., Anker*, 126 F.R.D. at 518 (applying Rule 26(b)(1)); *Farnsworth v. Proctor & Gamble Co.*, 101 F.R.D. at 357 (applying Rule 26(c)).

88. *Solarex*, 121 F.R.D. at 169, *quoting Plough v. National Academy of Sciences*, 530 A.2d 1152, 1155–56 (D.C.App. 1987).

89. *Dow*, 672 F.2d at 1276 n.25. *See also Anker*, 126 F.R.D. at 519; *Solarex*, 121 F.R.D. at 179 (non-party status "significant").

90. *Deitchman*, 740 F.2d at 563.

91. *Anker*, 126 F.R.D. at 518, *relying on Solarex*, 121 F.R.D. at 169–70.

92. *Kaufman*, 539 F.2d at 822.

93. *Solarex*, 121 F.R.D. at 167 n.2.

94. *Wright*, 547 F. Supp. at 874.

95. *In Re Snyder*, 115 F.R.D. at 214.

96. *Id.*

97. *Id* at 215.

98. *Id.* at 214.

99. *Buchanan v. American Motors Corp.*, 697 F.2d 151, 152 (6th Cir. 1983). *Compare R.J. Reynolds*, 518 N.Y.S.2d 729.

100. *Kaufman*, 539 F.2d at 821.

101. *Id.* at 813.

102. *Anker*, 126 F.R.D. at 521.

103. *Id.* at 521.

104. 880 F.2d at 1530.

105. *Id.* at 1529.

106. *See, e.g., In Re Snyder*, 115 F.R.D. at 215 ("The potential for a chilling effect on research appears great.").

107. *See Farnsworth*, 758 F.2d at 1547 (lay persons justifiably expect personal information will be kept confidential).

108. *See In Re Snyder*, 115 F.R.D. at 216.

109. *Dow*, 672 F.2d at 1276 n.25.

110. *Plough*, 530 A.2d at 1157.

111. *Id.* at 1159.

112. 21 F.R.D. 163, 175.

113. *Id.* at 164–65.

114. *Id.* at 168.

115. *Id.* at 171.

116. *Id.* at 179.

117. *Richards of Rockford*, 71 F.R.D. at 390. *See also In Re Consumers Union of the United States*, 495 F. Supp. 582 (S.D.N.Y. 1980) (quashing nonparty subpoenas to avoid deterring investigation of issues of public interest). *Accord Tahoe Insurance Co.*, 84 F.R.D. at 363 (government investigation should not be deterred by litigation).

118. 740 F.2d at 560.

119. *Id.*

120. 530 A.2d at 1157–58.

121. *Accord Doe*, 460 F.2d at 334 (grand jury context) (interest is not protecting the sources per se, but in preserving the flow of information).

122. *Kennedy*, 115 F.R.D. 497, 501 (D.Conn. 1987).

123. *Id.*

124. *Id.* at 498.

125. *Compare Wright*, 547 F. Supp. at 876 ("[T]he present case involves no attempt to compel the disclosure of confidential sources.").

126. *In Re Snyder*, 115 F.R.D. 211; *Dow*, 672 F. 2d 1262; *Plough*, 530 A.2d 1152.

127. *But see* Fed. R. Civ. Pro. 26(b) (1) (iii) (1990) (the court may take into account "limitations on the parties' resources").

128. *See In Re Snyder*, 115 F.R.D. at 215 (addressing "the quasi-fiction that [the party] seeks only [the expert's] first-hand account of historical events" as if "he [were] an ordinary 'actor or viewer' witness..."); *see also Tahoe Insurance Company*, 84 F.R.D. 362 (government investigatory panel members

characterized as ordinary witnesses, discovery limited to firsthand observations).

129.   106 F.R.D. 435 (W.D.N.Y. 1985).

130.   When an organization has been involved in a more direct manner in the events of the underlying litigation and potentially faces liability, it may be able to rely on Federal Rule of Evidence 407. The Rule prohibits introduction of evidence of subsequent remedial measures to make an event less likely to occur to prove negligence with regard to that event. Fed. R. Ev. 407 (1990).

131.   *Kennedy*, 115 F.R.D. 497; *Doe*, 460 F.2d 328.

132.   *Kennedy*, 115 F.R.D. at 498.

133.   *Id.* at 499.

134.   *Id.* at 330–31.

135.   *Id.* at 334.

136.   *See In Re Multi-Piece Rim Product Liability Litigation*, 653 F.2d 671, 674 (D.C. Cir. 1981); *Farnsworth*, 101 F.R.D. at 357. *But see Farnsworth*, 758 F.2d at 1547 (dicta indicating concern about hearsay).

137.   518 N.Y.S.2d at 733.

138.   *Id.*

139.   121 F.R.D. at 163.

140.   *Id.* at 179. *But see Deitchman*, 740 F.2d at 562–63 (expectation but not certainty that discovery will be futile does not justify forbidding it entirely).

141.   *See Anker*, 126 F.R.D. at 521–22.

142.   *Richards of Rockford*, 71 F.R.D. at 390.

143.   *See Deitchman*, 740 F.2d at 565 (suggesting protective order limiting disclosure).

5

Use of Credentialing Marks

In one manner or another, American lawyers, physicians, dentists, accountants, and other professionals have found ways to communicate information to the public regarding their qualifications and skills. Perhaps the most common approach is to inform actual and potential patients, clients, or customers about the nature of the professional's credentials. By displaying diplomas and certificates on the walls of offices, printing information on letterheads, and advertising their qualifications in such media as the yellow pages, newspapers, television, and radio, professionals market themselves by making representations to the public concerning their educational degrees, training, experience, and substantive expertise.

The state and federal governments, sometimes collaborating with private organizations, have at times sought to restrict the ability of professionals to use privately issued credentials as marketing devices. Such restrictions are chiefly justified as necessary to protect consumers from detrimentally relying on false or misleading communications. Frequently, however, restrictions are defended as necessary to preserve the "dignity" of a profession.

Likewise institutions that have achieved accredited status often use that accreditation to assist in attracting students, teachers, grants, and contributions. Occasionally challenges have been made on legal grounds to the ability of institutions to promote themselves by using references to accreditation.

Restrictions on the use of privately issued credentials in marketing by professionals raise serious legal and policy concerns. The Supreme Court's decisions on commercial speech make clear that representations by professionals concerning their skills or training enjoy First Amendment protection, albeit not as much protection as noncommercial speech. The Court has also held that when a professional association acts to restrict the business activities of its members, its actions will be subject to scrutiny under the antitrust laws. Because limitations on one's ability to utilize privately issued credentials in promotions manifestly restrict free competition, those limitations trigger antitrust considerations when they are imposed by a private organization.

Apart from antitrust issues, restrictions on the use of privately issued credentials raise important questions of regulatory policy. Such restrictions, though often justified as necessary to protect consumers, may have the effect of depriving consumers of useful information, and may stifle competition. The courts and the Federal Trade Commission (FTC) have frequently considered these problems when adjudicating challenges to restrictions on the use of privately issued credentials and related matters. Generally speaking, the more attention that the courts and Commission pay to the benefits that result from communications by professionals or institutions about their qualifications, the more likely they are to strike down a restriction on those communications.

This chapter considers court and FTC decisions involving restrictions on the use of privately issued professional or institutional credentials to promote services. The conclusion to which these decisions point is that, both constitutionally and as a matter of regulatory policy, one should be fully free to engage in public communications concerning credentials, as long as those communications are truthful and nonmisleading.

The Supreme Court's Decision in *Peel*

The Supreme Court, lower courts, and the FTC have each addressed the subject of marketing by attorneys, including marketing that uses privately issued credentials. In *Peel v. Attorney Registration and Disciplinary Comm'n*,[1] the Supreme Court adopted a generally expansive view of an attorney's First Amendment right to promote his services by exploiting a certification obtained from a private, nonprofit, voluntary organization. While *Peel* involves attorney specialty certification in particular, it establishes principles of law applicable to restrictions on use of privately issued credentialing marks in general.

The Plurality Opinion in *Peel*

Peel involved an attorney whose professional letterhead stated that he had been designated a "Certified Trial Specialist" by the National Board of Trial Advocacy, (NBTA) a nongovernmental professional certification organization, and that he was "[l]icensed" in Illinois, Missouri, and Arizona.[2] The Administrator of the Attorney Registration and Disciplinary Commission of Illinois, a state government agency, instituted disciplinary proceedings against the attorney on the grounds that these statements violated provisions of the Illinois Code of Professional Responsibility generally prohibiting an attorney from holding himself out as a certified legal specialist, among other things. The state agency's recommendation that the attorney be censured was adopted by the Illinois Supreme Court.

The U.S. Supreme Court reversed the censure in a five-to-four decision. In their plurality opinion, Justices Stevens, Brennan, Blackmun, and Kennedy, applying principles established in previous Supreme Court First Amendment cases involving commercial speech, concluded that the attorney could not be disciplined for his letterhead under the Illinois rules because 1) the letterhead had not *actually* misled anyone and was not *necessarily* (i.e., inherently) misleading; and 2) the state's categorical prohibition against claims of certification or specialization by lawyers could not be justified by any *potentially* misleading aspect of such statements.[3]

In concluding that the attorney's letterhead had not *actually* misled anyone, the plurality emphasized that there simply had been "no contention that any potential client or person was actually misled or deceived by petitioner's stationery."[4] The plurality also noted that "[t]he facts stated on petitioner's letterhead are true and verifiable" because it was "undisputed that NBTA has certified petitioner as a civil trial specialist and that three States have licensed him to practice law."[5]

The plurality then rejected the argument that the attorney's letterhead was *necessarily* misleading because of its "implied claim" as to the quality of his legal services.[6] The plurality again emphasized that a lawyer's certification by NBTA, the private certification organization, was a "verifiable fact," adding that the "predicate requirements" for NBTA certification—measures of trial experience and hours of continuing legal education—were also verifiable facts. The plurality reasoned that there is a sharp distinction between, on the one hand, an "unverifiable opinion of the ultimate quality of a lawyer's work or a promise of success," and, on the other, a claim of certification that might lead some consumers to infer that the certified lawyer's qualifications exceed that of non certified lawyers in the certified areas of practice. The latter type of claim was factual and verifiable while the former was not.[7]

The plurality cautioned, however, that a claim of certification could be deemed inherently misleading (and, therefore, subject to prohibition) if it were issued by an organization which had "made no inquiry" into the fitness of those it certified or which issued certificates "indiscriminately for a price."[8] The plurality warned that a state would be free to require an attorney who advertised a certification to "demonstrate that such certification is available to all lawyers who meet objective and consistently applied standards relevant to practice in a particular area of the law."[9] Hence, the plurality's conclusion that the attorney's letterhead was not inherently misleading depended on a finding that his claim of NBTA certification did not "suggest[ ] any greater degree of professional qualification than reasonably may be inferred from an evaluation" of NBTA's "rigorous requirements."[10]

The plurality then considered and rejected the argument by the State of Illinois that the categorical prohibition against lawyers' claims of certification or specialization was justified by the *potentially* misleading nature of such representations. The plurality stated that it would "assume" that such statements "may not be understood fully by some readers" but concluded that the statements posed "no greater potential of misleading consumers" than other kinds of truthful, nonmisleading attorney advertising that previous Supreme Court decisions had held to be constitutionally protected.[11] The plurality also noted that Illinois permitted lawyers to make claims of specialization in patent or admiralty law, undermining the state's claim that a "complete prophylactic against any claim of specialty" was required.[12] The plurality held that the state's blanket ban was, thus, "broader than reasonably necessary to prevent the perceived evil,"[13] and, therefore, unconstitutional.

Justice Marshall's Concurrence

In a concurring opinion joined by Justice Brennan, Justice Marshall agreed with the plurality's conclusion that the attorney's letterhead was neither actually nor inherently misleading and that the State of Illinois, therefore, could not ban outright the statements in the letterhead.[14] Justice Marshall, however, was prepared to find what the plurality had merely assumed: that the attorney's letterhead was potentially misleading.[15] Justice Marshall further concluded that, although the potentially misleading nature of the letterhead did not justify a total ban on specialization representations, it did justify "regulations other than a total ban" to ensure that the public was not misled by such representations.[16]

The only measure identified by Justice Marshall as permissible for regulating potentially misleading specialization claims was "some limited supplementation, by way of warning or disclaimer or the like, . . . so as to assure that the consumer is not misled."[17] The plurality opinion came close to embracing this position as well, stating that, although it was not necessary in this case to consider "whether a State might impose disclosure requirements . . . in order to minimize the possibility that a reader will misunderstand the significance of a statement of fact," the Court's holding did "not necessarily preclude less restrictive regulation of commercial speech."[18,19]

Significance and Limitations of *Peel*

Peel represents a significant victory both for professionals who wish to utilize privately issued credentials to market their talents and for the organizations to which professionals turn to earn certification. But such professionals and organizations should consider the limitations of *Peel* along with the benefits provided by the decision. In addition, the narrow margin of the vote in *Peel*, coupled with the replacements of Justices Brennan and Marshall subsequent to the issuance of the decision, is cause for caution.

For those involved in the use or creation of professional or institutional credentials, *Peel*'s principal significance lies in the plurality's application of the concept of misleadingness to certification claims. According to five of the Justices who participated in the *Peel* decision (Stevens, Brennan, Blackmun, Kennedy, and Marshall), a certification claim, if truthful and nonmisleading, cannot be prohibited outright,[20] and a certification claim is truthful and nonmisleading if the following factors are present: a) the claim itself is true, factual and verifiable; b) the bases on which certification was awarded are factual and verifiable; c) the certification in question is available to all professionals in the field who meet "relevant," "objective," and "consistently applied standards";[21] and d) the certification claim does not "suggest[ ] any greater degree of professional qualification than reasonably may be inferred from an evaluation" of the certification program's requirements.[22]

In effect, *Peel* constitutionalizes a common-sense approach to the regulation of certification claims, providing that such claims are constitutionally protected commercial speech if the certification itself is

awarded in a bona fide program and if the professional does not ex-
aggerate the significance of the certification. *Peel* recognizes, as previous
Supreme Court commercial speech decisions have, that consumers benefit from the public dissemination of information about a professional's
credentials.[23] Accordingly, *Peel* does *not* support prohibitions or restrictions on the use of privately issued credentials that are justified solely
on the ground that they are necessary to protect the "dignity" of a
profession or field, and it is unlikely that any regulations based solely
on such a rationale could survive First Amendment scrutiny.

Even truthful, nonmisleading credentialing representations are not
entirely immune from regulation under *Peel*, however. Potentially misleading representations, the Court held, may be regulated as long as the
regulation is not "broader than reasonably necessary to prevent the
perceived evil." As noted above, Justice Marshall would allow the state
to regulate potentially misleading representations in a manner short of
enacting a categorical prohibition, if such a regulation were necessary
to cure the potentially misleading features of the representation. As also
noted above, the *Peel* plurality, while not explicitly endorsing Justice
Marshall's views on this point, strongly suggested their agreement with
those views.

This regulatory power could be significant, as almost any kind of
credentialing claim can be deemed *potentially* misleading. The precise
kinds of regulations that might be enacted by a state in the category of
"less-than-categorical-ban" are difficult to discern. Justice Marshall focused on disclosure or disclaimer requirements designed to cure the
potentially misleading aspect of the credentialing claim; but it is not
clear whether he, let alone other members of the Court, would stop
there.

Pre-*Peel* Decisions on Attorney Certification

Although *Peel* is the most important decided case concerning the uti-
lization of privately issued credentials to promote services, judicial and
FTC decisions issued prior to *Peel* are also worth considering in order
to appreciate the way lower courts and the Commission have analyzed
restrictions on such uses of privately issued credentials. In particular,
two state court cases involving certification by the National Board of
Trial Attorneys, the same group involved in *Peel*, *Johnson v. Director
of Professional Responsibility*,[24] and *Ex parte Howell*,[25] show the extent
to which the principles ultimately expounded in *Peel* had gained acceptance prior to the issuance of the *Peel* decision, at least among some
courts.

Johnson invalidated a provision of the Minnesota Code of Professional Responsibility similar to the Illinois provision that would later
be struck down in *Peel*. The Minnesota provision prohibited a lawyer
from holding himself out as a specialist, even if the lawyer had been
certified as a specialist by a bona fide private credentialing organization.
The rule imposed a blanket prohibition on all commercial speech regarding specialization "unless and until" the Minnesota Supreme Court
promulgated rules describing what specialty designations would be ac-

cepted and how to obtain those designations.[26] The rule was challenged by a lawyer who had been certified by NBTA as a civil trial specialist and who had been disciplined for violating the rule.

The court, after reviewing previous Supreme Court commercial speech decisions, noted that a state may ban misleading commercial speech and "retains some authority to regulate" truthful, nonmisleading commercial speech if the state asserted a "substantial interest and the interference with speech" was "in proportion to the interest served."[27] But the court, taking notice of NBTA's "rigorous and exacting" standards, found that the NBTA certification of the lawyer in question was not misleading and therefore could not be banned, rendering the Minnesota rule unconstitutional.[28]

Howell also involved a provision of a state Code of Professional Responsibility which prohibited a lawyer from representing that he had been certified by NBTA as a civil trial specialist. The court held that such a blanket prohibition could be justified only to prohibit a representation that was actually false, deceptive, or misleading, not to ban a representation which was merely potentially misleading.[29] Potentially misleading certification claims, the court concluded, could be addressed by "restrictions which are no broader than necessary" to protect the public from the potentially misleading claim.[30] Finding that NBTA certification indicated a level of expertise with regard to trial advocacy "in excess of the level of expertise required for admission to the bar generally," the court found the lawyer's certification claim to be nonmisleading and the application of the bar's rule to be unconstitutional.[31]

The FTC, which during the Reagan and Bush Administrations generally opposed restrictions on commercial speech, has taken a position critical of state regulations on the use of privately issued credentials to promote services. In a March 31, 1987, letter to the Alabama Supreme Court, the Commission staff criticized proposed amendments to the Alabama Code of Professional Responsibility that would have sharply restricted the ability of lawyers to use privately issued certification marks. Alabama's proposed rule would have required a lawyer to obtain the approval of the Alabama State Bar's General Counsel before communicating that he was certified by an organization. The approval would be granted only if the General Counsel found that communicating the certification would "provide meaningful information that is not false, misleading, or deceptive."[32]

The FTC staff told the Alabama Supreme Court that the proposed rule threatened to harm consumers of legal services. The staff asserted that when nongovernmental certification programs were "reasonably related to assuring proficiency in the subject area certified," the advertising of certification could provide consumers with useful information about attorneys' special skills, and that a lawyer accordingly should be able to communicate, without prior approval by the state, any truthful, nonmisleading information about any certification that he had obtained.[33] The staff also contended that the proposed "meaningful information" standard was extremely vague and would require the General Counsel to determine what kinds of information the public as a whole would find "meaningful" when, in fact, individual consumers may place different values on different kinds of information.[34] In addition, the staff argued that the proposed rule could result in "inefficiency and injury to competition" because it would restrain the development of private certifying organizations, and that this in turn could discourage attorneys from acquiring training from organizations which the General Counsel had not approved.[35] Finally, the staff pointed out that the use of certificates that were not bona fide or that were issued by programs not related to improving skills in a subject area would already be prohibited under Alabama's existing rule against false or misleading advertising, rendering the new rule unnecessary.[36]

The March 31, 1987, letter from the FTC staff to the Alabama Supreme Court evinces hostility on the part of the Commission toward governmental restrictions on the use of certification to market professional services. The Commission's pro-consumer, pro-free enterprise orientation during the Reagan Administration and early Bush Administration is further evidenced by the FTC's filing of an *amicus* brief in *Peel* on behalf of the attorney challenging the state restrictions. Whether the Commission's defense of free market values will remain as vigorous in this area as time passes, is, however, uncertain.

Other Professions

Attorney certification has elicited the most explicit and considered judicial and Commission precedent concerning restrictions on the use of privately issued credentials. Although there are many court decisions involving the rights of nonlawyer professionals to engage in commercial speech,[37] relatively few of these decisions involve the promotion of services through the use of such credentials.

One frequently litigated question that does concern the use of credentials by professionals involves physicians who have received their training at osteopathic medical schools and who seek to use the term "M.D." rather than "D.O." to describe themselves, notwithstanding that they hold only the degree of Doctor of Osteopathy and that such degrees do not confer an "M.D." title. Courts have almost uniformly rejected the First Amendment, due process, and equal protection arguments advanced by D.O.'s in these cases, holding that a claim of M.D. status by a D.O. who does not have an M.D. degree would simply be false (notwithstanding the close similarity in the training that leads to the two degrees) and, hence, constitutionally unprotected.[38]

Buxton v. Lovell[39] raised a similar issue. In *Buxton*, the court held that a psychologist had a First Amendment and due process right to designate himself a "Ph.D." even though the Ph.D. degree he had received was from an unaccredited institution. The psychologist's constitutional victory was, however, a narrow one: he prevailed only because neither the state statute in question nor any regulation issued by the state regulatory board specifically authorized the board to ban the use of a "Ph.D." title earned at an unaccredited institution. The state, thereby, failed to provide constitutionally sufficient notice that psychologists with Ph.D. degrees from unaccredited institutions could not call themselves Ph.D.s. The court strongly suggested that if the statute or the board had clearly announced such a ban in advance, the ban would have been constitutional.[40]

Educational Accreditation

The FTC's opinion *In re Ohio Christian College (of Calvary Grace Christian Churches of Faith,) Inc.*,[41] which did not involve any constitutional issues, sheds additional light on the Commission's approach to restrictions on privately issued credentials. In *Ohio Christian College*, the Commission issued a cease-and-desist order requiring a correspondence school to, among other things, stop using the word "college" or similar words to describe itself, stop conferring academic degrees, and stop misrepresenting that it had been accredited or that its programs had been recognized by the State of Ohio or any other governmental body. The school, along with an "accreditation" organization and a "society" of alleged "psychological counselors," was actually a shell controlled by an individual named Alvin Langdon. The Commission found that the school was essentially a fraud: It had no faculty members trained and competent to teach accredited and recognized college courses, it had not been accredited by any recognized accrediting agency, it issued degrees that were not approved or accepted by any recognized educational institution or organization, and it offered courses that did not contain the materials or study requirements required by accredited colleges offering courses in the same areas. Langdon's "accrediting agency," styled the "National Educational Accrediting Association" and his counselors "society," which were both referred to in the promotional materials issued by Langdon in his efforts to recruit students, were also found to be chimerical.

Most of the opinion in *Ohio Christian College* is devoted to chronicling the objectionable statements of the Langdon entities and explaining why they were false and misleading and, hence, properly the subject of a cease-and-desist order. At several points, however, the Commission justified its order by asserting that the statements in question "may mislead," "place[ ] in the hands of others the means of misleading," and provide others with the "means and instrumentalities by and through which they may mislead and deceive others."

Under *Peel*, it is unlikely that any statement concerning private credentials may now be banned merely because it *may* mislead. But *Peel* does not address the question of whether a credential that, although truthful and nonmisleading when issued, may be banned on the grounds that the person issuing it is placing it into the hands of someone else who will use it as a means of misleading. Although the *Peel* plurality held that a professional could be banned from exaggerating the significance of his credentials,[42] *Ohio Christian College* goes further by suggesting that there are circumstances in which an organization issuing a credential that is truthful and nonmisleading on its face may be banned from doing so because the person to whom the credential is being issued plans to use it to mislead others.[43]

The precise circumstances under which the government may exercise the authority implied by *Ohio Christian College* are unclear.

Whether the issuing organization must know or have reason to know that a specific user of a credential it issues plans to misuse it or whether the mere fact that such misuse has occurred in the past suffices to justify a ban are issues that remain to be explored. If the First Amendment principles of *Peel* are to retain their force, however, it is likely that the circumstances justifying a ban will be narrowly limited.

Antitrust Issues

There is a dearth of precedent on the issue of *private* organizations' restrictions on the use of privately issued credentials. Such private restrictions do not trigger the First Amendment; they surely do, however, trigger antitrust considerations, because they restrict marketing and promotion, which manifestly constitute competitive activity. The courts have consistently held that when a nongovernmental organization such as an association restricts the competitive activities of individual members or non-members, its conduct is subject to scrutiny under the antitrust laws.[44] Under the holdings of these and other decisions, it is extremely likely that any organization that banned or severely limited the ability of professionals or institutions to utilize privately issued credentials to promote services could be held to have violated the antitrust laws.

Conclusion

The Supreme Court in *Peel* recognized that truthful, nonmisleading certification claims by attorneys are beneficial to consumers and held that such claims may not be banned outright. A majority of the Court also suggested that such claims may be regulated by means short of an outright ban, but only to the extent such regulation is necessary to cure a specific potentially misleading feature of a claim.

Pre-*Peel* decisions by courts and the Federal Trade Commission are generally consistent with the approach that was ultimately taken in *Peel*. The most significant issue not addressed in *Peel* that has been addressed elsewhere involves the circumstances in which a bona fide credential issued by one entity is placed into the hands of someone else with the risk that this person will misuse it. Though there is authority suggesting that the government could obtain an injunction against the issuance of the credential (or punish the issuing organization) in such circumstances, the circumstances justifying such governmental action must be narrowly construed by the courts if the First Amendment principles of *Peel* are to retain their force.

With respect to privately imposed restrictions on the use of credentials to promote services, where First Amendment protection is not available, the antitrust laws are likely to serve as an effective substitute, protecting the ability of professionals and institutions, as a matter of free competition, to use their credentials as promotional tools. There is a substantial body of antitrust case law clearly suggesting that the rights of the individual professional to compete freely will be protected against privately imposed restrictions on the use of credentials.

Endnotes

1. 110 S.Ct. 2281 (1990).
2. *Id.* at 2285.
3. 110 S.Ct. at 2287–2293.
4. *Id.* at 2288.
5. *Id.*
6. *Id.*
7. *Id.*
8. *Id.*
9. *Id.* at 2292.
10. *Id.* at 2288.
11. *Id.* at 2291.
12. *Id.*
13. *Id.* (quoting *Shapero v. Kentucky Bar Ass'n*, 486 U.S. 466, 472 (1988) and *In re R.M.J.*, 455 U.S. 191, 203 (1982)) (internal quotation marks omitted).
14. *Id.* at 2293 (Marshall, J., concurring).
15. *Id.*
16. *Id.*
17. *Id.* at 2296 (quoting *Bates v. State Bar of Arizona*, 433 U.S. 350, 384 (1977).
18. *Id.* at 2292 n.17.
19. In addition, Justice White, though dissenting and concluding that Peel's letterhead in its present form could be banned, agreed with Justice Marshall that a categorical ban on all specialization representations was unconstitutional but that "disclaimers" could be required to remedy the potentially misleading features of such representations. *Id.* at 2297. (White, J., dissenting).
20. Justice White also concluded that the state may not categorically prohibit truthful, nonmisleading representations by a professional concerning his credentials. But unlike the *Peel*-plurality and Justice Marshall, Justice White would effectively permit the state to apply such a categorical ban to a *potentially* misleading certification representation with the burden then placed on the professional to rewrite the representation so as to cure the potentially misleading aspect.
21. *Id.* at 2292.
22. *Id.* at 2288.
23. *See Id.* at 2293 ("Information about certification and specialties facilitates the consumer's access to legal services and thus better serves the administration of justice.") (footnote omitted).
24. 341 N.W.2d 282 (Minn. 1983).
25. 487 So.2d 848 (Ala. 1986).
26. 341 N.W.2d at 283.
27. *Id.* at 284.
28. *Id.* at 283–85.
29. *Id.* at 851.
30. *Id.*
31. *Id.*
32. March 31, 1987 letter from FTC staff to the Alabama Supreme Court ("FTC Letter") at 1–2.
33. *Id.* at 2.
34. *Id.* at 2–3.
35. *Id.* at 2.
36. *Id.*
37. *See, e.g., Virginia State Board of Pharmacy v. Virginia Citizens Consumer Council*, 425 U.S. 748 (1976) (price advertising by pharmacists); *Parker v. Kentucky Board of Dentistry*, 818 F.2d 504 (6th Cir. 1987) (holding unconstitutional a state statute banning general practicing dentists from including

the name of a dental specialty in their advertising); *Fane v. Edenfield*, No. TCA 88–40264–MMP (N.D. Fla. Sept. 13, 1990) (unpublished opinion) (in-person solicitation by accountants); *cf. Friedman v. Rogers*, 440 U.S. 1 (1979) (commercial optometrists' challenge to state requirement that majority of state optometry board be composed of optometrists belonging to particular optometrists' association).

38. *See, e.g., Brandwein v. California Board of Osteopathic Examiners*, 708 F.2d 1466 (9th Cir. 1983); *Maceluch v. Wysong*, 680 F.2d 1062 (5th Cir. 1982); *Eatough v. Albano*, 673 F.2d 671 (3d Cir.), *cert. denied*, 457 U.S. 1119 (1982); *Procario v. Ambrach*, 561 F. Supp. 804 (N.D.N.Y. 1983). *But see Oliver v. Morton*, 361 F. Supp. 1262 (N.D. Ga. 1973) (3–judge court) (rejecting various constitutional arguments but finding equal protection clause violation where state allowed foreign medical graduates to call themselves "M.D.s" even if their degree was not M.D. degree but prohibited graduates of U.S. osteopathy schools who did not have M.D. degrees from callings using "M.D." title).

39. 559 F. Supp. 979 (S.D. Ind. 1983).

40. *See Id.* at 990 ("[T]he use of a "Ph.D" title may be misleading or deceptive among other considerations if it has been conferred . . . by an institution not recognized as meeting a minimum standard of accreditation. However, the Board or the State Legislature must first define the regulation in this area.").

41. 80 F.T.C. 815 (1972).

42. *See* 110 S.Ct. at 2288.

43. The Commission's approach to this question also is found in cases involving product certification marks. *See In re National Association of Scuba Diving Schools.*, 100 F.T.C. 439 (1982) (ordering National Association of Scuba Diving Schools to, among other things, cease representing that any diving equipment or product bearing its seal meets an objective standard of safety or reliability unless such equipment has been adequately tested, and finding that association had improperly "place[d] in the hands of . . . users of the seal an instrumentality whereby such users are enabled to and do" mislead others); *In re Hearst Magazines*, 32 F.T.C. 1440 (1941) (ordering publishers of Good Housekeeping magazine to refrain from numerous specified false and misleading uses of its product approval seals and from allowing others to make such uses).

The area of product certification has also produced at least one FTC opinion where the Commission adopted an approach to disclosure requirements similar to that of Justice Marshall's concurring opinion in *Peel. See In re Revco D.S., Inc.*, 67 F.T.C. 1158 (1965) ("Where an advertiser uses the seal of an independent organization in order to represent to the public that such organization has endorsed or approved his product, and when the endorsing organization is not one with which the public can be expected to be familiar, we think that the advertiser has an obligation to explain completely and clearly just what the significance of the endorser's seal is.").

44. *See, e.g., Patrick v. Burget*, 486 U.S. 94 (1988) (subjecting physicians peer-review committee's exclusion of physician from privileges at town's only hospital to federal antitrust analysis); *Federal Trade Comm'n v. Indiana Federation of Dentists*, 476 U.S. 447 (1986) (holding that dental association rule forbidding members to submit x-rays to dental insurers in connection with insurance claims was unreasonable restraint of trade under Sherman Act); *National Society of Professional Engineers v. United States*, 435 U.S. 679 (1978) (holding that rule of professional engineers association prohibiting competitive bidding by its members violated Sherman Act).

6

Protecting Credentialing Marks

To enable credentialed individuals or institutions to distinguish their goods and services from those of others, private credentialing organizations often issue credentialing designations. Sometimes, the organization merely allows credentialed individuals or institutions to use the organization's acronym. These designations assure the public that those using the designation possess specific qualifications or meet certain criteria in connection with their goods and services. Because credentialing designations generate good will for the owning organizations and those allowed to use them, credentialing organizations have an interest in protecting the credentials they bestow.

Federal Registration

The most important method of protecting credentialing designations is federal registration. Federal registration conveys a number of advantages. First, a registrant's right to use a mark in commerce may become incontestable following registration if the registrant meets certain conditions.[1] Second, registration provides constructive notice to other persons of a registrant's ownership rights in a mark.[2] Constructive notice prevents an infringer from alleging lack of knowledge of prior ownership of a mark as a defense in an infringement action. Finally, federal registration entitles a mark to nationwide protection.

Types of Marks

The federal Trademark Act of 1946, commonly referred to as the Lanham Act, permits parties to register the following four types of marks: trade, service, certification, and collective marks.[3] A trademark or service mark is a word, name, or symbol that its owner uses to distinguish his goods or services from those of another or to indicate their source.[4]

On the other hand, a certification mark is a word, name, or symbol used by a party other than its owner "to certify regional or other origin, material, mode of manufacture, quality, accuracy, or other characteristics of such person's goods or services or that the work or labor on the goods or services was performed by members of a union or other organization."[5] Examples of certification marks include the Good Housekeeping "Seal of Approval" and Underwriters' Laboratories' "UL" designation. Unlike trade and service marks, the owner of a certification mark cannot use the mark in connection with goods or services that the owner produces. This requirement prevents the conflict of interest that would arise if a certifying organization could certify its own goods and services.

A collective mark is a trade or service mark "used by the members of a cooperative, an association, or other collective group or organization . . . and includes marks indicating membership in a union, an association, or other organization."[6] Three types of collective marks exist: collective trademarks, collective service marks, and collective membership marks. Typically, members of an organization use collective trade and service marks to identify goods and services with the organization rather than with the individual producers of these products. The difference between a collective trade or service mark and a collective membership mark is that a collective membership mark does not identify particular goods or services, but rather signifies membership in a group.[7] Although a membership organization that owns a collective membership mark can use the mark, its members also must use the mark in a manner that indicates membership.

Generally, an organization engaged in professional certification should register a credentialing designation as a certification mark because certified individuals will want to use the designation in connection with their professional services to indicate that the certified individuals possess specific qualifications. For example, the Trademark Trial and Appeal Board ("Board") in *In re Institute of Certified Professional Business Consultants*[8] held that an applicant organization correctly sought to register a credentialing designation as a certification mark where the applicant certified that the parties using the mark were individuals who met its standards of experience, expertise, competency, and professional conduct.

Credentialing designations usually do not function as trade or service marks because certified individuals, rather than the bestowing organizations, will use them. However, if a credentialing organization intends to use a credentialing designation in connection with goods or services that it produces and offers, it should register the designation as a trade or service mark. Furthermore, if an organization plans to use a mark to denote membership in it, it should register the mark as a collective membership mark.

Credentialing organizations may also reserve certification marks that they intend to use in commerce. To enable parties to protect marks they expect to use in the future, the Trademark Law Revision Act of 1988 ("TLRA") amended the Lanham Act to permit a party not only to register a mark it is currently using in commerce but also to reserve a mark it intends to use in commerce.[9] The primary requirement for reserving a mark under TLRA's intent-to-use provisions is that an applicant have a "bona fide intention, under circumstances showing the good faith of such person, to use [it] in commerce."[10] Parties can register certification marks under the new intent-to-use provisions because certification marks are "registrable under [the Lanham Act] . . . in the same manner and with the same effect as are trade-marks."[11]

Registering a Mark

To register a credentialing mark, a credentialing organization must comply with the requirements for registering a trademark to the extent that
those requirements apply.[12] Generally, a person may register a mark as
a trademark unless the mark:

1. contains scandalous, immoral, or deceptive matter;
2. consists of a government insignia or symbol;
3. refers to a living person without his consent or to a deceased President
   of the United States without his widow's consent;
4. falsely suggests a relationship with any institution, belief, national symbol,
   or persons, living or dead;
5. is likely to cause confusion with another mark already in use; or
6. generically describes the goods or services associated with it.[13]

In addition, the Patent and Trademark Office may require an applicant
to disclaim any unregistrable component of a mark it seeks to register.[14]

   The primary procedural requirements for registering a trademark
include:

1. filing an application, a drawing of the mark, and specimens of the mark;
2. paying the registration fee; and
3. complying with any rules or regulations which the Commissioner of Pat-
   ents and Trademarks promulgates.[15]

In addition to the rules and regulations that apply to all marks, the
Patent and Trademark Office has issued regulations applying only to
the registration of collective and certification marks.

Certification Mark Registration

To register a certification mark, federal regulations require an applicant
to "specify the manner in which and the conditions under which the
certification mark is used . . . [and to] allege that the applicant exercises
legitimate control over the use of the mark and that the applicant is not
engaged in the production or marketing of the goods or services to
which the mark is applied."[16] If an applicant wants to register a certification mark under TLRA's intent-to-use provisions, it must phrase the
allegations noted above in the future tense.[17]

   A person may register a certification mark if it exercises "legitimate
control" over the mark it seeks to register.[18] This requirement ensures
that a credentialing body will allow only qualified individuals to use its
credentialing designation. If a registrant fails to police the use of his
mark, an interested party may petition the Patent and Trademark Office
to cancel the mark.[19]

   To register a credentialing designation as a certification mark for
services, the individuals authorized to use the mark must use it as if it
were a service mark and display it "in the sale or advertising of the
services rendered."[20] Similarly, a party may register a certification mark
for goods only if qualified users use the mark as if it were a trademark
and display it "on the goods or their containers or displays associated
therewith or on the tags or labels affixed thereto."[21]

In determining whether a credentialing designation functions as a certification mark, the Patent and Trademark Office will examine "the manner and context in which the term is used, as revealed by the specimens and other literature of record, and the significance which the term is likely to have to members of the public because of the manner in which it is used."[22] However, a registrant does not have to show that the public will instantly recognize the designation as a certification mark. The registrant need only show that "that the circumstances surrounding the use or promotion of the mark will give certification significance to the mark in the marketplace."[23]

A credentialing designation does not function as a certification mark if the certified individuals use the mark as a title or to indicate the attainment of an educational degree.[24] Thus, a certifying organization should make sure that individuals qualifying to use its credentialing designation do not display it as if it were a title or degree.

One way for a credentialing organization to avoid the possibility that the Patent and Trademark Office will determine that the organization's certification designation is generic or functions as a title is to register a design instead of the credentialing designation. For example, in *In re National Institute for Automotive Service Excellence*, the Trademark Trial and Appeal Board registered a design comprised of two meshed gears as a certification mark for services, because the design neither followed a name nor was a combination of letters.[25] In registering this design, the certifying organization did not seek to register the terms "National Institute for Automotive Service Excellence" and "Certified General Mechanic," which qualified users superimposed on the mark when they displayed it. Unlike a designation composed solely of words or letters, which an applicant must show are not generic or descriptive, "a background design used for the display of a word or letter mark . . . [is registrable] without any evidence of secondary meaning if it is distinctive or unique enough to create a commercial impression as an indication of origin separate and apart from the remainder of the mark."[26]

Federal law does not require an applicant seeking to register a certification mark to certify the quality of goods or services; rather an applicant need only certify that individuals meeting its standards performed the labor involved in producing a good or service.[27] Moreover, "[i]f the services rendered by persons certified by [an] applicant are not in fact of high quality, such fact may affect the value of the mark, but not its function."[28]

Enforcement: Infringement Actions

Federally registered certification marks are protected under federal law to the same extent as registered trademarks.[29] However, federal law does not protect a certification mark used "to represent falsely that the owner or a user thereof makes or sells the goods or performs the services on or in connection with which such mark is used."[30] The owner of a federally registered certification mark may bring an action for infringement under § 32 of the Lanham Act against a person using a confusingly similar mark or reproducing such a mark with the intent to use it in commerce.[31] The remedies available to an owner in such an action include injunctive relief, monetary relief, or both, depending on the circumstances of infringement.[32]

While federal registration of a certification mark applies most specifically to circumstances of professional certification, Lanham Act challenges may be suitable as well for organizations engaged in academic accreditation.

Enforcement: Federal Unfair Competition Actions

Owners of federally registered and unregistered credentialing marks may also be entitled to bring an action under § 43(a) of the Lanham Act.[33] Under § 43(a):

> Any person who, on or in connection with any goods or services, or any container for goods, uses in commerce any word, term, name, symbol, or device, or any combination thereof, or any false designation of origin, false or misleading description of fact, or false or misleading representation of fact, which
>
> (1)   is likely to cause confusion, or to cause mistake, or to deceive as to the affiliation, connection, or association of such person with another person, or as to the origin, sponsorship, or approval of his or her goods, services, or commercial activities by another person, or
>
> (2)   in commercial advertising or promotion, misrepresents the nature, characteristics, qualities, or geographic origin of his or her or another person's goods, services, or commercial activities, shall be liable in a civil action by any person who believes that he or she is or is likely to be damaged by such act.[34]

The provisions of § 43(a) are most relevant for owners of credentialing marks are those prohibiting persons or entities from falsely affiliating themselves or their goods and services with another party. The types of relief available in a § 43(a) action are the same as those available in an infringement action under § 32.[35]

Section 43(a) also protects unregistered credentialing marks from infringement because it does not require that one own a registered mark in order to bring an action under it.[36] Violations of § 43(a)'s prohibition of false designations of affiliation, connection, or association are likely to injure owners of credentialing marks. The court in *State of Florida v. Real Juices, Inc.*[37] held that an owner of an unregistered certification mark could bring an action under § 43(a) to prevent unauthorized use of the mark. The remedies available in a § 43(a) action are identical to those available to the owner of a registered mark in a federal trademark infringement action under § 32 of the Lanham Act.[38]

Enforcement: State Statutes

Credentialing organizations may be able to rely on state antidilution statutes and deceptive trade practices acts to protect their credentialing designations. Antidilution statutes typically allow an owner of a mark to enjoin the conduct of others that is likely to injure the owner's business reputation or to dilute the distinctiveness of business marks.[39] State trademark registration acts often contain antidilution provisions. For example, the Model State Trademark Bill ("Model Bill"), which serves as the basis for most state trademark registration statutes, contains an antidilution provision.[40] Because the Model Bill applies only to trade and service marks, whether registered or unregistered, an owner of a certification mark cannot bring a dilution action under the Model Bill's antidilution provision.[41]

However, if a state permits parties to register certification marks, its antidilution statute, if it has one, may apply to such marks. For example, owners of certification marks can bring dilution actions under Florida law because Florida's trademark registration provision, which defines "mark" to include certification marks, also applies to Florida's antidilution statute.[42] Thus, whether a credentialing organization can seek injunctive relief under a state antidilution statute depends on the particular language of the statute and the circumstances of dilution.

The second type of state statute a credentialing organization body may use to protect its credentialing designations is a deceptive trade practices statute. The Uniform Deceptive Trade Practices Act ("UDTPA"), which the National Conference of Commissioners on Uniform State Laws approved in 1964 and 1966, serves as the basis for most statutes of this type.[43] Although the UDTPA does not provide substantive protection for marks, it allows a party likely to be injured by another's deceptive trade practices to enjoin such misleading conduct.

Under the UDTPA, "deceptive trade practices" include:

1. caus[ing] likelihood of confusion or of misunderstanding as to the source, sponsorship, approval, or certification of goods or services;
2. caus[ing] likelihood of confusion or of misunderstanding as to affiliation, connection, or association with, or certification by, another; [and]
3. represent[ing] that goods or services have sponsorship, approval, characteristics, ingredients, uses, benefits, or quantities that they do not have or that a person has a sponsorship, approval, status, affiliation, or connection that he does not have.[44]

Given the UDTPA's broad definition of deceptive trade practices, a credentialing organization should be able to prevent another person or entity from using its credentialing designation or a similar designation if such use would falsely suggest that the credentialing organization had certified or accredited a person or institution when it had not done so.

Because the UDTPA does not require a party to own a registered mark to have standing to sue, owners of registered or unregistered credentialing marks can seek injunctive relief under it.

Enforcement: Common Law Unfair Competition

Both federally registered and nonregistered credentialing marks may also be entitled to protection from infringement under state common law. Under state unfair competition law, owners of trade and service marks can acquire common law rights in their marks. The law is based on:

[the] notions that business should be conducted fairly; that the good will and

other property of a business should be protected; that a competitor should not be allowed to trade on another's good will, palm off his goods as those of another, or be unjustly enriched by such conduct; and that the public is entitled to be protected from various kinds of deceptive business practices.[45]

Thus, the protection of trademarks against infringement is only one function of unfair competition law. State common law allows a trademark owner to acquire rights in a mark to protect the commercial goodwill which a mark generates.[46] Whether owners of credentialing designations can acquire common law rights in such marks is uncertain; however, a few cases suggest that they can.

The court in *State of Florida v. Real Juices, Inc.*[47] held that the Florida Department of Citrus acquired common law certification mark rights in the words "Sunshine Tree," which the Department allowed citrus producers to use to certify that their products contained citrus grown in Florida. Similarly, the Trademark Trial and Appeal Board in *Stabilisierrungsfonds fur Wein v. Zimmermann-GraeffKG*[48] held that a person opposing another person's trademark registration application could rely on common law credentialing mark rights to support its notice of opposition. Whether state courts will also extend common law protection to credentialing marks is unclear; however, they should be willing to do this because the reasons for protecting trademarks equally support the protection of credentialing marks.

Although the decisions in these two cases are predicated on the existence of common law rights in certification marks, their precedential value at the state level is uncertain because they both interpret federal law. However, given the similarity between the policies for protecting trade and service marks and certification marks, owners of certification marks can argue forcefully that the common law should protect credentialing designations.

State Registration

Generally, credentialing organizations may not register their credentialing designations under state trademark registration statutes. The Model State Trademark Bill only provides for the registration of trade and service marks.[49] However, some states permit parties to register certification marks. For example, as noted above, Florida expressly provides for the registration of certification marks.[50] The substantive requirements for registering a certification mark under Florida law are similar to those for registering the same mark under federal law.[51] Given this similarity, a credentialing designation that is registrable as a certification mark under federal law is likely to be registrable under Florida law and vice versa. However, state registration may be of limited value to an owner of a federally registered certification mark because it ordinarily does not enlarge an owner's substantive rights in a mark beyond those existing at common law.[52]

With the exception of an action under § 32 of the Lanham Act, the owner of a state registered mark is generally entitled to bring any enforcement action the owner of a similar federally registered mark may bring. Thus, depending on the circumstances of infringement, the owner of a state-registered mark may be able to bring actions under § 43(a) of the Lanham Act, state antidilution and deceptive trade practices statutes, and state unfair competition common law. In addition, the owner of a state-registered mark may often have a statutory claim for infringement under state law.[53]

Conclusion

A credentialing organization has available a number of methods at the federal and state level to protect its credentialing designations. To obtain the highest degree of protection, the organization should explore registration of its credentialing designations under federal law.

A single act of infringement will often provide an owner of a mark with multiple causes of action. Although the case law is unclear as to whether owners of "certification marks," as defined under federal law, are entitled to bring all of these claims, no persuasive reason exists for denying certification marks the rights and protection federal and state law grants to trademarks. Both types of marks provide the public with information about the goods and services associated with them. They both generate good will for their owners and users. Moreover, allowing persons who did not meet a credentialing organization's criteria and standards to use its credentialing designation would be inequitable.

Endnotes

1. 15 U.S.C. § 1065 (1988).
2. 15 U.S.C. § 1072 (1988).
3. Trademark (Lanham) Act of 1946, ch. 540, Pub. L. No. 489, 60 Stat. 527 (codified as amended in 15 U.S.C. §§ 1051–1127).
4. 15 U.S.C. § 1127 (1988).
5. *Id.*
6. *Id.*
7. *In re International Institute of Valuers*, 223 U.S.P.Q. (BNA) 350, 350 (T.T.A.B. 1984).
8. 216 U.S.P.Q. (BNA) 338 (T.T.A.B. 1982).
9. Trademark Law Revision Act of 1988, Pub. L. No. 100-667, 102 Stat 3935 (codified as amended in scattered sections of 15 U.S.C.).
10. 15 U.S.C. § 1051(b) (1988).
11. 15 U.S.C. § 1054 (1988).
12. 15 U.S.C. § 1054 (1988).
13. *See* 15 U.S.C. § 1052 (1988).
14. 15 U.S.C. § 1056 (1988).
15. *See* 15 U.S.C. § 1051 (1988).
16. 37 C.F.R. § 2.45(a) (1990).
17. *See* 37 C.F.R. § 2.45(b) (1990).
18. 15 U.S.C. § 1054 (1988).
19. 15 U.S.C. § 1064 (1988).
20. *In re Professional Photographers of Ohio, Inc.*, 149 U.S.P.Q. (BNA) 857, 858 (T.T.A.B. 1966).
21. *Id.*
22. *In re Institute for Certification of Computer Professionals*, 219 U.S.P.Q. (BNA) 372, 373 (T.T.A.B. 1983).
23. *In re Institute of Certified Professional Business Consultants*, 216 U.S.P.Q. (BNA) 338, 339 (T.T.A.B. 1982) (Board found that the designation "CPBC" did

not have certification significance where the designation followed a certified individual's name on a business card and was printed in the same size of type as the name).

24. *See, e.g., Professional Photographers*, 149 U.S.P.Q. at 859 (Board refused to register "Certified Professional Photographer" as a certification mark for services because the applicant's specimens showed that the certified individuals merely used the mark as a title following their names); *Certified Professional Business Consultants*, 216 U.S.P.Q. at 340 (Board refused to register "CPBC" as a certification mark for services where the designation followed a certified individual's name on a business card and was printed in the same size of type as the name).
25. *Id.* at 746.
26. *Id.* at 745.
27. *In re National Institute for Automotive Service Excellence*, 218 U.S.P.Q. (BNA) 744, 747 (T.T.A.B. 1983).
28. *Id.*
29. 15 U.S.C. § 1054 (1988).
30. *Id.*
31. 15 U.S.C. § 1114 (1988).
32. *Id.*
33. 15 U.S.C. § 1125(a) (1988). Under § 43(a):
34. *Id.*
35. 15 U.S.C. §§ 1116–1118 (1988); *see generally* 1 J. Gilson, *Trademark Protection and Practice*, § 7.02[8][b] (1991) (explains the effect of the 1988 amendments on the remedies available in a § 43(a) action).
36. 15 U.S.C § 1125(a)(1988).
37. 330 F. Supp. 428 (M.D. Fla. 1971).
38. 15 U.S.C. §§ 1116–1118 (1988).
39. *See, e.g.*, Model State Trademark Bill § 12 (United States Trademark Association 1964); Fla. Stat. Ann. § 495.151 (West 1988).
40. Model State Trademark Bill § 12.
41. *See id.* §§ 1(C), 12.
42. *See* Fla. Stat. Ann. §§ 495.011, 495.151 (West 1988 & Supp. 1991).
43. Unif. Deceptive Trade Practices Act (1966).
44. *Id.* § 2(a)(2)–(3), (5).
45. 1 J. Gilson, *Trademark Protection and Practice*, 1991, § 1.04[2].
46. 87 C.J.S. *Trade-marks, Trade-names, and Unfair Competition* § 4 (1954).
47. 330 F. Supp. 428 (M.D. Fla. 1971).
48. 199 U.S.P.Q. (BNA) 188 (T.T.A.B. 1978).
49. Model State Trademark Bill § 1 (United States Trademark Association 1964).
50. Fla. Stat. Ann. § 495.021(2) (West 1988).
51. *Compare* Fla. Stat. Ann. § 495.021 (West 1988 & Supp. 1991) *with* 15 U.S.C. § 1052 (1988).
52. See, e.g., 1 J. Gilson, Trademark Protection and Practice, 1991, § 1.04[5].
53. *See, e.g.*, Fla. Stat. Ann. § 495.131 (West 1988).

7

Tax Exemption

Credentialing organizations frequently seek to qualify for federal income tax exempt status under § 501(c) of the Internal Revenue Code. Section 501(c) lists various categories of tax exempt organizations, and each category has somewhat different tax exemption ramifications. For instance, § 501(c)(3) status—for charitable, educational, or scientific organizations—entitles the exempt organization to solicit contributions that are assured federal individual or corporate tax deductibility for the contributors as charitable contributions. On the other hand, § 501(c)(6) status—for business organizations such as trade associations or professional societies—does not allow a contributor to deduct contributions to the organization as charitable contributions (although many kinds of payments to (c)(6) organizations may be deductible as business expenses). With respect to the organization itself, neither a (c)(3) not a (c)(6) organization pays federal income tax on income related to its exempt activities, but either will be taxed on its business-related income.

Professional certification and academic accreditation organizations have frequently failed to qualify as charitable, educational, or scientific organizations under § 501(c)(3). Instead, these organizations are more often granted exception as "business leagues" under § 501(c)(6). Credentialing organizations have often had difficulty qualifying for § 501(c)(3) status because their activities may seem to the Internal Revenue Service to advance primarily the business interests of the individual credentialed constituents of the organizations rather than the public interest. Most kinds of private, nonprofit, voluntary certification or accreditation organizations that provide their credentialing services throughout an entire field of endeavor can qualify relatively easily for an IRS determination of federal income tax exempt status as business leagues under § 501(c)(6). These organizations would generally prefer (c)(3) exemption, however, because it: 1) denotes a primarily public interest goal that many credentialing organizations foster; 2) permits charitable deductions by donors; 3) may be required to obtain grants from other (c)(3) organizations and foundations; and 4) enhances the opportunity to enjoy preferential nonprofit postal rates under criteria separately administered by the U.S. Postal Service.

Because (c)(3) status is usually preferred, this chapter discusses the requirements for qualifying as a charitable, educational, or scientific organization under § 501(c)(3) and how a certifying or accrediting organization might structure its purposes and activities to qualify for the benefits inherent in § 501(c)(3) status.

Qualifying For Section 501(c)(3) Status

To qualify for tax-exempt status under § 501(c)(3), an organization must be both organized and operated exclusively for exempt purposes, it may not be formed or operated to benefit private individuals, no substantial part of its activities may constitute lobbying, and it may not engage in any campaigning.[1] In general, an organization will not qualify for § 501(c)(3) status, unless it is acting primarily in the public interest and conferring a public benefit.

If an organization fails to meet either the organizational test or the operational test of the regulations, it will not qualify for (c)(3) IRS exemption. The determination of whether an organization meets the requirements of § 501(c)(3) is highly fact-specific, and many factors are considered. First, to meet the organizational test, an organization must have an exempt purpose in its articles of organization, and it must limit the purposes of the organization to exempt purposes.[2] Furthermore, an organization is not organized "exclusively" for an exempt purpose if its articles empower it to carry on activities that are more than an insubstantial part of its activities and are in furtherance of a nonexempt or "commercial" purpose.[3] The operational test provides that an organization is regarded as "operated exclusively" for one or more exempt purposes only if it engages *primarily* in activities that accomplish one or more exempt purposes and its net earnings do not inure in whole or in part to the benefit of private shareholders or individuals.[4] While an exempt organization does not have to operate solely exempt programs to meet this test, if more than an insubstantial part of its activities is in furtherance of a nonexempt purpose it will not qualify for the § 501(c)(3) tax exemption.[5] The uncertainty surrounding what is "more than an insubstantial part of its activities" that are not in furtherance of an "exempt purpose" is demonstrated by the number of administrative rulings and cases that have addressed this issue over the years. For instance, in *Copyright Clearance Center, Inc. v. Commissioner of Internal Revenue*,[6] a corporation organized to provide a service through which public and private libraries, commercial organizations, and others could centrally pay license fees for reproducing copyrighted materials was found to be organized and operated for a substantial nonexempt purpose because the main purpose of the organization was to ensure that publishers could exploit copyrights. In another case, an organization had a substantial nonexempt purpose because it failed to demonstrate that it had a *bona fide* educational purpose and its promotional brochures emphasized recreational and sightseeing activities without including course descriptions.[7] Finally, a nonprofit corporation that operated a pharmacy, selling drugs to elderly and handicapped persons at cost, was not operated exclusively for exempt purposes. The court found that it had a substantial commercial purpose because it competed with other discount pharmacies and did not attempt to provide drugs below cost or at no cost to indigent customers.[8] Thus, the operational test is the biggest stumbling block a nonprofit organization will encounter in attempting to qualify for tax exempt status under § 501(c)(3).

Passing the Operational Test

Professional certification and academic accreditation activities may present a particular problem because those endeavors can be construed as advancing the commercial purposes of those who receive credentials. In general, such activity is regarded by the IRS as policing the field in order to advance its economic gain directly or to advance such gain indirectly by avoiding governmental regulation.

The more "commercial" a credentialing program seems to IRS, the less likely it is to obtain (c)(3) status. In one ruling in 1928,[9] the IRS found that an organization whose activities included the inspection, testing, and safety certification of cargo shipping containers, as well as research, development, and reporting of information in the field of containerization, was not operated exclusively for the purposes of testing for public safety or for scientific purposes. Thus, the organization did not qualify for § 501(c)(3) status. The IRS found that the testing and certification programs served the private interest of container manufacturers and other manufacturers and shippers by facilitating their operations and international commerce, and only incidentally the public interest. Additionally, because the testing and certification activities did not test consumer products for safe use by the general public, any public interest flowing from the certification and testing activities was deemed to be incidental.

Obviously, the kind of program reviewed in that IRS ruling is significantly different from typical professional certification and academic accreditation programs; but the ruling demonstrates the risk of being too "commercial." For organizations formed primarily to certify professionals, the IRS has found that such certification contributes to the development of the practice of an individual professional practitioner and that the benefit to the consumers of the professional services may be merely incidental, as discussed later. In another ruling,[10] a medical specialty board devised written examinations and administered them to physicians; it then issued certificates to successful candidates. This organization was held not exempt under § 501(c)(3). However, if services are provided by a private, nonprofit, voluntary credentialing organization primarily to the general public, or the organization performs services that relieve the government of a recognized burden, the organization may well qualify for § 501(c)(3) tax-exempt status.

Benefit to the Public

Where the services provided by a private, nonprofit, voluntary credentialing organization benefit the public and are not provided primarily to promote, protect, or enhance a profession or field, an organization is entitled to § 501(c)(3) status. In the *Kentucky Bar Foundation* case,[11] a nonprofit corporation whose stated purpose was to foster, promote, and carry on certain educational, literary, scientific, and charitable purposes was initially denied (c)(3) tax exempt status by the IRS. The Foundation was raising money to buy property and build a Bar Center that would house various activities of the Bar including a library that would be open to the public. The IRS contended that the Bar Foundation had a "substantial nonexempt purpose" of promoting the interest and reputation of the legal profession.

The court looked to the nature of the activities to be conducted at the Bar Center to determine whether the Bar Foundation had a substantial nonexempt purpose.[12] In doing so, the court found that the following activities served an exempt educational purpose: the continuing legal education program, the public law library, and the publication of the "Kentucky Bench and Bar." The lawyer referral service was found to serve a charitable purpose. In addition, the Client Security Fund and inquiry tribunal were found to serve the public interest and did not interfere with exempt status because any possible benefit to lawyers, by improving their reputation, was incidental and did not accrue to any one particular lawyer. Finally, the court found that the fee arbitration plan was carried out for a charitable purpose, contrary to the IRS assertion that it was merely a low-cost method for collecting disputed fees. The court also noted that any benefit accruing to the legal profession was only incidental to the educational and charitable purposes. Thus, the court held that the Kentucky Bar Foundation was operated for an exempt purpose and qualified for tax exemption under § 501(c)(3).

Similarly, in the *Fraternal Medical* case,[13] a nonprofit corporation that engaged in various activities to promote health, including: the publication of a newsletter; sponsorship of a community health fair; arranging for speakers to discuss health-related matters with community groups; and operation of a medical and dental referral service, was found to be tax exempt under § 501(c)(3). As in *Kentucky Bar Foundation*, the court found that the referrals served a broad charitable purpose and any benefit to individual service providers was merely incidental to that exempt purpose. It is important to note that any member of the public could subscribe to the information services provided by the organization for a nominal fee. Thus, the court held that the organization was not operated to serve a substantial commercial purpose and that a public rather than a private interest was served. The corporation qualified for § 501(c)(3) treatment.

An organization that conducted a voluntary accreditation program for animal care facilities qualified for tax-exempt status under § 501(c)(3).[14] In that ruling, the accreditation program was intended to educate and furnish guidance to those who maintained and operated laboratory animal care facilities and to upgrade the standards for those facilities. All organizations that have animal care facilities and use animals for research purposes were invited to apply for accreditation. The accreditation organization was funded by contributions, and the fees charged were for accreditation. The accreditation fees did not cover the full cost of administering the accreditation program.[15] The organization qualified for exemption under § 501(c)(3) because, the IRS ruled, it supported and advanced education and science and promoted humane care of animals.

It appears that an organization that performs a broad range of educational, scientific, or charitable services generally available to the public, and do not directly benefit a group of professionals or institutions, will more easily qualify for § 501(c)(3) status. Thus, an organization that conducts professional certification or academic accreditation activities may be more successful in qualifying for § 501(c)(3) tax exempt status if it can demonstrate that it provides a broad range of charitable and educational activities to the general public. In that way, even if the IRS finds that the certification or accreditation activities also serve a nonexempt purpose by benefitting the credentialed individuals or institutions, an argument can be made that such purpose is insubstantial and is only incidental to the public-directed educational and charitable purpose served by the organization.

Activities That Serve Exempt Purpose

There are signs that, in some instances, the IRS will not look for a direct benefit to the public, but will instead scrutinize the nature of the activities of an organization to determine whether they serve a (c)(3) exempt purpose undertaken by the organization. First, in a 1978 IRS General Counsel Memorandum,[16] the General Counsel rejected use of a "direct benefit" approach in favor of an approach that judges § 501(c)(3) status based on whether services provided by an organization further an exempt purpose. In the pertinent area of academic accreditation, an organization established to accredit educational institutions qualified for § 501(c)(3) status in a 1974 ruling.[17] There the IRS found that the accreditation activities advanced an exempt purpose because the program fostered excellence in education and contributed to the general welfare by ensuring that the educational community had access to the various criteria and standards for improvement. It disregarded the fact that a few of the accredited institutions were proprietary and therefore, arguably "commercial."

In contrast, a medical peer review organization did not qualify for (c)(3) status, but rather for (c)(6) status, because the IRS found that the organization was operated primarily to advance the interests of the individual members of the medical profession.[18] In that matter, the IRS found that the primary purpose of the medical review board was to police the medical field and not to educate the public. In another ruling, a city medical society that directed most activities to promoting the local medical profession did not qualify for § 501(c)(3) status.[19]

While medical society activities are suspect under § 501(c)(3) criteria, the IRS has ruled that organizations that promote improvements in health care facilities are exempt under (c)(3). In its ruling in this matter,[20] the IRS distinguishes another ruling concerning medical peer review groups. The IRS found that the medical research organization merited (c)(3) status because it was formed to develop scientific methods for diagnoses, prevention, and treatment of diseases, and to disseminate the results of its developmental work and research to members of the medical profession and the general public. Additionally, it had a professional research staff to conduct social science research and made those results available to the general public. The IRS stated that § 501(c)(3) organizations that were exclusively concerned with the research and study of existing health care facilities, the dissemination of results of such studies, and discovery and determination of methods and practices that would provide medical services to the general public would qualify for § 501(c)(3) status.

On the other hand, the IRS emphasized that a state medical association formed to operate peer review boards and to carry on other related research and oversight functions for the primary purpose of establishing and maintaining standards for quality, quantity, and reasonableness of cost of medical services does not qualify for exemption under § 501(c)(3). Apparently, the IRS regards any benefit to the public in this context as merely incidental to the primary purpose of aiding professional members of the association. This conclusion is further supported by an earlier medical society ruling.[21] In that ruling, after evaluating various educational and charitable activities in which a medical society was engaged, the IRS concluded that nonexempt purposes involving the interests of members were more than insubstantial and, thus, the organization did not qualify for § 501(c)(3) status.

Relieving Governmental Burden

Unlike the medical peer review organizations set up by local medical societies to monitor quality of care, those organizations that provide a public benefit and relieve the government of a recognized governmental burden have achieved exempt status under § 501(c)(3). In a key certification case, *Indiana Crop Improvement Assoc.*,[22] a corporation was delegated by an Indiana university the responsibility of seed certification in accordance with Indiana and federal law. The corporation also conducted other research and educational activities. The court found that it was organized for charitable, educational, and scientific purposes within the meaning of § 501(c)(3).

Likewise in a medical review case,[23] a nonprofit organization, called a "Professional Standards Review Organization," was authorized by the federal Department of Health, Education, and Welfare to establish a physician-sponsored organization in its geographic area to certify the medical necessity of hospital admissions, the appropriateness of the level of care, and the quality of care rendered for all federally subsidized patient care. This PSRO accomplished the same types of activities as medical review boards that were established by state medical societies, which the IRS had previously found were not exempt under § 501(c)(3).

The controlling factor that distinguished this case from the previous IRS revenue rulings was that the PSROs were set up to serve a particular Congressional mandate to improve delivery of health care services to Medicare and Medicaid beneficiaries. In another PSRO case,[24] the IRS acknowledged that, because the PSROs served the interests of particular federal beneficiaries and not primarily the interests of the physicians, they were distinguishable from the medical peer review boards. Thus, the PSROs were tax exempt under § 501(c)(3), whereas peer review boards set up voluntarily by medical societies were not, because the latter were policing bodies viewed as primarily advancing the interests of the individual members of the society.

Certainly if professional certification or academic accreditation activities are accomplished pursuant to a direct or indirect governmental mandate, they should have a better chance of being exempt under § 501(c)(3). If instead, they are part of a movement to discourage or avoid further governmental regulation or intrusion in the profession or field, they will more likely not receive favorable treatment under § 501(c)(3). In the middle ground where the organizations provide credentialing and other types of services that enable or assist a governmental body to meet its governmental mandate, then such activity should be deemed to further one of the exempt purposes listed in § 501(c)(3) and might qualify for that status.

Providing Benefits to Constituents

Even if an organization seeking § 501(c)(3) status provides a benefit to the general public and the organization also provides particular benefits to its constituents, such as individuals who are professionals, then the constituent services cannot be more than an incidental benefit, or the organization will be unable to obtain (c)(3) status. In the *Colorado State Chiropractic Society* case,[25] after finding that the Society met the organizational test of the regulations, the court found that a mobile educational unit, which was used approximately 30 times in connection with grand openings or open houses held by the Chiropractic Society's members at their individual chiropractic offices, was used in furtherance of commercial purposes and not exempt purposes. The court noted that such uses were not related to the general imparting of information to the public about the importance of chiropractic health care, but rather were concerned with promoting the practices of the Society's member constituents and, therefore, furthered commercial purposes. It should be noted that the court went on to find that the frequency of use of the mobile educational unit was insubstantial, so that the organization still qualified for § 501(c)(3) based on its other education-oriented activities, such as continuing professional education seminars.

Conclusion

In general, organizations engaged in professional certification or academic accreditation activities ordinarily can easily qualify for § 501(c)(6) status as "business leagues" because their activities are generally believed to further a common business interest of constituents. However, such organizations may alternatively be able to qualify under § 501(c)(3) if their activities are designed primarily to provide charitable, educational, or scientific services that benefit the public in general.

In addition, organizations that primarily pursue policing activities of their respective professions or fields, such as peer review boards, or primarily contribute to increased quality of services or products, generally are not found to be exempt under § 501(c)(3). Thus, certification and accreditation organizations that are organized and operated for the purpose of improving the quality of their credentialed constituents may be found to be analogous to policing activity and not exempt under § 501(c)(3). However, if the certification or accreditation activities are carried out by organizations whose primary activities serve the public interest, the organizations may qualify for § 501(c)(3) status. Even if the certification or accreditation activities are viewed as policing, if those policing activities are incidental to a primary public exempt purpose, the organization may qualify for § 501(c)(3) status.

Endnotes

1. *Fraternal Medical Specialist Services, Inc. v. Commissioner*, 49 T.C.M. 289, 291 (1984); Reg. § 1.501(c)(3)-1(a).
2. Reg. § 1.501(c)(3)-1(b)(1).
3. Reg. § 1.501(c)(3)-1(b)1(iii).
4. Reg. § 1.501(c)(3)-1(c)(2).
5. *Better Business Bureau v. United States*, 326 U.S. 279 (1945).
6. 79 T.C. 793 (1982)
7. *International Postgraduate Medical Foundation v. Commissioner*, 56 T.C.M. 1140 (1989).
8. *Federation Pharmacy Services, Inc. v. Commissioner of Internal Revenue*, 72 T.C. 687 (1979) *aff'd* 625 F.2d 804 (8th Cir. 1980).
9. Revenue Ruling 78-426, 1978–2 C.B. 175,
10. Revenue Ruling 73-567, 1973–2 C.B. 178,
11. *Kentucky Bar Foundation, Inc. v. Commissioner of Internal Revenue*, 78 T.C. 921 (1982),
12. *Id.* at 923.
13. *Fraternal Medical Specialist Services, Inc. v. Commissioner*, 49 T.C.M. 289 (1984),
14. Revenue Ruling 66-359, 1966–2 C.B. 219,
15. *Id.*
16. General Counsel Memorandum 37661, dated August 30, 1978.
17. Revenue Ruling 74-146, 1974–1 C.B. 129.
18. Revenue Ruling 74-553, 1974–2 C.B. 168.
19. Revenue Ruling 71-504, 1971–2 C.B. 231.
20. Revenue Ruling 76-455.
21. Revenue Ruling 71-504, 1971–2 C.B. 231.
22. *Indiana Crop Improvement Assoc. v. Commissioner of Internal Revenue*, 75 T.C. 394 (1981),
23. *Professional Standards Review Organization of Queens County, Inc. v. Commissioner of Internal Revenue*, (CCH) Dec. 36,947 (1980) *acq.* 1980-2 C.B. 2,
24. Revenue Ruling 81-276, 1981-2 C.B. 128,
25. *Colorado State Chiropractic Society v. Commissioner of Internal Revenue*, 93 T.C. 487 (1989).

8

Americans With Disabilities Act

The Americans with Disabilities Act (ADA), enacted in 1990, provides sweeping protection for disabled persons against discrimination in areas of employment, public accommodations, state and local government services, and telecommunications, regardless of whether such entities receive any federal funds.[1] The U.S. Department of Justice (DOJ) has issued final regulations interpreting the public accommodations provisions in Title III of the Act.[2] The rules set forth specific requirements for private entities that conduct examinations and courses related to applications, licensing and certification, or credentialing for educational, professional, or trade purposes. These provisions are likely to be of particular interest to private, nongovernmental, nonprofit credentialing organizations.

They apply directly to the operations of professional certification organizations, because they dictate specific and extensive accommodations that must be made for disabled persons in connection with professional certification programs. They also have applicability in the area of academic accreditation, because they specify requirements for those who offer courses of study or education to disabled persons in certain instances. Many accrediting organizations will want to consider whether the ADA requirements should be reflected in accreditation criteria.

The first section of this chapter discusses the general requirements of Title III of the Act as interpreted by the DOJ regulations. The next section describes the provisions for examinations and courses. The impact of the new rules on professional certification organizations is then discussed. Last, there is a discussion of the enforcement provisions and effective date of the rules.

General ADA Rules

Title III of the ADA, Section 302, states the Act's general rule against discrimination in public accommodations:

> No individual shall be discriminated against on the basis of disability in the full and equal enjoyment of the goods, services, facilities, privileges, advantages or accommodations of any place of public accommodation by any person who owns, leases (or leases to), or operates a place of public accommodation.

The ADA broadly defines disabilities to include a physical or mental impairment, or any record or perception of that impairment, that substantially limits one or more of the major life activities of an individual. For example, individuals with physical or mental impairments include physiological disorders, cosmetic disfigurements, visual, speech, or hearing impediments, cerebral palsy, epilepsy, heart disease, diabetes, mental retardation, HIV disease, and so forth. Environmental, cultural, or economic disadvantages, age, or sexual preferences are not included; likewise, disorders from the current use of illegal drugs are not included.

The rules define a "public accommodation" to mean a private entity that owns, leases (or leases to), or operates a place of public accommodation. The ADA contains a long list of places of public accommodation that are covered by the Act. The list includes hotels, convention centers, restaurants, auditoriums, lecture halls, bakeries, dry cleaners, professional offices of health-care providers, hospitals, and other places of public gathering or service establishments.

Title III generally requires public accommodations to make reasonable modifications in policies, practices, or procedures to accommodate individuals with disabilities, unless making the modifications would fundamentally alter the nature of the goods, services, facilities, and so forth, that are provided. In certain instances, "auxiliary aids and services," such as interpreters, note takers, videotext displays, or braille materials may be required, unless those aids and services would fundamentally alter the nature of the goods, services, facilities, and so forth, that are offered, or impose an undue burden; that is, significant difficulty or expense. Likewise, a public accommodation must remove architectural or other structural barriers in existing facilities to the extent that those steps are "readily achievable;" that is, easily accomplishable and able to be carried out without much difficulty or expense. In addition, any alteration or new construction after July 26, 1993 to places of public accommodation or any "commercial facilities" must be made to ensure that they are "readily accessible" to persons with disabilities. Guidelines for accessibility have been published with the regulations.

It is not clear whether the headquarters or office space of private, nonprofit, voluntary credentialing organizations would qualify as places of public accommodation under Title III or the DOJ's rules. To the extent that credentialing bodies sponsor or cosponsor conferences or seminars that are not considered to be examinations or courses, the meetings are covered by the general requirements of Title III.[3] However, the requirements of the Act most directly applicable and of most interest to credentialing organizations are the rules governing examinations and courses.[4]

Examinations and Courses

Section 309 of Title III imposes separate and specific requirements for private organizations offering "examinations and courses." These requirements are restated in Section 36.309 of the DOJ final rules as follows:

> Any private entity that offers examinations or courses related to applications, licensing, certification, or credentialing for secondary or postsecondary education, professional, or trade purposes shall offer such examinations or courses in a place and manner accessible to persons with disabilities or offer alternative accessible arrangements for such individuals.

dentialing would clearly fall within the scope of this provision. These rules are designed to fill the gap created when private credentialing organizations or other testing authorities are not covered by Section 504 of the Rehabilitation Act (because they receive no federal funding) or Title II of the ADA (because they are not state or local agencies).[5]

The DOJ Title III regulations have several additional provisions elaborating the requirements for entities that offer examinations and courses. These standards seem to be designed to track the general requirements for public accommodations. However, they are more specific and, in some ways, more stringent than the general rules for public accommodations.

Examinations

The regulations provide that any private entity offering an examination must satisfy the following conditions.

1. The examination must be selected and administered to an individual with a disability that "impairs sensory, manual, or speaking skills" in a way that best ensures that the examination results accurately reflect the individual's aptitude or achievement level, or other relevant factor, rather than the individual's impaired sensory, manual, or speaking skills, except where those are the skills that the examination is intended to measure.
2. An examination designed for individuals with impaired sensory, manual, or speaking skills must be offered at equally convenient locations, as frequently, and in as timely a manner as the regular examination.
3. The examination must be accessible to individuals with disabilities, or alternative accessible arrangements must be made.

Examples of required modifications to the examination procedure include changing the length of time permitted for completion of the test and adaptation of the manner in which the examination is given, such as reading the examination to the individual. In some cases, the form of the exam may need to be changed; for example, from multiple choice to essay.

The entity offering the test is also required to offer appropriate auxiliary aids to persons with the specified impairments, including but not limited to taped examinations, interpreters, brailled or large print examinations and answer sheets, readers, transcribers, and other similar services and actions. These auxiliary aids are not required if the entity can show that providing them would "fundamentally alter the measurement of the skills or knowledge the examination is intended to test or would result in an undue burden [that is, significant difficulty or expense]." The rules provide several factors to consider in determining whether an action would result in an undue burden, including, for example, the nature and cost of the action needed and the overall financial resources of the entity or parent entity sponsoring the examination.

The rules specifically state that one example of an alternative accessible arrangement is to provide the examination at an individual's home with a proctor if the test cannot be given in an accessible facility with appropriate equipment. The regulations require that any alternative arrangements must provide comparable conditions to those provided for nondisabled individuals. The preamble to the DOJ rules, for example, states that the alternative examination cannot be offered in a cold, poorly lit basement if the regular examination is provided in a warm, well-lit classroom.[6]

To the extent that examinations are offered in an educational institution, lecture hall, or other "place of public accommodation," the test must be provided in the most integrated setting appropriate to the needs of individuals with disabilities, as required by the general rules for public accommodations. In other words, disabled individuals must be given the opportunity to take all or part of examinations with non-disabled persons wherever it is appropriate and feasible to do so.

The cost of any modifications, auxiliary aids, or alternative arrangements for examinations and courses may not be charged to the disabled individuals.

Courses

The rules for courses are similar to those for examinations. They generally require that modifications must be made in courses offered by private entities to ensure that the place and manner in which the course is given are accessible to individuals with disabilities. Significantly, this provision of the rules for courses broadly refers to "individuals with disabilities," whereas the rules for examinations and other parts of the rules for courses protect only individuals with "impaired sensory, manual, or speaking skills."

Modifications in courses may include changes in the length of time allowed for completing the course, substitution of course requirements, or adapting the manner in which the course is conducted or materials are distributed. Advance notice of the opportunity to obtain materials in alternative formats must be provided to disabled individuals.

As with the rules for examinations, private entities offering courses must provide appropriate auxiliary aids and services for persons with impaired sensory, manual, or speaking skills similar to those required for examinations. Here again, auxiliary aids are not required if it can be shown that providing them would fundamentally alter the course or create an undue burden.

If courses cannot be administered in a facility accessible to individuals with disabilities, alternative arrangements must be made. Such arrangements may include offering the course through videotapes, cassettes, or prepared notes. The selection or choice of courses available to individuals with disabilities may not be restricted. As with the rules for examinations, alternative arrangements must provide comparable conditions to those provided for nondisabled individuals. Here again, to the extent that a course is offered in a place of public accommodation listed in the rules, it must be conducted in the most integrated setting appropriate to the needs of disabled individuals. Finally, of course, the costs of complying with the Act cannot be charged just to disabled individuals.

Impact Of ADA Requirements

Theoretically, the impact of the ADA rules should be relatively limited. The Rehabilitation Act of 1973 prohibits private licensing and certifying entities that receive federal funding from discriminating on the basis of disability. So organizations that receive federal funding are already familiar with similar legal requirements. It is already the usual practice of many, if not most, credentialing organizations to provide reasonable auxiliary aids, offer examinations in facilities that are physically accessible to disabled persons, and provide other special arrangements.[7]

However, the DOJ rules seem to be more detailed and exacting than existing Rehabilitation Act regulations. In some respects, the specific rules for examinations and courses are even more stringent than those for public accommodations generally. At the same time, the DOJ rules leave open several questions for private certification organizations regarding the definition of disability and extent to which the needs of disabled individuals must be accommodated.

The rules give a fairly extensive list of examples of the type of disabilities that are covered. Nonetheless, the definition of disability—a physical or mental impairment that substantially limits one or more of the major life activities, or a record or perception of such an impairment—is so broad that private, nonprofit, voluntary credentialing organizations could be encountered with a flood of issues or problems relating to individuals seeking special arrangements for conditions that are not normally considered to be disabilities for the purposes of examinations or courses. For instance, a candidate with "anxiety neurosis" could claim entitlement to extra time on the examination due to stress and anxiety.[8] There has also been some speculation as to whether the DOJ rules cover pregnancy as a temporary disability.[9] The DOJ regulations generally provide insufficient guidance to determine whether specific disabilities not listed in the rules are covered by the law.

In addition to the broad definition of disability, the rules impose an unqualified requirement that credentialing organizations modify exams or courses and provide alternative arrangements to ensure accessibility and fairness to disabled individuals. The open-ended nature of this rule is in direct contrast to the rule for auxiliary aids, which states that auxiliary aids need not be provided if to do so would fundamentally alter the examination/course or create an undue burden. There is no comparable limitation on the duty to modify an examination/course or provide accessible arrangements.[10]

In this respect, the requirements for examinations and courses are even tougher than those for public accommodations generally. As noted above, public accommodations need not make modifications in their policies, practices, and procedures if those modifications would fundamentally alter the nature of the goods, services, facilities, and so forth.

Ultimately, future judicial review of the DOJ rules may result in the imposition of an overall reasonableness requirement on the duty to modify and provide accessibility. But, until then, the DOJ rules could cause private, nonprofit, voluntary credentialing organizations to incur significant expense and administrative hassles to comply with requests for special arrangements. These costs and burdens are in addition to the following that will be incurred to provide auxiliary aids.

1. There will almost certainly be an increase in requests for special accommodations arising out of the ADA rules. Unfortunately, not all of these requests will be made by persons with legitimate disabilities.
2. In many cases, special tests and course materials will have to be produced, and alternative testing sites will have to be provided.
3. Conceivably, some credentialing organizations may be forced to drop or waive certain requirements for licensure to accommodate individuals with special needs.
4. Some undeserving requests for special arrangements may be granted to avoid costly disputes.
5. The overall validity of examination results may be threatened by a reduction in standardization of the examination process.
6. The application fee for examinations and course fees will likely increase to cover the higher costs of developing and administering exams and courses.[11]

Professional certification organizations should also take note that they may not refuse to administer an examination to individuals with disabilities on the grounds that, because of those disabilities, the individuals would be unable to perform the essential functions of the profession or occupation for which the examination is given, or the disability would otherwise be an obstacle to the organization's certification or ultimate state licensure. DOJ specifically states that an individual may not be barred from taking an examination merely because he or she might be unable to meet other requirements of the credentialing process. However, if the examination is not the first stage in the qualification process, an applicant may be required to complete earlier stages before being admitted to the examination. Certification organizations that utilize a combined cognitive and practical examination program will find these requirements perplexing.

The DOJ rules do attempt to meet some of the concerns previously expressed to DOJ by professional certification interests. For example, DOJ has concluded that it is permissible for organizations that administer tests "to require individuals with disabilities to provide advance notice and appropriate documentation, at the applicant's expense, of their disabilities and of any modifications or aids that would be required."[12] Those requirements may not be unreasonable, and the deadline for providing the notice must be no earlier than the deadline for others applying to take the exam. According to the rules, "appropriate documentation might include a letter from a physician or other professional, or evidence of a prior diagnosis or accommodation, such as eligibility for a special education program."[13]

Finally, all credentialing organizations should note that the Title III rules do not supplant other applicable state, federal, or local laws forbidding discrimination against disabled persons.[14] For instance, private entities receiving federal funds would be covered by the Rehabilitation

Act and Title III of the ADA and would have to comply with the applicable regulations issued under each law.

The two federal agencies most likely to distribute federal funds to private, nonprofit, voluntary credentialing organizations are the Department of Education and the Department of Health and Human Services. These agencies have issued virtually identical Rehabilitation Act regulations governing admission tests for postsecondary education programs and related activities receiving federal assistance.[15] Certain sections of the Title III regulations for examinations and courses were adopted directly from these Rehabilitation Act rules on admission tests, but the Title III rules are generally more comprehensive and detailed than the corresponding Rehabilitation Act rules. For the most part, therefore, compliance with the Title III rules on examinations and courses would seem to satisfy the admission test requirements of the Rehabilitation Act rules. The converse is not true: compliance with the Rehabilitation Act rules will not necessarily satisfy the requirements of Title III for examinations and courses.

In any case, to limit the risk of liability, credentialing organizations that receive federal funds should review their policies and procedures to ensure that they reflect the relevant requirements of both the Rehabilitation Act and Title III of the ADA.

Enforcement Provisions

Section 308 of the ADA provides for private suits seeking damages, injunctive relief, and attorneys' fees to be brought against persons or entities that discriminate against the disabled in violation of the Act. This relief is modeled after remedies provided under other civil rights laws. The statute also gives DOJ the power to seek injunctive relief and civil penalties of up to $50,000 for an initial violation and up to $100,000 for each subsequent violation of the Act.

Effective Date

The effective date of the Title III provisions is January 26, 1992. However, DOJ has stated that no civil enforcement actions will be brought under these provisions before July 26, 1992 against organizations with 25 or fewer employees and gross receipts of one million dollars or less, or before January 26, 1993 against organizations with 10 or fewer employees and gross receipts of $500,000 or less. Nonetheless, it would be advisable for all credentialing organizations to evaluate their policies, practices, and procedures for administering examinations and courses and take steps as soon as possible to ensure compliance with the ADA.

Endnotes

1. The Act was intended to fill a gap left by existing nondiscrimination statutes, such as the Rehabilitation Act of 1973, which apply only to entities receiving

federal funds. As discussed more fully below, because nothing in the ADA preempts these other laws, private credentialing bodies that receive federal funds must still comply with the requirements of other applicable nondiscrimination statutes and regulations.

2. *See* 56 Fed. Reg. 35544 (July 26, 1991). DOJ has also issued rules interpreting Title II of the ADA governing nondiscrimination against the disabled in the provision of public services by governmental entities. 56 Fed. Reg. 35694 (July 26, 1991). In addition, the Equal Employment Opportunity Commission has promulgated rules interpreting Title I of the Act, which prohibits employment discrimination against the disabled. 56 Fed. Reg. 35726 (July 26, 1991). This chapter focuses solely on the DOJ rules interpreting Title III.

3. The preamble to the DOJ rules clearly states:

An entity that is not in and of itself a public accommodation, such as a trade association or performing artist, may become a public accommodation when it leases space for a conference or performance at a hotel, convention center, or stadium. . . . As a public accommodation, the trade association or performing artist will be responsible for compliance with [the regulations]. Specific responsibilities should be allocated by contract, but, generally, the lessee [the association] should be responsible for providing auxiliary aides (which could include interpreters, braille programs, etc.) for participants in its conference or performance as well as for assuring that displays are accessible to individuals with disabilities. 56 *Fed. Reg.* at 35556.

4. It is clear that private, nonprofit, voluntary credentialing organizations having more than the specified number of employees would be subject to the employment provisions under Title I of the Act. Although these provisions are not discussed here, credentialing organizations are advised to review these rules to ensure they are in compliance.

5. The requirements of DOJ's Title II rules are similar, but not identical, to those of Title III. See 56 Fed. Reg. 35694.

6. 56 *Fed. Reg.* at 35573.

7. *See* Comments of National Organization for Competency Assurance on ADA Proposed Regulations, April 15, 1991, at 1. *See also* Zeitlin and Dorn, *Accommodation to Candidates with Disabilities: Are the "New" Rules New*, CLEAR Exam Review (Summer 1991) at 10 ("Certain accommodations during test administration, which are required now by the ADA and Title III regulations, already have become routine").

8. *See* Comments of National Organization for Competency Assurance on ADA Proposed Regulations, April 15, 1991, at 2.

9. *See* Zeitlin and Dorn, *supra* n.7, at 11.

10. The only boundary on the duty to modify exams is that no change need be made if the exam is designed to test the very sensory, manual, or speaking skill in which the individual has an impairment—that is , there would be no duty to modify a vision test to accommodate a blind person where vision was an essential requirement of a profession.

11. *See* Comments of National Organization for Competency Assurance on ADA Proposed Regulations, April 15, 1991, at 3.

12. 56 *Fed. Reg.* at 35573.

13. 56 *Fed. Reg.* at 35573.

14. *See* Section 36.103 of the DOJ final rules, 56 *Fed. Reg.* at 35593.

15. *See* 34 C.F.R. § 104.42(b) (1990) (Education); 45 C.F.R. § 84.42(b) (1989) (HHS).

Cases on Credentialing

The following is a list of pertinent cases relating to the credentialing process as discussed principally in Chapter 2, The Legal Framework.

Marjorie Webster Jr. College v. Middle States Association of Colleges and Secondary Schools, Inc., 432 F.2d 650, 655 (D.C. Cir. 1970), cert. denied, 400 U.S. 965

Goldfarb v. Virginia State Bar, 421 U.S. 733 (1975)

Parker v. Brown, 317 U.S. 341 (1943)

Bates v. Arizona State Bar, 433 U.S. 350 (1977)

Cantor v. Detroit Edison Co., 428 U.S. 579 (1976)

California Retail Liquor Dealers Association v. Midcal Aluminum, Inc., 445 U.S. 97, 105 (1980)

Berhagen v. American Basketball Association of the US, 884 F.2d 524 (10th Cir. 1989)

Maple Flooring Mfrs. v. United States, 268 U.S. 563 (1925)

Schachar v. American Academy of Ophthalmology, Inc., 870 F.2d 397 (7th Cir. 1989)

Federal Prescription Service v. American Pharmaceutical Association, 663 F.2d 253 (D.C. Cir. 1981), cert. denied, 102 S.Ct. 1293 (1982)

Sherman College of Straight Chiropractic v. American Chiropractic Association, 654 F. Supp. 716 (N.D. Ga. 1986)

Allied Tube & Conduit Corp. v. Indian Head, Inc., 108 S.Ct. 1981 (1988)

Virginia Academy of Clinical Psychologists v. Blue Shield of Virginia, 624 F.2d 476 (4th Cir. 1980)

Wickard v. Filborn, 317 U.S. 111, 125 (1942)

Veizaga v. National Board for Respiratory Therapy, 1977–1-CCH Trade Cases 61, 274 (N.D. Ill. 1977)

Boddicker v. Arizona State Dental Association, 549 F.2d 626, 629 (1977)

Parsons College v. North Central Association of Colleges and Secondary Schools, 271 F. Supp. 65, 75 (N.D. Ill. 1967)

Medical Institute of Minnesota v. National Association of Trade and Technical Schools, 817 F.2d 1310 (8th Cir. 1987)

Falcone v. Middlesex County Medical Society, 34 N.J. 582, 170 A.2d 791 (1961)

Salter v. New York State Psychological Association, 248 N.Y. 2d 867, 872 (Ct. App. 1964)

Treister v. Academy of Orthopedic Surgeons, 78 Ill. App. 3d 746, 396 N.E.2d 1225 (N.D. Ill. 1979)

Hawkins v. North Carolina Dental Society, 230 F. Supp. 805 (W.D.N.C. 1964), *rev'd on other grounds*, 355 F.2D 718 (4th Cir. 1966)

Pinkser v. Pacific Coast Society of Orthodontists, 12 Cal. 3d 541, 526 P.2d 253 (1974)

Arizona v. Maricopa County Medical Society, 102 S. Ct. 2466 (1982)

National Society of Professional Engineers v. United States, 435 U.S. 679 (1978)

Blalock v. Ladies PGA, 1973-1 CCH Trade Cases par. 74,597 (N.D.Ga. 1973)

Eliason Corp. v. National Sanitation Foundation, 614 F.2d 126, 128-28 (6th Cir. 1980), *cert. denied*, 449 U.S. 826 (1980)

Chicago Board of Trade v. United States, 246 U.S. 231, 238 (1918)

Paralegal Inst., Inc. v. American Bar Ass'n, 475 F. Supp. 1123, 1128 (E.D.N.Y. 1979), *aff'd*, 662 F.2d 575 (2d Cir. 1980)

U.S. Trotting Association v. Chicago Downs Ass'n, Inc., 665 F.2d 781, 790 (1981)

Zavaletta v. American Bar Ass'n, 721 F. Supp. 96 (E.D. Va. 1989)

Bogus v. American Speech & Hearing Ass'n, 582 F.2d 277, 286 (3rd Cir. 1978)

MacHovec v. Council for National Register of Health, 616 F. Supp. 248 (E.D.Va. 1985)

Hester v. Martindale-Hubbel, Inc., 659 F.2d 433 (4th Cir. 1981)

Wilk v. American Medical Ass'n, 719 F.2d 207 (7th Cir. 1983)

Hatley v. American Quarter Horse Ass'n, 552 F.2d 646, 653 (5th Cir. 1977)

E.A. McQuade Tours, Inc. v. Consolidated Air Tour Manual Committee, 467 F.2d 178 (5th Cir. 1970), *cert. denied*, 409 U.S. 110 (1973)

Bishara v. American Board of Orthopedic Surgery, No. 85 c 3400, slip op. (N.D. Ill. Dec. 30, 1986)

Watson v. Maryland, 218 U.S. 173 (1910)

Kreuzer v. American Academy of Periodontology, 558 F. Supp. 683, 685 (D.D.C. 1983), *aff'd in part, rev'd in part on other grounds*, 735 F.2d 1479 (D.C. Cir. 1984)

Dietz v. American Dental Ass'n, 479 F. Supp. 554, 560-61 (E.D. Mich. 1979)

Hannah v. Larche, 363 U.S. 420, 422 (1960)

Kronen v. Pacific Coast Society of Orthodontists, 237 Cal. 2d 289, 572 P.2d 32 (1977)

Medical Institute of Minnesota v. Nat'l Ass'n of Trade and Technical Schools, 817 F.2d 1310 (8th Cir. 1987)

Transport Careers, Inc. v. Nat'l Home Study Council, 646 F. Supp. 1474 (N.D. Ind. 1986)

Higgins v. American Society of Clinical Pathologists, 51 N.J. 191, 238 A.2d 665 (1968)

Deesen v. Professional Golfers Ass'n of America, 358 F.2d 165 (4th Cir. 1966), *cert. denied*, 385 U.S. 846 (1966)

Northwest Wholesale Stationers v. Pacific Stationery and Printing Co., 472 U.S. 284 (1985)

Appendix A
Sample Certification Procedures with License Agreement

Introduction

A professional _____ who is certified as having attained compliance with the professional competency standards identified and adopted by the Council of _____ (the "Council") demonstrates to members of the _____ profession, the public, and governmental authorities a commitment and interest in providing only the highest quality professional _____ services available. The Council's Certification Program, which is voluntary, provides more than an ordinary assurance of professional quality services; the certification designation " _____ " is recognized as the sign of achievement of excellence. The professional _____ who participates in the Council's Certification Program publicly endorses the Program's Standards of Professional Conduct and standards of excellence and offers professional services knowing that the _____ profession, the public, and governmental authorities realize that established Council standards serve as the certified professional's own starting point in delivering professional quality services.

To ensure the administration of the Council's Certification Program in a uniform and equitable manner, a Procedural Guide has been prepared for the information and guidance of the participants. The Certification Program Participant's License Agreement is the basic governing document for operation of the Certification Program. This Procedural Guide, which is incorporated by reference into that document, is designed to describe the basic procedures and administration of the Certification Program and may be updated and amended from time to time. Changes relating to program policy matters will be published in Certification Program communications.

A. The Council's Certification Program Concept

The Council's Certification Program is based upon the philosophy that any standard of professional quality services is only as good as the application of, and continuous adherence to, the requirements of that standard by those who claim to comply with its provisions.

To the profession, the public, and governmental authorities, the " _____ " designation offers assurance that professional _____ services are provided through attaining and continuously maintaining high standards of excellence.

In short, the mission of the Certification Program is to advance and help assure a high overall quality of professional services in the _____ field. To that end, the three specific goals of the Certification Program are:

1. To improve professional practice in the _____ field through the establishment of professional development goals;
2. To identify a body of knowledge and skills necessary to the practice of the _____ profession; and
3. To recognize those individuals who have demonstrated a level of excellence in the practice of the _____ profession.

B. Eligibility

Any individual who meets the criteria defined below is eligible, on a voluntary basis, to apply for certification. The specific Program eligibility criteria are as follows:

1. A person is eligible to apply if he or she, as a prescribed or ongoing part of his or her job, engages in the providing of professional services in the _____ field;
2. The applicant must be a full-time _____ professional with three years minimum experience in the _____ field; and
3. The applicant must hold a bachelor's degree in any major issued by a regionally accredited college or university.

No "grandfathering" process exists with respect to professional practice prior to the inception of the program.

C. Who Conducts the Program

The Council of _____ is the sponsor of the Program. The _____ Certification Board ("Certification Board" or "Board") is an arm of the Council and is Administrator of the Certification Program. The Board's Chairman and members are appointed by the Council.

   The Certification Board considers Program applicants and provides for review and testing as follows. The Board and its representatives develop education, experience, and communication services performance standards. The Board appoints several three-person Portfolio Review Committees that evaluate Certification Program applicants' portfolio submissions. These Review Committees are composed equally of representatives of academia, national leaders of the _____ profession, and of Certified _____ . The Board and its representatives oversee development and administration of competency examinations, review test data and perform other administrative services.

D. A Certified Professional's Representations to the Public

A certified professional in the Program represents publicly that he or she meets or surpasses the educational, experience, and professional competency standards of the Council's Certification Program.

E. How the Certification Program Works

The Program provides for simple, equitable administration and enforcement through the following procedures.

1. Professional competency standards

The Certification Board acts as follows.

   a. The Board recommends standards of education, experience, performance, competency, or other reasonable criteria for certified professionals to the Council for consideration and approval.
   b. The Board implements professional standards approved by the Council as the basis for the grant of professional certification, including standards as to length of education or professional experience, quality and quantity of any continuing professional education programs completed, quality of applicants' work sample submissions (which are specifically reviewed by three-person Portfolio Review Committees that reports to the Board), and any other approved professional standards that have a reasonable relationship to the capacity of a _____ professional to serve the profession, the public and the government.
   c. The Board administers written examinations whose contents are developed and validated by an impartial and independent third-party professional testing service.
   The professional standards for certification of _____ professionals are reviewed by the current Board and the Council at least once every year to ensure they are current and up-to-date. Questions as to the applicability of any standard to a professional are to be referred to the Board.

2. Standards of professional conduct

The Certification Board and the Council may develop, periodically review, and publish standards of professional conduct that all participants in the Certification Program agree to respect. A copy of the Standards of Conduct is attached.

3. Professional competency portfolio and examination

Within two years after the submission and approval of a Program applicant's portfolio by a Portfolio Review Committee, an applicant _____ professional must complete and pass a written competency examination administered by the Certification Board as a prerequisite to obtaining certification. If an applicant's portfolio does not achieve the minimum point requirement, he or she may appeal the decision. The contents of the professional competency written examination are validated by an impartial and independent third-party testing service. If an applicant passes the portfolio review but fails the written examination, he or she may retake the written examination, provided this is done within the two-year application period.

4. Continuing professional education

The Certification Board may adopt in the future a certification maintenance requirement that could include participation in continuing professional education courses.

5. Certified professional's directory

Certified professionals in the Program are listed in an annual Certification Directory. The Certification Directory is available to various members of the _____ profession, government regulatory agencies, and interested members of the public. Directory listings contain the participant's name, office address, and description of professional services rendered. The Directory is updated periodically to reflect the participation of new participants in the Certification Program.

F.   The Formal Certificate of Competency and Compliance with Voluntary Professional Standards

An applicant who successfully complies with the standards and procedures of the Certification Program is entitled, under the provisions of the license agreement with the Board, to certify that:
1.   He or she is a Certification Program participant, and a member in good standing in the certification program.
2.   He or she meets the professional standards of the Certification Program sponsored by the Council.

The _____ professional who certifies his or her voluntary compliance with the standards of the program is entitled, under the provisions of the Program license agreement.
1.   To use the terms " _____ ".
2.   To publicly display a formal certificate of Certification Program good standing, participation, and standards compliance.
3.   To use any other Certification Program trademarks owned by the Council and whose nonexclusive use is licensed to the program participant.

G.   Assuring Compliance with Certification Standards

1. Decertification

Any individual certified in the Certification Program found to be not in compliance with the Program's procedures or professional standards is subject to removal of certification. Following a certified professional's receipt of a notice of noncompliance, the professional enjoys a 30-day grace period in which corrective action to the satisfaction of the Board may be taken. If satisfactory corrective action is not accomplished by the end of the 30-day period, pursuant to his or her license, the certified professional automatically is no longer entitled to claim he or she is certified under the Council's Program, and he or she thereafter is excluded from the Program.

2. Notice of directory delisting

If, 30 days after the certified professional's receipt of notice of noncompliance, required corrective action is not taken, the Board will notify the professional of certification delisting in accordance with the terms of the License Agreement. The Board will remove that individual's name and listing from the next issue of the Certification Directory and disclose the decertification in the next Certification Program bulletin.

3. Notice of exclusion

If, after 10 business days from date of mailing a certified mail notice of noncompliance to the certified professional, the Board has received no notice or other evidence from the certified professional of his or her intent to take required corrective action, the Board will exclude that individual from the Program.

4. Complaints of noncompliance

Information on a certified professional supporting a complaint of noncompliance may be submitted from any source, including other certified professionals. Complaints in writing will be received by the Board, which will investigate the complaint on the following basis. The complainant will provide to the Board a minimum surety deposit of $100, which will be assessed at rate of $50 per day, plus out-of-pocket expenses, to cover all costs of the investigation, with any unused balance to be refunded to the complainant. If the Board makes a finding of noncompliance and upholds the complaint (and the Board's decision is upheld following any subsequent due process appeal as noted below), the expense of the investigation will be assessed to the certified professional found in noncompliance and the complainant's original surety deposit will be completely refunded.

H. Program Responsibility

1. The Council (Sponsor of the Certification Program)

The Council, composed of nine members, has full responsibility for the sponsorship, development, and guidance of the Certification Program and formulation of general policy to ensure the uniformity and equity of its administration on a continuing basis. Actions relating to Program policy matters are delegated by the Council to the Certification Board (which administers the Certification Program), which makes appropriate recommendations to the Council and implements matters adopted by the Council.

2. The certification board

The Certification Board shall:
- a. Establish, implement, and review all administrative procedures for the Certification Program.
- b. Conduct any review of questions raised by participants. Actions taken in the name of the Board shall be by majority vote.

3. Due process appeals review

A participant in the Certification Program may appeal in writing to the five-person independent Certification Program Appeals panel for review of the Board's interpretation of applicable certification standards, review of the Board's determination of an applicant's noneligibility or nonadmittance to, or a participant's exclusion from, the Certification Program, or for a hearing on any other complaint pertaining to the Board's final actions. A decision affirming an action or determination of the Board adverse to a Certification Program participant shall be by a three-fifths vote, provided that a statement of the factual record on which the Certification Appeals panel is acting, together with copies of any documents to be considered by the Appeals Panel, shall have been mailed to the Certification Program participant at least 15 days before any hearing and vote. This statement shall be accompanied by a notice of the time and place of the meeting of the Appeals Panel and the applicant or Program participant shall have the opportunity to appear in person and/or to be represented by counsel and to present any defense or explanation before action is taken by the Appeals Panel. The decision of the Appeals panel shall be final in the matter under consideration.

I. Certification Program Documents

This guide sets forth the operational procedures in the operation of the Program that are intended first, to ensure its integrity, and second, to maintain the uniformity and equity of its administration impartially.

Sample License Agreement

Sponsor: Council of _____
Administrator: _____ Certification Board
CERTIFICATION PROGRAM LICENSE AGREEMENT entered into this _____ day of
_____, 19_____, by and between the COUNCIL OF _____
(hereinafter "Council" or "Licensor") and _____ (hereinafter "Licensee").

WITNESSETH:

WHEREAS, the Council has established the _____ Certification Program
(hereinafter "Program"), administered by the _____ Certification Board (hereinafter "Board"), to improve the quality of professional services in the _____
field. The Program provides for the certification of professionals who voluntarily participate
in the Program and whose competency meets the Program's educational, experience, and
performance quality standards; and

WHEREAS, a formal certificate of professional competency in accordance with Program
standards shall be provided by the Council to Program participant licensees for use in
certifying a licensee's participation in the Program and voluntary attainment and compliance
with the standards thereof; and

WHEREAS, Licensee desires to participate in the Program under the terms and conditions hereinafter set forth;

Now, THEREFORE, for valuable consideration, the sufficiency of which is hereby
acknowledged, it is agreed by and between Licensor and Licensee as follows:

1. PROFESSIONAL CERTIFICATION STANDARDS AND PROCEDURES

Licensor, through the _____ Certification Board, shall review and approve
professional education, experience, and performance quality standards and review the implementation and administration thereof, as a benchmark measure of competency and
quality in the provision of professional services in the _____ field.

2. CERTIFICATION PROGRAM ADMINISTRATOR

Licensor has designated the Certification Board as the administrator of the Program.
The Board, through its established review and testing procedures, shall determine subject
to any due process appeal by Licensee to the Certification Program Appeals Panel whether
Licensee and other licensees meet the Program's professional standards. The Board's duties
shall include, but not be limited to, the following:

A. Develop and recommend for approval by the Council various certification standards
and procedures concerning education, experience, performance, or other reasonable criteria
relating to competency of professionals in the _____ field and the maintenance
of certification;

B. Implement certification standards approved by the Council that have a reasonable
relationship to the capacity of professionals in the _____ field to serve the
profession, the public, and the government;

C. Administer periodic written competency examinations for professionals in the
_____ field. The contents of these examinations shall be developed and validated by an independent third-party professional testing service;

D. Authorize, withdraw, or deny to any Licensee or applicant to the Program the right to designate himself or herself as a "_____" and to display a formal certificate of competency in accordance with Program standards. The Licensee or applicant may appeal to the Certification Program Appeals Panel for a due process review of the Board's interpretation and application of the applicable standards in accordance with procedures set forth in the Certification Procedures.

3. LICENSEE'S CERTIFICATION DUTIES

Licensee voluntarily agrees to accept the Program's certification standards and to submit the necessary information for participation in the Program in accordance with the Procedures set forth in the Certification Procedures. Failure to submit necessary supporting information and abide by Program standards shall be due cause for revoking this Agreement.

4. CERTIFICATION DETERMINATION

Licensee shall be deemed "certified" when the Board has determined that the Licensee meets Program standards and has issued a formal certificate to Licensee enabling Licensee to publicly stipulate his or her compliance with Program procedures and standards. Licensee may publicly display said certificate only during such period as Licensee is in compliance with Program procedures and standards and is a registered participant in the Program. Licensee shall not display the certificate when the necessary Administrator's finding of compliance has been withheld or withdrawn. Subject to the right of due process appeal specified hereinafter, Licensee shall abide by the decision of the Board as to the compliance or noncompliance of Licensee with applicable Program standards. Licensee shall not permit the display or use of the certificate other than as permitted by the Board and the terms of this Agreement and the Certification Procedures. Use of the certificate in contravention of this Agreement will be due cause for Licensor to revoke this Agreement and to issue a public announcement to this effect in accordance with the provisions of the Certification Procedures.

5. CERTIFICATION PROGRAM DIRECTORY

Licensor shall prepare and publish periodically, as it deems appropriate, a Certification Directory containing a list of all who are certified at the time of each publication. Licensor shall publish periodic bulletins to include any additions to or deletions from the Certification Directory.

6. PROGRAM CERTIFICATION PROCEDURES

Both the Licensee and Licensor shall follow and be controlled by the procedures and rules regarding the formulation of standards, the administration of competency examinations, reporting of information, complaints, display of formal certificates of participation in the Program, and due process appeals from decisions of the Board and other matters to which this Agreement refers, as set forth in the Certification Procedures developed and periodically reviewed and updated by the Board.

7. LICENSEE'S GOOD FAITH COMPLIANCE

Licensee shall use all practical means at his or her disposal continuously to assure that the services he or she provides fully comply with applicable Program standards at all times.

8. CHARGES OF LICENSEE NONCOMPLIANCE

Licensee agrees that if a claim of noncompliance with Program procedures or standards is filed against Licensee, he or she will promptly comply with any requests of the Board for necessary information. Licensee agrees to reimburse Licensor for any expenses related thereto, unless the claim was filed by another Licensee and is found to be without merit, in which case the charging Licensee shall so reimburse Licensor. Licensee agrees to reimburse Licensor for expenses incurred in connection with a meritless charge that he or she files. Licensee agrees that if the Board provides notice to Licensee that he or she is in noncompliance, he or she will enjoy a 30-day grace period in which Licensee may take corrective action to the satisfaction of the Board, but if satisfactory corrective action is not taken by the end of the 30-day grace period Licensee then will discontinue public representations of certification until the board again approves Licensee for certification, or the Board's decision is reversed on a due process appeal taken in accordance with procedures set forth in the Certification Procedures.

9. CERTIFICATION STATUS REPRESENTATION

When reference is made to Program certification by Licensee at any time, only the term "_____", or an official certificate issued by Licensor, or a Program logo and trademark owned by Licensor and whose nonexclusive use by Licensee is hereby licensed by Licensor to Licensee, shall be referred to or used, and such certificate, if referred to or used, shall be printed in full, without alteration of any kind. Licensor shall have the right to notify Licensee of any material used or issued by Licensee that Licensor considers to be misleading to the public in regard to any reference to Licensor or to Licensee's certification, and Licensee agrees on receipt of notice from Licensor to terminate use of such materials and take such other steps as Licensor may deem appropriate in the public interest.

10.   INDEMNIFICATION AND HOLD HARMLESS

Licensee agrees to indemnify and hold harmless Licensor, the Board and their directors, officers members, employees, and agents from and against any and all liability, loss, damages, costs, or expenses, including reasonable attorneys fees, which they may incur, suffer, or be required to pay by reason of, or in consequence of, Licensee's actions, or breach of this Agreement or any acts or omissions of Licensor or the Board in respect to the right granted hereunder to obtain and to represent certification status or to display formal certification certificates, or that may be sustained or incurred in making any investigation on account of any claim, loss, cost, damage, or expense, or in defending or prosecuting any action, suit, or other proceeding that may be brought in connection therewith, or in enforcing any of the obligations herein contained, or in obtaining a release from liability in connections therewith.

11.   DURATION AND TERMINATION OF AGREEMENT

Licensee agrees that Licensor may, on ten days written notice to licensee, terminate this Agreement for any of the causes set forth in this Agreement and in accordance with the due process procedures of the Certification Program. Otherwise, this Agreement shall be effective on the date of execution and shall be renewed automatically with the signature of the licensee of same agreement every three years.

12.   DECERTIFICATION

Procedures for decertification, and due process appeals thereof, shall be as set forth in the Certification Procedures and this license. Licensor, in the event it shall be necessary to exclude Licensee from participation in the Program in accordance with the provisions of this Agreement, may do so by giving Licensee ten days written notice of Licensor's termination of the License Agreement.

13.   GOVERNING LAW: ENTIRE AGREEMENT: AMENDMENTS

The interpretation of this Agreement and the parties' performance thereunder shall be governed by the laws of the District of Columbia. This Agreement, together with the Program Certification Procedures, which is incorporated herein, constitutes the entire Agreement between the parties and all of the terms agreed upon by the parties with respect to the subject matter of this Agreement and supersedes all prior agreements, arrangements, and communication between the parties concerning such subject matter, whether oral or written.

14.   WAIVER

Waiver by either party of any term or condition of this Agreement or any breach thereof shall not constitute a waiver of any other term or condition or other breach.

15.   NON-ASSIGNABILITY

Licensee may not assign, transfer, or otherwise dispose of this Agreement to any other person.

16.   COUNTERPARTS

This Agreement may be executed in one or more counterparts, each of which shall be considered an original, and all of which taken together shall be considered one and the same instrument.

In WITNESS WHEREOF, the parties hereto have caused this Agreement to be executed and delivered as of the date and year first above written.

LICENSEE

_____

(Print name)

_____

(Signature)

LICENSOR

By _____

(Signature)

_____

(Print Name)

Its _____

(State office)

Appendix B
Sample Accreditation Procedures

1. Purpose of Accreditation.   The Council on Accreditation of the American _____
_____ Association ("Council") accredits educational and training programs at the
_____ levels in certain professional areas of the field of _____. The
purpose of accreditation is to promote excellence in programs designed to educate and
train professionals and to provide a valid and objective evaluation of these programs as a
service to the public, prospective students, and the profession.

2. Standards for Accreditation.   All actions with respect to accreditation taken by
the Council shall be governed by the Criteria for Accreditation ("Criteria") in force at the
time an application for accreditation is made to the Council. The Criteria are developed,
adopted, and promulgated by the Council in a separate document. Advance notice of six
to twelve months is given of all proposed substantive changes of the criteria and evaluating
policies, providing the opportunity for comment by affected persons, institutions, and
organizations.

3. Procedures.   These procedures outline the functions of the Council and the major
actions that occur in the operation of its accreditation process. This document identifies
the functions of the Council, its volunteers and staff, and prescribes general rules and
procedures for the operation of its accreditation program in a manner that promotes the
availability of due process throughout.

4. Categories and Duration of Accreditation

a. There are three categories of accreditation:

   (1) Full Accreditation is granted to any program that, in the exclusive judgment
       of the Council, meets the Criteria in a satisfactory manner.

   (2) Provisional Accreditation is granted to programs making initial application
       that, in the exclusive judgment of the Council, do not meet all the Criteria,
       but for which the Council believes there is a reasonable expectation that they
       will be met within a foreseeable period of time from the date of the initial
       site visit.

   (3) A program that has been awarded full accreditation may be placed on *Pro-
       bation* when the Council has evidence that it is not currently in satisfactory
       compliance with the Criteria.

b. Normal Intervals Between Site Visits.   At the time of award of any of the three
categories of accreditation, the Council specifies the academic year during which the next
site visit to the program is expected to occur, under the presumption that the program will
maintain its degree of compliance with the Criteria during the intervening period as reflected
in the annual report specified in Section 4.c. below. For fully accredited programs, this is
normally the fifth year following the last site visit; for provisionally accredited programs,
it is the third year. Probationary status continues for a minimum of one year after the site
visit.

c. Annual Reaffirmation of Accreditation: Annual Reports.   Each accredited program files an annual report with the Council, in accordance with guidance furnished by the Council, which presents a limited self-study by the program and provides evidence of the program's continued compliance with the Criteria at the level of its accredited status. If this report is acceptable to the Council, the program's current accredited status is reaffirmed for the next academic year. If it is not, the Council may request additional information or an invitation for a site visit, stating to the program the reason that such a visit is necessary. In either case, the current accredited status of the program is maintained until the Council takes action, in accordance with Section 9.b. below.

5. The Council on Accreditation

a. Functions.   The principal function of the Council is to exercise professional judgment in making decisions on programs as specified in Section 9.b. below. It also develops guidance documents and data-gathering instruments necessary to carry out this principal function, institutes programs for the training of site visitors, provides consultation to programs, interacts with other elements of the governance structure of American _____ Association on matters related to accreditation, and takes such actions as required to enable it to carry out its functions.

b. Membership.   The Council consists of not fewer than ten members appointed by the American _____ Association, for staggered three-year terms, from these one member is elected by the Council as chairperson. The membership of the Council includes at least two public members who are not members of the _____ profession. Members of the _____ profession who serve on evaluation committees or other bodies that recommend the award of funds to education or training programs that have or may seek Council accreditation may not accept concurrent membership on the Council.

c. Quorum.   Two-thirds of the members constitute a quorum for the purpose of making a decision on a program (see Section 9.b. below). When a Council member has withdrawn from a portion of the meeting (as in Section 5.d. below), that position is not counted in determining a quorum. The vote of the majority of the Council members at a meeting at which a quorum is present is required to make a program decision.

d. Avoidance of Conflict of Interest.   Should a member of the Council be in possible conflict of interest with respect to any program scheduled for review by the Council at any particular meeting, that member is excused during discussion and decision on that program. Furthermore, the Council may, in its judgment, determine that a member is in possible conflict of interest and ask that member to withdraw from discussion of, and decision on, a particular program.

e. Executive Committee.   An Executive Committee is appointed by the chairperson of the Council, including at least one member each in the third, second, or first year on the Council, to act for the Council between meetings on accreditation matters other that the making of program decisions as outlined in Section 9.b. below.

f. The Exercise of Professional Judgment.   A high degree of professional judgment in the application of the Criteria is required in the review of applications, in the conduct and reporting of site visits, and in the deliberations of the Council. Professional judgment must be used not only in evaluating the extent of compliance by a program with each individual criterion but also by the site-visiting team in making its overall recommendation to the Council and by the Council in reaching its final decision. Thus, there is no minimum "score" of the number of criteria with which a program must be in compliance to be accredited. Rather, an overall judgment is exercised as to whether, in light of the mode and degree of compliance with each criterion, the program is fulfilling acceptable, publicly stated objectives.

6. The Process of Applying for Accreditation

a. Governing Principle.   Because the accreditation process is initiated by the program that submits itself for review, the burden of proof of compliance with the Criteria rests with the applicant. Therefore, an application must be prepared with that degree of thoroughness that will satisfy detailed review by staff, by a site-visiting team, and by the Council.

b.   The Council provides oral and written *consultive guidance* to programs undergoing the accreditation process.

c.   The Application constitutes a report of the results of a self-study made by the program, organized in accordance with guidelines furnished by the Council. The topics in these guidelines follow the sequence of the Criteria and afford the program the opportunity to document in detail how it complies, in its own unique fashion, with the several items in the Criteria.

d.   Signatories of the Application.   A completed application, accompanied by payment of the application fee (see Section 12 below), may be forwarded to the office of the Council at any time. An application from a program must be signed by the director(s) of the program and the director(s) of any academic department wherein the program may be located.

e.   Acceptance of the Application.   In order to expedite processing, the staff of the Council reviews each application and may schedule initial site visits to programs that, from the application alone, seem to meet a substantial number of the Criteria. Before making this decision, staff may request additional information from a program when the application seems to be incomplete in its response to one or more criteria-related topics in the application guidelines. Staff refers to the Council all applications from programs that may not clearly meet enough of the Criteria to warrant a site visit. The Council decides, by vote of the majority of the Council members at which a quorum is present, to:

(1)   accept the application and schedule a site visit; or

(2)   reject the application because it seems on the face of the application that the applicant does not meet the Criteria for accreditation; or

(3)   request additional information.

f.   Notice of Rejection.   In the event the application is rejected by the Council, it advises the program in writing of the reasons for its rejection. The program may appeal the rejection to the Board of Directors of the American _____ Association as provided in Section 11 below.

g.   Withdrawal of Application.   At any time before the Council takes final action to grant or refuse accreditation to an applicant program, the senior signatory may withdraw the application without prejudice.

7.   Site Visits

a.   Purpose.   The site visit constitutes an essential and unique step in the award and renewal of accreditation because it provides for collegial interaction between experienced professional members of the visiting team and professionals associated with the program, as well as with any appropriate administrative officials of the host institution. The Council has the responsibility to provide for the training of site visitors. In addition, periodic evaluations of site visitors and their written reports are conducted by the Council. Visitors are provided in advance with self-study reports by the program. By discussions with members of the educational and training staff, students and support personnel, and by inspection of facilities and equipment, the visitors are able to form professional judgments about the program's degree of compliance with the Criteria. In addition to providing the Council with a report of the team findings, the visit is expected to be of benefit to the program in its quest for excellence.

b.   Arrangements for the Visit.   When a site visit is required, the Council requests an invitation from the chief executive officer of the institution in which an educational or training program is located. If an invitation is not forthcoming from an accredited program, it will be dropped from the list of accredited programs. Upon receipt of the invitation, the program selects, from a list of names drawn from a pool of visitors approved by the Council, a visiting team. No fewer than three persons constitutes a team to visit a program, except by mutual agreement between the Council and the program. Detailed arrangements for the visit are made through direct contact between the program and the chairperson of the visiting team.

c.   Report of the Visiting Team.   Within 30 days of the completion of the visit, the team forwards a written report ("Report") in a format prescribed by guidance furnished by the Council. The Report includes a recommendation to the Council of the accreditation status to be awarded the program. This recommendation is advisory to, but not binding on, the council. The recommendation of the visiting team is transmitted to the program along with the report. The written Report of the site visitors should clearly distinguish between statements about actual or potential deficiencies in meeting criteria and statements offering consultative recommendations to the institution or program.

d. Response by the Program. The program acknowledges receipt of, and may file with the Council a written response ("Response") to, the Visiting Team's Report. The Response is filed within 30 days of receipt by the institution of the Report; however, upon written request, the period for responding may be extended for an additional 30 days. The program includes in its Response any objections, corrections, additional facts, exhibits, or comments it has to the Report of the Visiting Team. Any statement of facts in the Report that are not disputed in the Response are considered by the Council to be undisputed.

8. Complaints

a. About the Operation of an Accredited Program. To be considered by the Council, a complaint about the operation of an accredited program must:

(1) be written and signed;

(2) identify the individual group or legal entity represented by the complainant;

(3) present substantial evidence that the subject program is not in compliance with one or more of the criteria in use at the time referred to in the complaint;

(4) demonstrate, when reasonably possible, that serious effort has been made to pursue all review procedures provided within the institution in which the program is located; and

(5) grant permission to send the complaint, in its entirety, to the program.

Receipt of a complaint meeting these requirements is acknowledged by Council staff and sent to the program for comment. Both complaint and comment are placed on the Council agenda for its next scheduled meeting. The Council may reach a decision at that meeting wherein the matter is resolved and so inform the program. The Council may vote to pursue the matter further, either by further correspondence with the program or by means of a special site visit to provide additional information on which to reach a decision on the accreditation status of the program, as outlined in Section 9. below. The program is afforded the opportunity to comment on any additional information provided to the Council by means of a special site visit. The Council communicates the disposition of the complaint, in writing, to the complainant and the program.

b. Against Actions of Site Visitors. The chief executive officer of the host institution may file a complaint regarding the actions of site visitors. That official must notify the Council of the institution's or program's intent to file a complaint within 14 days after completion of the site visit. Subsequently, the complaint should be addressed to the council and must:

(1) be written and signed;

(2) be sent *before* the host institution has received the written report from the site visit team and within 30 days after completion of the site visit;

(3) provide a clear description of the critical incident(s) in question; and,

(4) grant permission to send the complaint, in its entirety, to the site visiting team.

Receipt of a complaint meeting these requirements is acknowledged by the Council's staff and held until the Report of the site-visiting ream is received. The complaint is sent to all members of the site-visiting team with request for comment within 30 days. At the same time, the site visit Report is sent to the program for comment. On receipt of (1) the comments by site visitors on the complaint and (2) the Response of the program to the site visit report, both sets of papers that pertain to the visit to a particular program are placed on the Council's agenda for its next scheduled meeting.

In mailing the agenda to the Council members, the complaint is covered separately and not bound with the site visit report and program's response in the main agenda book. In preparation for the meeting of the procedures, members are requested to observe the following procedures. Each member is asked to review the complaint and site visitors' comments and then to review the site visit Report and Response to it and form an opinion as to whether the action(s) of the site visitors were such as to void the site visit report.

Based upon its review of the relevant materials, the Council may reach the following decisions by a majority vote:

(1)   Deny the complaint, thereby sustaining the site visitor(s);

(2)   Sustain the complaint, thereby requiring a reprimand of the site visitor(s), which may include deletion from the list of potential site visitors maintained by the Council; or

(3)   May vote to pursue the matter further, either by further correspondence with the parties involved, or by means of a special fact-finding group, to provide additional information on which to reach a decision.

In the event the Council votes to sustain the complaint, it then must determine whether the critical incident(s) influenced the content of the site visit report. If the incident is determined to have influenced the site visit report, the Council voids the site visit Report and request from the host institution an invitation to revisit at Council expense. If the incident is determined not to have influenced the site visit Report, the Council proceeds with its decision regarding the program's compliance with the Criteria presented in Section 9. below.

In no case is the Council's decision regarding the program's compliance with the Criteria made until the complaint has been disposed of by the Council.

The Council communicates the disposition of the complaint, in writing, to the chief executive officer of the host institution of a program and to the site visitor(s).

c.   Processing an Accreditation Complaint that is in Litigation.   If, in the course of processing a complaint, the Council finds that the party against which the complaint is filed is involved in litigation over the same issue, the Council, upon advice from legal counsel, may exercise its discretion in determining the most appropriate action to take in the case before it. That discretion can be guided by a number of factors, including whether the complainee is willing to cooperate with the Council, how protracted the litigation is likely to be, whether the failure to initiate action against the program immediately might damage the public interest, and the impact on the confidentiality of the Council's deliberations if its files are subpoenaed during the course of litigation. In all instances, the Council should consider the potential effect of its action upon the interests of the public and the profession.

9.   Council Decisions on Accreditation

a.   Documentary Bases for Decisions.   Before rendering a decision on the award, denial, renewal, placing on probation, or revocation of accreditation, the Council reviews the current self-study by the program (application or annual report), the most recent site visit report, the program's Response to that Report, and other relevant materials and the program's comments on these materials. The Council may make a decision or it may defer action until its next scheduled meeting in order to obtain more information on which to base a decision. The decision of the Council is recorded in the minutes and transmitted not later than one month following the decision to the chief executive officer of the institution housing the program, together with a statement of the factual basis for the decision and, in the case of an adverse decision, the criteria the program did not meet. That communication of the final accrediting decision clearly distinguishes between statements speaking to actual or potential deficiencies in meeting criteria and statements offering consultative recommendations to the institution or program. In the decision letter, the Council encourages the program and its host institution to share information about its accredited status appropriately.

b.   Award, Renewal, or Denial of Accreditation.   Four types of decisions may be made by the Council to award, renew, or deny accreditation

(1)   In the case of a new program applying for accreditation, the Council first votes whether to grant *full* accreditation. If the Council votes not to grant full accreditation, then the Council votes whether to grant *provisional* accreditation. Programs that receive neither provisional nor full accreditation are denied accreditation.

(2)   In the case of a provisionally accredited program, the Council first votes whether to grant *full* accreditation. If the Council votes not to grant full

accreditation, the Council votes whether to renew *provisional* accreditation for a specified period. Programs that receive neither full accreditation nor continued provisional accreditation have their provisional accreditation revoked (see Par. 9.d. below).

(3)   In the case of a fully accredited program, the Council votes whether to renew full accreditation. A program whose full accreditation is not renewed is automatically placed on *probation* for a period of not less than one year.

(4)   In the case of a program on *probation,* the Council votes first whether to reinstate full accreditation. If the Council votes against reinstatement, it then votes whether to continue probation for a specified period. A program that is neither reinstated nor granted continued probation has its accreditation revoked.

c.   Effective Date of a Decision and its Public Announcement.   Award of full or provisional accreditation, in accordance with Section 9.b. above, is effective as of the last day of the site visit, the Report of which was among the documents used by the Council in reaching its decision. Other decisions are effective as of the adjournment of the meeting of the Council when the decision was made. The next site visit is scheduled from this same date. There is an annual listing of accredited programs in an appropriate professional journal selected by the Council, with a mid-year update of the listing, to reflect the latest decisions of the Council, including revocations, except that no change in the status of a program is reflected in these listings if the program has filed an appeal that has not been decided. In the same public listing, notice is given of programs that voluntarily withdraw from accredited status. The Council takes action to correct any errors of fact or possibly misleading statements in its public listing in a timely manner.

d.   Revocation of Accreditation.   A provisionally approved program that receives neither full accreditation nor continued provisional accreditation has its provisional accreditation revoked.

A program on probation that is neither reinstated on full accreditation nor granted continued probation has its accreditation revoked.

A program on full accreditation that does not have its full accreditation continued is automatically placed on probationary status for a period of not less than one year. The placing of a program on probation is a clear warning that, if it does not substantially correct the deficiencies noted by the Council, the program will have its accreditation revoked at the end of the probationary period.

The Council has the authority to delete a program from the list of approved programs when the Council has sufficient documentary evidence that the program is no longer a functional entity. At a subsequent time the program may reapply for accreditation without prejudice.

10.   Voluntary Withdrawal from Accredited Status.   The chief executive officer of the institution in which a program is located may request the removal of a program from the published list of accredited programs. The Council will comply with that request and delete the program. At a subsequent time the program may reapply for accreditation without prejudice.

11.   Appeal of Decision of the Council

a.   Filing an Appeal.   The chief executive officer of the host institution of a program may appeal any of the decisions of the Council specified in Section 11.b. below within 30 days of receipt of written notice of the Council's decision. The appeal must specify the grounds on which the appeal is made. The appeal should be addressed to the President of the American _____ Association. The burden of presenting the argument initially, and or persuading the appeals body, rests with the program filing the appeal.

b.   Appealable Decisions.   Only the following decisions of the Council may be appealed:

(1)   In the case of a program applying for an initial site visit, a denial of the initial visit;

(2)   In the case of a program applying for accreditation, a denial of full or provisional accreditation;

(3)   In the case of a program applying for accreditation, the award of provisional instead of full accreditation.

(4)   In the case of a provisionally accredited program, a denial of full accreditation, continued provisional accreditation, or revocation of provisional accreditation.

(5)   In the case of a fully accredited program, a decision to place the program on probation.

(6)   In the case of a program on probationary status, a decision to continue probation or to revoke accreditation.

(7)   In the case where the Council decides to request the next site visit in a fewer number of years than the normal intervals defined in Section 4.b. above.

c.   Formation of *ad hoc* Appeal Panel.   Within 30 days of receipt of the appeal, the Board of Directors of the American _____ Association names three members of an *ad hoc* Appeal Panel, and three alternates, no one of whom shall have had affiliation with the program filing the appeal or with the accreditation process relating to that program. Staff of the Council determines the willingness of the designated principals and alternates to serve and notifies the program of the names of the three principals. If the program shows good cause why a named principal is unacceptable, an alternate is selected who is acceptable to both parties.

d.   The Meeting of the Appeal Panel.   The Appeal Panel meets within 90 days of the date on which the program is notified of the adverse decision by the Council or on a date mutually acceptable to the program, the Appeal Panel, and the Council representative. The program may have one or more representatives appear before the Panel to make an oral and/or written presentation and to respond to questions from the Panel. The Chairperson of the Council designates a representative to appear before the Appeal Panel to support the decision of the Council and to respond to questions of the Appeal Panel. Either party may be represented by counsel; however, the proceeding is conducted on an informal basis. The Appeal Panel may request the assistance of counsel to provide guidance in the interpretation and resolution of legal or procedural problems that may arise in the context of an appeal.

e.   Documents To Be Considered by the Appeal Panel.   The issues addressed by the Appeal Panel are limited to those included in the appeal made by the program. The panel, the appellant, the Council's representative, and legal counsel will be furnished with all the documents reviewed by the Council in making its decision and the letter notifying the program of the Council decision. Changes that may have been made by the program that would alter the nature of the program as described in these documents may not be considered by the Appeal Panel.

f.   Decisions of the Panel.   The function of an Appeal Panel in a given case is to review the decision of the Council based on the record that was before the Council at the time of its decision. In the event that the decision of the Council is not upheld, the case will be remanded to the Council for disposition in a manner not inconsistent with the findings of the Appeal Panel.

g.   Reporting of the Decision of the Panel.   The report of the Panel, including the decision and the reasons for it, is prepared within 30 days and is addressed to the President of the American _____ Association. Copies are forwarded to the chief executive officer of the host institution of the program and to the chairperson of the Council.

12.   Financial Support of the Accreditation Program.   The costs of the accreditation program are met by application and annual fees, by charges for site visits paid by programs, and by contributions from the American _____ Association or others. The Council may accumulate a reasonable surplus for future contingent needs. The Council sets fees on a three-year basis and site visit charges on an annual basis. Current schedules of fees and site visit charges are available from the Council.

13.   Confidentiality of Records.   The records of the Council and of *ad hoc* Appeal Panels used in making decisions on the accreditation of programs and recommendations

on all applications before it, and all records of the Council relating to accreditation, shall be kept confidential except:

a.   Listings of all categories of accredited programs are published, as determined by the Council and specified above.

b.   Disclosure is made in those instances in which the Council is legally required to disclose information.

c.   At the request of the chief executive officer of the institution where a program is located, information on a specific program may be made available upon request to other accrediting agencies by which the institution has been accredited or whose accreditation it is seeking.

d.   In the case of an appeal, the Council's decision as recorded in the minutes is available to the Board of Directors of the American _____ Association.

Appendix C
Sample Bylaws of Incorporated Certification or Accreditation Board

ARTICLE I.   NAME

The name of this Corporation shall be referred to as the Board.

ARTICLE II.   PURPOSE

The Board shall exist to serve the public and the field of _____ through the establishment and maintenance of criteria and procedures for certification (accreditation).

ARTICLE III.   LIMITATIONS

The Board is a private, nonprofit, tax-exempt, autonomous, voluntary credentialing organization. No part of the net earnings of the Board shall inure to the benefit of, or be distributable to, its Directors, officers, or other private persons, except that the Board shall be authorized to pay reasonable compensation for services rendered and to make payments and distributions in furtherance of the purposes set forth in Article II, above.

The Board shall not engage in any activities relating to election campaigns for candidates seeking political office.

ARTICLE IV.   BOARD OF DIRECTORS

Section 1. Director: The Board shall be composed of _____ voting members representing the following organizations:
(*List organizations and number of attributable Board Members for each*).

Section 2. Selection and Appointment: The (name organization) shall appoint _____ Director(s) who shall (state criteria). The at-large population of Board certificants (accredited programs) shall elect, by majority vote, the balance of the Directors who shall be Board certificants (Accredited program directors).

The Board of Directors shall itself appoint one Director representing the public. That appointee shall be chosen from a list of nominees provided by nonprofit organizations.

Additional qualifications shall be determined by the organization or group appointing or electing the respective Directors.

Section 3. Term of Office: Directors shall serve a term of three (3) years from the date of their entrance into office, or until their successors are seated. A full three (3) year term shall be considered the passage of three (3) annual meetings. After designation by an appointing organization, the term of a Director may not be reduced, except for cause as specified in these bylaws. No Director shall serve more than two (2) terms. Directors shall take office at the close of the annual meeting at which they are appointed.

Section 4. Vacancies: In the case of a vacancy, resignation, or removal of a Director, the appointing organization shall designate a person to fill the unexpired portion of the previous Director's term; in the case of an at-large Director vacancy, the chairman of the Board shall fill the vacancy for the unexpired portion of the term.

Section 5. Resignation: A Director may resign at any time by filing a written resignation with the chairman of the Board.

Section 6. Duties and Functions of the Board: The Board shall have full authority to establish policies, rules, regulations, and requirements for the certification (accreditation) program. The Board shall circulate proposed relevant changes in policies, rules, regulations, and requirements, to the organizations represented on the Board at least sixty (60) days prior to the meeting at which the Board will vote on the proposed changes, for their review and comment. Upon Board approval, reasonable advance notice will be given prior to implementation.

The Board shall establish and maintain fee structures for its certification (accreditation) program.

The Board shall direct the establishment and implementation of certification (accreditation) criteria and procedures for its certification (accreditation).

The Board may remove any Officer or Director for cause by two-thirds (2/3) vote of the entire Board of Directors at any regular or special meeting of the Board, provided that a statement of the reason or reasons for removal shall have been mailed by Registered Mail to the Officer or Director proposed for removal at least thirty (30) days before any final action is taken by the Board. This statement shall be accompanied by a notice of the time when, and the place where, the Board is to take action on the removal. The Officer or Director shall be given an opportunity to be heard and the matter considered by the Board at the time and place mentioned in the notice.

The Board shall employ a Board Executive Director to carry out the administration of Board policy and programs, and the Board shall have the power to remove the Executive Director, in conformance with the procedures set out in the paragraph above.

The Board shall elect the officers of the Board and may appoint consultants whose specialized knowledge and ability would be of value in the furtherance and conduct of the affairs of this organization.

The Board shall maintain a policy manual.

The Board shall carry out any other lawful activities deemed necessary to further the objectives of the Board.

ARTICLE V.   MEETINGS OF THE BOARD OF DIRECTORS

Section 1. Regular Meetings: The annual meeting of the Board shall be at a time and place designated by a majority of the Board for the election of officers and, where applicable, a Director representing the public, and the transaction of business that comes before the Board. There shall be one other regular meeting of the Board each year at a place designated by a majority of the Board for the transaction of such business as may come before the Board. Agendas of all items to be discussed at Board meetings shall be circulated at least thirty (30) days prior to the meeting. The agenda will be mailed to Directors as well as to the central offices of the organizations represented on the Board.

Section 2. Special Meetings: Special meetings may be called by a majority of the Board or by the Chairman, filing a written request for such a meeting with the Secretary and stating the object, date, and hour therefore, due notice having been given each director ten (10) days prior to date of meeting.

Section 3. Notice: Notice of all regular and special meetings of the Board and an agenda of all items to be discussed at such meetings shall be given to all Directors by the Executive Director no less than sixty (60) days prior to the meeting.

Any Director may waive notice of any meeting. The attendance of a Director at any meeting shall constitute a waiver of notice of such meeting, except where a Director attends a meeting for the express purpose of objecting to the transaction of any business because the meeting is not lawfully called or convened.

Section 4. Quorum: A majority of the Directors shall constitute a quorum of any meeting of the Board. Such majority shall be capable of transacting such business as may be provided in these Bylaws.

Section 5. Mail Votes: When not in meeting, should a matter requiring a vote of the Board arise, a ballot by mail, authorized by the Chairman, may be taken. A two-thirds (2/3) vote of the entire Board will be necessary to carry.

Section 6. Telephone Conference: The Chairman may authorize a telephone conference meeting of the Board when deemed necessary, and ten (10) days notice of such conference call shall be given each Director. Such notice shall include object, date, and hour of conference. Should an item of business need immediate attention and action by the Board, a telephone conference may be called without previous notice, as long as all of the Directors have been contacted. A two-thirds (2/3) roll call vote of the entire Board will be necessary to carry.

Section 7. Proxies: Voting by proxies shall not be permitted.

ARTICLE VI.   OFFICERS

Section 1. Elective Officers: Elective officers of the Board shall be three (3): Chairman, Vice-Chairman, and Secretary-Treasurer.

Section 2. Appointive Officer: The appointive officer of the Board shall be the Executive Director.

Section 3. Nominations and Elections: A Nominating Committee, elected by the Board, shall present a slate of officers. The elections shall be held at the Annual Meeting of the Board. Elections shall be by written ballot and the majority of the ballots cast shall elect, *provided* a quorum of directors is present. In the event of a tie on the first ballot, run-offs between the candidates in contention shall be conducted until a majority vote for one candidate can be achieved.

Section 4. Term of Office: The newly elected officers shall take office at the close of the meeting at which they are elected and the term of office shall be one year, or until respective successors assume office. A Director may serve more than one (1) term in the same office. The term of office of the appointive officer shall be determined by the Board.

Section 5. Vacancies: In the event the office of Chairman becomes vacant, the Vice-Chairman shall become Chairman for the unexpired portion of the term. In the event the office of Vice-Chairman or Secretary-Treasurer becomes vacant, the Chairman shall appoint interim officers to fill such vacant offices until a scheduled meeting of the Board can be held.

ARTICLE VII.   COMMITTEES

Section 1. Appointment: The Chairman shall appoint committees of the Board, except the Nominating Committee. Such committees may be composed of Directors or of consultants, or of both. The Board may prescribe the need and/or the composition of such committees.

Section 2. Standing Nominating Committee:

    A.   Composition, election, and term in office: This Committee shall be composed of three (3) members elected by the Board who shall serve for a term of one (1) year. The Committee shall select its own Chairman. The Board shall elect this committee at the annual Board meeting to serve for the following fiscal year.

    B.

Duties: It shall be the duty of this Committee:

      i.   To study the qualifications of Board members and select the best qualified as nominees for officers.

     ii.   To present a slate of nominees for officers at the Annual meeting.

   iii.   To present a slate of one or two Board nominees for the at-large positions on the Board when such positions are open for election. Such slate to be circulated to all who are entitled to vote at least thirty (30) days prior to the annual meeting and shall allow for write-in candidates. The candidate with the most votes shall be elected, and the results of the election shall be announced at the annual meeting.

ARTICLE VIII. GOVERNMENT

Section 1.:   The Board shall in all respect be autonomous in the matter of its credentialing criteria, finances, policies, administration, time, place, and frequency of its meetings, election and appointment of officers and representatives, and all other lawful activities.

Section 2.:   No member of the Board, elected officers, or employees of the Corporation may act on behalf of the Board or hold himself or herself out to the public as authorized to act on behalf of the Board without the express consent of the Board.

Section 3.:   The fiscal year of the Board shall begin on ＿＿＿＿＿＿＿＿ and terminate on ＿＿＿＿＿＿＿＿.

Section 4.:   *Roberts Rules of Order*, New Revised Edition, shall be the parliamentary authority for the conduct of all meetings of the Board, except as otherwise provided in these bylaws.

ARTICLE IX.   AMENDMENTS

These bylaws may be adopted, amended, or repealed at any meeting of the Board by a two-thirds (2/3) vote of the Board, *provided* that proper notice of proposed bylaw changes is given to each Director at least thirty (30) days prior to the meeting.

ARTICLE X.   DISSOLUTION

Upon the dissolution of the Board, the Board shall, after paying or making provisions for the payment of all liabilities, dispose of all assets of the corporation exclusively for the purposes of the Board in such a manner, or to such organization or organizations, as shall at the time qualify as an exempt organization or organizations under the Internal Revenue Code, as the Board shall determine.

Appendix D
Sample Policy on Conflicts of Interest

A nongovernmental self-regulation organization that fails to provide "fair procedure" may be held liable for damages under the common law. "Fair Procedure" requires notice and an opportunity to be heard. It also requires a process free from unlawful conflicts of interest.

The basic conflicts rules are simple enough. No *actual conflict* can be tolerated. Thus, potential official participants who are in fact biased must be excluded. Further, no *appearance of conflict*, as defined, may be allowed. Specifically, whether or not they could put aside their conflict and "be fair," refusal is mandated for a) persons with a tangible pecuniary interest in the outcome of the matter; b) persons who have been the target of personal abuse by any party directly concerned; c) persons "enmeshed" in other matters with any party; and d) persons who have previously been involved in the case in another capacity.

Self-regulating organizations responsible in any of these circumstances—and in particular where members of the adjudicatory body were direct competitors of the subject or otherwise stood to gain from a sanction against the subject and where members of the adjudicating body had been involved in the initial decision to find the subject not in compliance.

CONFLICTS POLICY[1]

I. General Guidelines[2]

    A. Persons with actual bias must be disqualified from any official involvement in the matter being resolved.[3]

    B. No person may serve in more than one capacity (i.e., staff member, board member, or appeals panelist) in connection with any matter being reviewed.

    C. Any person not otherwise required by these rules to recuse him/herself, but who feels for other reasons incapable of adequately performing his/her responsibilities, should disqualify him/herself.

    D. The fact that the application of these rules would prevent investigation or adjudication of a particular matter shall *not* result in the waiver or disregard of these requirements.

    E. Refusal should be formally noted in the record where not to do so would raise an inference that the individual in issue did participate.

II. Guidelines for Investigatory Staff

    A. No staff member should play any role as a board member or appeal panel member, in connection with a matter to be resolved in the office at the time he or she was a member of the staff.

    B. No staff member should share information concerning any matter to be resolved with members of the board or appeal panel, except as specifically authorized in the procedures promulgated by the organization.

III. Guidelines for Board Members and Appeal Panelists

A. Disqualification is required for:

1. Those with prior involvement in the case—whether within the self-regulation organization or any other body considering the same accused or matter;

2. Those who might be called upon to serve as witnesses in the matter;

3. Those with substantial personal or professional relationships to the subject;

4. Those with an appreciable pecuniary interest in the outcome. This would mandate the recusal of anyone in direct economic competition with the subject; and

5. Those who have had previous disputes with the subject or who have been a target of abuse by the subject.

B. Factual determinations should be based solely upon the record presented consistent with procedures promulgated by the organization and not on any information extrinsic to the process specified in the procedures.

COMMENT

These guidelines may be adopted as the official policy of the self-regulating organization. This may be preferable to incorporating them into the official procedures of the organization because that may increase the possibility that these policies are enforceable by subjects. In fact, the policy itself need not be shared with subjects and can bear the footnote disclaiming any intent to be bound by a standard higher than the common law standard pertinent to a particular matter to be resolved.

One state, California, has gone further than any other jurisdiction regarding conflicts of interest by self-regulating organizations. It has also held that the process must permit the subject to examine his or her judges concerning their biases. As a matter of policy, such questioning should perhaps be allowed in matters where a subject shows some basis for concern regarding the impartiality of a panelist.

NOTES

1. This policy is solely for the guidance of official participants in the self-regulation process and is not intended to create any rights enforceable against the self-regulation organization in any person or entity.

2. These guidelines apply to all official participants in the self-regulation process—staff, consultants (including outside counsel, who is governed by legal conflicts of interest rules as well), board members, and appeals panelists.

3. "Official involvement" means involvement as a representative of the self-regulating organization. Individuals with a conflict of interest may serve as witnesses or complainants, but must be treated in such capacity exactly as they would have been had they had no other connection with the organization. Individuals with conflicts of interest must otherwise separate themselves entirely from the matter with respect to which the conflicts exist.

Appendix E
National Commission for Certifying Agencies Criteria for Approval of Certification Programs

A certifying agency responsible for attesting to the competency of practitioners has a responsibility to the individuals desiring certification, to the employers of those individuals, to those agencies that may reimburse for the services and to the public. The National Commission for Certifying Agencies was formed to identify how these varying responsibilities can be met and to determine if a certification program meets those responsibilities. Approval of a certification program by the Commission indicates that the certification program has been evaluated by the Commission and deemed to meet all of the established criteria. In order to be "approved" by the Commission, a certification program* shall meet the following criteria.

1. Purpose of Certifying Agency

   a. shall have as a primary purpose the evaluation of those individuals who wish to enter, continue and/or advance in the professions, through the certification process, and the issuance of credentials to those individuals who meet the required level of competency.

2. Structure

   a. shall be nongovernmental, unless the certification is for government employees;

   b. shall conduct certification activities that are national in scope.

   c. shall be administratively independent** in matters pertaining to certification, except appointment of members of the governing body of the certifying agency. A certifying agency that is not a legal entity in and of itself shall provide proof that the agency's governing body is administratively independent in certification matters from the organization of which it is a part;

---

*The term "certifying program" as used in this document means a certification offered by an independent not-for-profit certifying agency or a not-for-profit association with a certifying component. As of January 1, 1982, the certifying component of a not-for-profit association must be administratively independent.

**Administratively independent means that all policy decisions relating to certification matters are the sole decision of the certifying body and not subject to approval by any other body and that all financial matters related to the operation of the certifying component are segregated from those of the professional association.

d. shall have a governing body that includes individuals from the discipline being certified. A certifying agency that certifies more than one discipline or more than one level within a discipline shall have appropriate representation for each on the governing body.

e. shall require that members of the governing body who represent the certified profession shall be selected by the certified profession or by an association of the certified profession and such selection shall not be subject to approval by any other individual or organization;

f. shall have formal procedures for the selection of members of the governing body that shall prohibit the governing body from selecting its successors;

g. shall provide evidence that a public member and a supervising professional (if this relationship exists) have input into the policies and decisions of the agency through membership on the governing body.

h. the certifying body of a professional organization shall be separate from the accrediting body of the professional association (see Guideline on Education and Certification).

i. shall have completed at least two national examination administrations.

3. Resources of Certifying Agencies

a. shall provide evidence that the agency has the financial resources to conduct the certification activities properly;

b. shall provide evidence that the staff possesses the knowledge and skill necessary to conduct the certification program or has available and make use of nonstaff consultants and professionals to supplement staff knowledge and skill sufficiently.

4. Evaluation Mechanism

a. shall provide evidence that the mechanism used to evaluate individual competence is objective, fair, and based on the knowledge and skills needed to function in the profession (see Guideline on Validity);

b. shall have a formal policy of periodic review of evaluation mechanisms and shall provide evidence that the policy is implemented to ensure relevance of the mechanism to knowledge and skills needed in the profession (see Guideline on Validity);

c. shall provide evidence that appropriate measures are taken to protect the security of all examinations;

d. shall provide evidence that pass/fail levels are established in a manner that is generally accepted in the psychometric community as being fair and reasonable (see Guideline on Cut-Off Scores); and

e. shall provide evidence that the evaluation mechanisms include evidence of attempts to establish both reliability and validity for each form of the examination (see Guideline on Reliability and Guideline on Validity).

5. Public Information

a. shall publish a document that clearly defines the certification responsibilities of the agency and outlines any other activities of the agency that are not related to certification;

b. shall make available general descriptive materials on the procedure used in test construction and validation and the procedures of administration and reporting of results (see Guideline on Validity);

c. shall publish a comprehensive summary or outline of the information, knowledge, or functions covered by the test (see Guideline on Validity); and

d. shall publish, at least annually, a summary of certification activities, including number tested, number passing, number failing, number certified, and number recertified (if the agency conducts a recertification program).

6. Responsibilities to Applicants for Certification or Recertification

    a. shall not discriminate among applicants as to age, sex, race, religion, national origin, handicap, or marital status and shall include a statement of nondiscrimination in announcement of the certification program (see Guideline on Bias and Guideline on Validity);

    b. shall provide all applicants with copies of formalized procedures for application for, and attainment of, certification and shall provide evidence to the Commission that such procedures are uniformly followed and enforced for applicants;

    c. shall have a formal policy for the periodic review of application and testing procedures to ensure that they are fair and equitable and shall give evidence to the Commission of the implementation of the policy;

    d. shall publicize nationally appropriate data concerning certification program including eligibility requirements for certification, basis of examination, dates and places of examination;

    e. shall provide evidence that competently proctored testing sites are readily accessible in all areas of the nation at least once annually;

    f. shall publicize nationally the specific educational background or employment background required for certification;

    g. shall give evidence that a means exists for individuals who have obtained a skill or knowledge outside the formal educational setting to be evaluated and obtain certification, or, in the absence of such means, provide reasonable justification for exclusion. These means employed should be consistent with the evaluation standards (see Guideline on Eligibility and Guideline on Validity);

    h. shall provide evidence of uniformly prompt reporting of test results to applicants;

    i. shall provide evidence that applicants failing the examination are given information on general areas of deficiency (see Guideline on Validity);

    j. shall provide evidence that each applicant's test results are held confidential (see Guideline on Education and Certification);

    k. shall have a formal policy on appeal procedures for applicant's questioning examination results and shall publish this information in examination announcements; and

    l. shall have a formal policy, acceptable to the Commission, delineating grounds, based on applicant's prior or current conduct, for refusing applicant's eligibility to take the certification examination and shall provide applicants the opportunity to present their cases to an impartial decision maker in the event of denial of eligibility or denial of certification.

7. Responsibilities to the Public and to Employers of Certified Personnel

    a. shall strive to ensure that the examination adequately measures the knowledge and skills required for entry, maintenance and/or advancement into the profession (see Guideline on Validity);

    b. shall provide evidence that the agency awards certification only after the skill and knowledge of the individual has been evaluated and determined to be acceptable (see Guideline on Validity);

    c. shall periodically publish or maintain in an electronic format a list of those persons certified by the agency;

    d. shall have formal policy and procedures for discipline of certificants, including the sanction of revocation of the certificate, for conduct that clearly indicate incompetence, unethical behavior and physical or mental impairment affecting performance that is acceptable to the Commission. These procedures shall incorporate due process (see Report on Discipline);

    e. any title or credential awarded by the credentialing body shall appropriately reflect the practitioner's daily occupational duties and shall not be confusing to employers, consumers, related professionals, and/or other interested parties.

The Commission may consider the following factors in determining whether practitioner's titles or credentials comply with this criterion:

1) educational background;
2) function of profession;
3) occupational duties and breadth of these activities;
4) level of supervision by other practitioners, or of any other practitioners; and
5) various titles already in the field, other titles considered, and a justification of why these titles were not utilized or why they were changed.

8. Recertification* (see Guideline on Continuing Competence)

   a. shall have in existence or shall be in the process of developing a plan for periodic recertification;

   b. shall provide evidence that any recertification program is designed to measure continued competency or to enhance the continued competence of the individual.

9. Responsibilities to Commission

   a. shall provide the Commission on a regular basis with copies of all publications related to the certifying process;

   b. shall advise the Commission of any change in purpose, structure, or activities of the certifying agency;

   c. shall advise the Commission of substantive change in test administration procedures;

   d. shall advise the Commission of any other major changes in testing techniques or in the scope or objectives of the test;

   e. shall undergo re-evaluation by the Commission at five year intervals;

   f. shall submit to the Commission the report requirements information specified for all approved certification programs; and

   g. shall annually complete and submit to the Commission information requested on the current status of the certification program and agency.

10. Recommendations

   a. All certification programs are encouraged to review the Equal Employment Opportunity Commission (EEOC et al.) guidelines "The Uniform Guidelines on Employee Selection Procedures" (1978) and Standards for Educational and Psychological Testing (1985) produced by the American Educational Research Association, the American Psychological Association, and the National Council on Measurement in Education, to be sure that certification examinations comply with these statements, which are frequently referred to in legal challenges of examinations.

---

*In this document, the term "recertification" includes periodic renewal or revalidation of certification based on re-examination, continuing education, or other methods developed by the certifying agency.

Appendix F
Council on Postsecondary Accreditation Provisions for Becoming Recognized as an Accrediting Body

As the nongovernmental organization dedicated primarily to the improvement of postsecondary education in the United States through voluntary accreditation, the Council on Postsecondary Accreditation (COPA) reviews the accrediting practices of those bodies desiring recognition by the Council. Such review and recognition acknowledge accreditation's broad public responsibilities as well as the specific interests of the many groups affected by accreditation by: 1) helping to ensure the integrity and consistency of accreditation policies and procedures; 2) encouraging continual improvement of accrediting practices; 3) providing guidance to institutions and programs about the status of bodies in the accrediting community; and 4) providing assurance about the accreditation status of institutions and programs to students, employers, state and federal agencies, and other interested groups.

Recognition by the Council on Postsecondary Accreditation as an accrediting body for postsecondary educational institutions or programs is dependent on compliance with the following Provisions:

A. To be considered for COPA recognition, an accrediting body

A1. Is a nongovernmental body;
A2. Conducts specialized accreditation on a national basis, or conducts institutional accreditation on a national or regional basis;
A3. Applies for recognition of the full scope of the postsecondary accrediting activities for which it assumes responsibility;
A4. Accredits entire institutions that are primarily postsecondary, are properly licensed and chartered to operate, and confer postsecondary degrees, diplomas, or certificates; or accredits programs that are generally accepted as preparing for the entry level(s) into a profession or occupation; or accredits units* in which such programs are offered;
A5. Describes in official public documents its full accrediting scope, evaluative criteria, and procedures;

---

*A unit is the college, school, department, or other administrative body within an institution that is officially responsible for a program or programs.

A6.   Defines each accreditation status, including accreditation and any available preaccreditation status;

A7.   Has written procedures for each possible action that affects the accreditation of an institution or program;

A8.   Is responsible for formulating its accrediting policies, procedures and criteria; and

A9.   Is solely responsible for the final decision on accreditation of an institution or program.

B.   To carry out its activities in the public interest, an accrediting body

B1.   Provides evidence that its accreditation protects the interests of students, benefits the public, and improves the quality of teaching, learning, research, and professional practice;

B2.   Provides evidence that its policies, evaluative criteria, procedures, and evaluative decisions are accepted by the appropriate communities of interest such as educators, educational institutions, other accrediting bodies, practitioners, employers, and public agencies;

B3.   Develops and interprets its evaluative criteria to encourage institutional freedom and autonomy, the improvement of institutions and programs, sound educational experimentation, and constructive innovation;

B4.   Has effective, impartial, and objective public representation in its evaluation, policy, and decision-making processes;

B5.   Makes public a current listing of the accreditation or candidacy of all institutions or programs affiliated with it;

B6.   Makes public all final decisions granting or withdrawing the accreditation (or candidacy for accreditation) of institutions or programs, including decisions by institutions or programs to withdraw voluntarily from accreditation (or candidacy);

B7.   Provides appropriate and fair procedures for considering and acting upon applications from institutions or programs;

B8.   Provides appropriate and fair procedures for appeals from decisions refusing or terminating accreditation (or candidacy) of an institution or program, such procedures to include consideration by a body whose members did not participate in the original decision, and maintains the accreditation (or candidacy) status of the institution or program until completion of the appeal process;

B9.   Has adopted policies defining what information about an institution or program it will reserve or keep confidential and what information it will make available to the public;

B10.   Has mechanisms to provide public correction of incorrect or misleading statements about the accreditation status of an accredited (or candidate) institution or program, the contents of reports of site visitors and/or its accrediting actions;

B11.   Responds to inquiries from the public about its activities and about its accredited (or candidate) institutions or programs;

B12.   Makes available on request the academic and professional qualifications of individual participants in its activities, including the members of its policy and decision-making bodies and its administrative personnel;

B13.   Undertakes timely and appropriate analysis of its own objectives, criteria, policies, and procedures to ensure that they contribute to the purposes of accreditation and modifies them to achieve these purposes better and meet changing conditions;

B14.   Provides advance notice of proposed changes in its objectives, criteria, and evaluating policies, giving opportunity for comment by affected persons, institutions, and organizations;

B15.   Permits an institution or program to withdraw an application for any status of accreditation (or candidacy) at any time before a final decision is made on that request; and

B16.   Permits an institution or program to withdraw from any status of accreditation (or candidacy) at any time.

C.   To follow accepted practices of postsecondary accreditation, an accrediting body

C1.   Recognizes the right of an institution or program to be evaluated in the light of its own stated purposes, so long as these are consistent with purposes generally accepted as appropriate to postsecondary education and to the recognized scope of the accrediting body;

C2. Utilizes evaluative criteria and processes that judge (a) the appropriateness of institutional or program purposes, (b) the adequacy of resources and organization to meet those purposes, (c) educational outcomes that indicate that those purposes are met, and (d) the reasonable assurance of continued meeting of those purposes;

C3. Provides to institutions and programs appropriate consultative guidance about the accrediting process;

C4. Evaluates an institution or program for candidacy or initial accreditation only at the invitation of the chief executive officer of the institution involved; however, it will initiate a review of the accredited status of the institution or program when required;

C5. Requires as an integral part of its accreditation process a self-analysis of the institution or program and an on-site review by a visiting team, or a validated equivalent of an on-site review;

C6. Provides in its evaluation, policy, and decision-making processes an appropriate balance between academic and administrative personnel (if an institutional accrediting body), or an appropriate balance between educators and practitioners (if a specialized accrediting body);

C7. Confines its requests for data from institutions or programs to data directly related to the evaluation and accreditation processes;

C8. Collects data from institutions or programs by means that stimulate self-assessment and improvement and that make maximum use of information already available in the institutions or programs;

C9. Consults with the institution or program about the number and selection of site visitors and about the length of the visit;

C10. Provides evidence that its practices respecting the number of site visitors and visit length appropriately reflect the complexity of the institution or program being visited and the purposes of the visit;

C11. Appoints site visitors using procedures developed to select visitors who are: (a) qualified by academic training, professional experience, and knowledge of the accrediting process; (b) sensitive to the uniqueness of individual institutions and programs; and (c) impartial, objective, and without conflict of interest;

C12. Provides for the training and evaluation of site visitors;

C13. Encourages discussion during the on-site visit between site visitors and the faculty, staff, administrators, students, and other interested parties;

C14. Provides opportunity and a reasonable period for the institutional chief executive and, in the case of a specialized accrediting body, the director of the program to comment on the report of the site visitors before final action is taken on the accreditation status of an institution or program;

C15. Provides to the institutional chief executive and, in the case of a specialized accrediting body, the director of the program a written evaluation report that the institution is free to distribute;

C16. Provides to the institutional chief executive and, in the case of a specialized accrediting body, the director of the program written notification of any decision affecting the status of the institution or program not later than one month following the decision, giving reasons for the action;

C17. Clearly distinguishes in the written report of the site visitors and in the communication of the final accrediting decision between: (a) statements speaking to actual or potential deficiencies in meeting criteria, and (b) statements offering advice to the institution or program;

C18. Provides reasonable checks and balances in its procedures to guard against: (a) accrediting an institution or program that does not meet its criteria; and (b) refusing to accredit an institution or program that does not meet its criteria; and

C19. Has the staff and financial resources to implement and maintain effective accrediting procedures.

D. To meet its obligations as a COPA-recognized body, an accrediting body

D1. Advises COPA before effecting any change that will alter its status of COPA recognition;

D2.   Provides evidence of continuing efforts to work with other COPA-recognized accrediting bodies in cooperative accrediting practices; and

D3.   Files regularly with COPA materials pertaining to its activities and complies with requests by COPA for other data or information.

In considering the above Provisions, the following COPA policy statements are most relevant. The full texts of these policies are found in Part II of this handbook.

- Bylaws of the Council on Postsecondary Accreditation (adopted April 17, 1987)
- Public Meetings
- Evaluation of Accrediting Activities by Institutions
- Disclosure, Confidentiality and the Integrity of the Accrediting Process
- Interagency Cooperation
- Accreditation and the Public Interest
- Joint Statement on Transfer and Award of Academic Credit
- Off-Campus Credit Programs
- Accreditation of Graduate Education
- Trustee Involvement in the Accreditation Process
- Rights and Responsibilities of Accrediting Bodies and Institutions in the Accrediting Process
- Principles of Good Practice in Institutional Advertising, Student Recruitment, and Representation of Accredited Status
- Accreditation and Authorization of Distance Learning Through Telecommunications
- Validity and Reliability of Accrediting Body Standards and Process

Appendix G
United States Department of Education 34 Code of Federal Regulations 602 Procedures and Criteria for Recognition of Accrediting Agencies

AUTHORITY: 20 U.S.C. 1058, 1061, 1085, 1088, 1141, 1401, 2471, and 3381, unless otherwise noted.

SOURCE: 53 FR 25096, July 1, 1988, unless otherwise noted.

Subpart A—General Provisions

§ 602.1   Purpose.

(a) This part establishes procedures and criteria for the Secretary's recognition of accrediting agencies. Recognition is based on the Secretary's determination that accrediting agencies are reliable authorities concerning the quality of education or training offered by the postsecondary educational institutions or programs within the agencies' respective scopes of operation.

(b) Accreditation of postsecondary institutions or postsecondary programs by agencies recognized by the Secretary is a prerequisite to eligibility for many types of Federal financial assistance for those institutions or programs and for the students enrolled in those institutions or programs.

(Authority: 20 U.S.C. 1058 *et al.*)

§ 602.2   Definitions.

The following definitions apply to terms used in this part:

(a) *Definitions in the Education Department General Administrative Regulations.* The following terms used in this part are defined in 34 CFR 77.1:

Department

Secretary

(b) *Definitions that apply to this part.* The following definitions also apply to this part:

Accrediting and accreditation refer to the status of public recognition which an agency grants to an educational institution or program which meets the agency's established qualifications and educational standards.

Accrediting agency and *agency* mean a legal entity, including an association, council, commission, or corporation, or a part of that entity, which conducts accrediting activities.

Act means the Higher Education Act of 1965, as amended.

Educational program or *program* means a legally authorized program of instruction or study, offered by an educational institution or other organization, that leads to an academic or professional degree, vocational certificate, or other recognized educational credential.

Preaccreditation means an agency's formal grant of status to an educational institution or program that signifies that the agency has determined that the institution or program is progressing towards accreditation within a reasonable period of time.

Recognized agency means an accrediting agency currently recognized by the Secretary under this part.

State means a State of the Union, American Samoa, the Commonwealth of Puerto Rico, the District of Columbia, Guam, the Trust Territory of the Pacific Islands, the Virgin Islands, and the Commonwealth of the Northern Mariana Islands.

(Authority: 20 U.S.C. 1058 *et al.*)

§ 602.3   Recognition procedures.

(a) An accrediting agency that desires to be recognized by the Secretary under this part shall apply in writing to the United States Department of Education, Office of Postsecondary Education, Washington, DC 20202.

(b) For initial recognition and for renewal of recognition, the accrediting agency will furnish information establishing its compliance with the criteria set forth in Subpart B by the submission of written materials and by affording the Secretary access to the agency's accreditation site visits and proceedings.

(c) To the extent that the documentation submitted by an agency under paragraph (b) of this section does not demonstrate to the satisfaction of the Secretary that the agency meets one or more of the criteria in Subpart B, an agency nontheless wishing to be recognized shall, at the Secretary's request—

(1) Make its personnel available for interviews; and

(2) Submit additional records and information.

(d) The Secretary does not deny or withdraw recognition of an agency, or limit recognition of an agency to a scope narrower than that requested, without first giving the agency an opportunity to show cause why that action should not be taken.

(e) The Secretary re-evaluates each recognized agency at the Secretary's discretion, but at least once every five years.

(Authority: 20 U.S.C. 1058 *et al.*)

§ 602.4   Participation of National Advisory Committee

In making determinations under this part, the Secretary considers the recommendations of the National Advisory Committee on Accreditation and Institutional Eligibility.

(Authority: 20 U.S.C. 1058 *et al.*, 1145)

§ 602.5   Publication of list of recognized agencies.

The Secretary periodically publishes in the FEDERAL REGISTER a list of recognized agencies, including the scope of recognition of each agency.

(Authority: 20 U.S.C. 1058 *et al.*)

Subpart B—Criteria for Secretarial
Recognition

§602.10   Criteria for recognition.

(a) The Secretary recognizes an accrediting agency only if the Secretary determines that the agency is a reliable authority as to the quality of the education or training offered by postsecondary educational institutions or programs within the agency's scope of activity, taking into account the degrees or certificates offered and the education or specific occupational training offered. In making this determination, the Secretary decides whether the agency possesses the characteristics and follows the procedures described in this subpart.

(b) To be recognized by the Secretary, an agency must satisfactorily meet each of the criteria in §§ 602.11–602.19 unless it can demonstrate to the Secretary's satisfaction why one or more criteria should not appropriately be applied.

(c) For purposes of the determination in paragraph (b) of this section, each section, taken as a whole, constitutes a criterion.

(Authority: 20 U.S.C. 1058 *et al.*)

§ 602.11   Experience.

An accrediting agency must demonstrate sufficient experience with respect to both—

(a) The geographical scope of activity for which it seeks recognition; and

(b) The specific degress, certificates, and programs which would be covered by its recognized accreditation and preaccreditation activities.

(Authority: 20 U.S.C. 1058 *et al.*)

§ 602.12   Scope of activity.

The Secretary determines whether an accrediting agency—

(a)(1) Is national in the scope of its operation; or

(2) Includes in its geographical scope of operation at least three States that are contiguous or that otherwise constitute a distinct geographic region, and defines its accrediting activity as the accreditation of entire institutions; and

(b) Accredits types and academic levels of institutions or programs that must be accredited by an accrediting agency recognized by the Secretary in order for those institutions or programs, or their students, to be eligible for participation in one or more Federal programs.

(Authority: 20 U.S.C. 1058 *et al.*)

§ 602.13   Clarity of purpose, scope, and operational information.

The Secretary determines whether an accrediting agency maintains, and makes publicly available, current written material clearly describing each of the following matters:

(a) Its purposes and objectives.

(b) The geographical area and the types and academic levels of educational institutions or programs covered by the agency's accrediting activity.

(c) The definition of each type of accreditation and preaccreditation status, including probationary status, if any, that the agency grants.

(d) The criteria and procedures used by the agency for determining whether to grant, reaffirm, reinstate, deny, restrict, or revoke each type of accreditation and preaccreditation status that the agency grants.

(e) The standards to which an agency holds an educational institution or program for the purpose of making determinations respecting each of the criteria referred to in paragraph (d) of this section.

(f) The procedures established by the agency for appeal of its denials or withdrawals of accreditation or preaccreditation status.

(g) The procedures followed by the agency for the timely review of complaints pertaining to institutional or program quality, as these relate to the agency's criteria, in a manner that is fair and equitable to the person making the complaint and to the institution or program.

(h) The current accreditation or preaccreditation status publicly conferred on each educational institution or program within the agency's scope of operation, and the date of the next currently scheduled review or reconsideration of accreditation of each of those institutions or programs.

(i) The names and relevant employment and organizational affiliations of the members of the agency's policy and decision-making bodies responsible for the agency's accrediting activities, and the names of the agency's principal administrative staff.

(j) Provisions for the inclusion of representatives of the public in its policy and decision-making bodies, responsible for its accrediting activities or for the retention of advisors who can provide information about issues of concern to the public.

(k) With regard to institutions or programs of study that admit students on the basis of their ability to benefit from the education or training offered, any criteria established by the agency with respect to nationally recognized, standardized, or industry-developed tests designed to measure the aptitude of prospective students to complete successfully the program to which they have applied.

(Authority: 29 U.S.C. 1058 *et al.* and 1091(d))

§ 602.14   National recognition.

The Secretary determines whether an accrediting agency demonstrates that its policies, evaluation methods and decisions are accepted throughout the United States by, as appropriate—

(a) Educators and educational institutions;

(b) Licensing bodies; practitioners, and employers in the professional or vocational fields for which the educational institutions or program within the agency's jurisdiction prepare their students; and

(c) Recognized agencies.

(Authority: 20 U.S.C. 1058 *et al.*)

§ 602.15   Resources.

The Secretary determines whether an accrediting agency has, and will be likely to have sufficient resources to carry out its accreditation function in light of its requested scope of recognition, including—

(a) Administrative staff and financial resources; and

(b) Competent and knowledgeable personnel responsible for on-site evaluation, policy-making and decisions regarding accreditation and preaccreditation status.

(Authority: 20 U.S.C. 1058 *et al.*)

§ 602.16   Integrity of process.

The Secretary determines whether an accrediting agency adheres to the following practices and procedures in making its determinations concerning accreditation and preaccreditation status:

(a) As an integral part of its accrediting activity, it—

(1) Requires self-analysis by each subject educational institution or program in accordance with guidance provided by the agency; and

(2) Conducts an on-site review of the institution or program, conducts its own independent analyses and evaluations of the data furnished by the institution or program, and provides a written report on the review to the institution or program concerning—

(i) The strengths and weaknesses of the institution or program (both at the main campus and branch campus or off-campus locations), including areas needing improvement; and

(ii) The institution's or program's performance respecting the assessment of student achievement as described in § 602.17.

(b) It re-evaluates at reasonable intervals the institutions or programs to which it has granted accreditation or preaccreditation status.

(c) It bases its decisions regarding the award of accreditation or preaccreditation status upon its published criteria and provides advance public notice of proposed new or revised criteria, providing interested parties adequate opportunity to comment on such proposals prior to their adoption.

(d) With regard to the award of preaccreditation status, it applies criteria and follows procedures that are appropriately related to those used to award accreditation status.

(e) It offers appropriate and fair written procedures for appeals of its denial or withdrawal of accreditation or preaccreditation status. Such written procedures shall be made promptly available to the chief executive official of any institution or program affected by such a change in status.

(f) It maintains a written policy under which it notifies the Secretary within 30 days of any final decision—

(1) To withdraw accreditation or preaccreditation status from an institution or program; or

(2) To place an accredited or preaccredited institution or program on a publicly announced probationary status.

(g) Its organization, functions, and procedures include effective controls against conflicts of interest and against inconsistent application of its criteria and standards.

(h) If the institution or program elects to make public disclosure of its status, it requires that each institution or program to which it has granted accreditation or preaccreditation status disclose that status accurately, including the academic or instructional programs covered by that status.

(i) It maintains a systematic program of review designed to assess the validity and reliability of its criteria, procedures, and standards relating to its accrediting and preaccrediting activity and their relevance to the educational and training needs of affected students.

(j) It maintains complete and accurate records of its last two reviews of each institution or program, and accurate permanent records of its decisions with respect to preaccreditation, accreditation, and adverse actions.

(Authority: 20 U.S.C. 1058 *et al.*)

§ 602.17 Focus on educational effectiveness.

The Secretary determines whether an accrediting agency, in making its accrediting decisions, systematically obtains and considers substantial and accurate information on the educational effectiveness of postsecondary educational institutions or programs, especially as measured by student achievement, by—

(a) Determining whether an educational institution or program maintains clearly specified educational objectives consistent with its mission and appropriate in light of the degrees or certificates it awards;

(b) Verifying that satisfaction of certificate and degree requirements by all students, including students admitted on the basis of ability to benefit, is reasonably documented, and conforms with commonly accepted standards for the particular certificates and degrees involved, and that institutions or programs confer degrees only on those students who have demonstrated educational achievement as assessed and documented through appropriate measures;

(c) Determining that institutions or programs document the educational achievements of their students, including students admitted on the basis of ability to benefit, in verifiable and consistent ways, such as evaluation of senior theses, reviews of student portfolios, general educational assessments (e.g., standardized test results, graduate or professional school test results, or graduate or professional school placements), job placement rates, licensing examination results, employer evaluations, and other recognized measures;

(d) Determining that institutions or programs admitting students on the basis of ability to benefit employ appropriate methods, such as preadmissions testing or evaluations, for determing that such students are in fact capable of benefiting from the training or education offered;

(e) Determining the extent to which institutions or programs broadly and accurately publicize, particularly in representations directed to prospective students, the objectives described in paragraph (a) of this section, the assessment measure described in paragraph (c) of this section, the information obtained through those measures, and the methods described in paragraph (d) of this section; and

(f) Determining the extent to which institutions or programs systematically apply the information obtained through the measures described in paragraph (c) of this section toward steps to foster enhanced student achievement with respect to the degrees or certificates offered by the institution or program.

(Authority: 20 U.S.C. 1058 *et al.*)

§ 602.18 Regard for adequate and accurate public disclosures.

The Secretary determines whether an accrediting agency, in making its accrediting decisions, reviews elements of institutional or program integrity as demonstrated by the adequacy and accuracy of disclosures of information that do not mislead the public (and especially prospective students) as to—

(a) The institution's or program's resources, admission policies and standards, academic offerings, policies with respect to satisfactory academic progress, fees and other charges, refund policies, and graduation rates and requirements;

(b) The institution's or program's educational effectiveness as described in § 602.17;

(c) Employment of recent alumni related to the education or training offered, in the case of an institution or program offering training to prepare students for gainful employment in a recognized occupation, or where the institution or program makes claims about the rate or type of employment of graduates; and

(d) Data supporting any quantitative claims made by the institution with respect to any matters described in paragraphs (a), (b) and (c) of this section.

(Authority: 20 U.S.C. 1058 *et al.*)

§ 602.19   Regard for decisions of States and other accrediting agencies.

The Secretary determines whether an accrediting agency, in making its decisions, shows regard for the decisions of States and of other recognized accrediting agencies by conforming with the following practices:

(a) Recognizing only those institutions or programs that are legally authorized under applicable State law to provide a program of education beyond secondary education.

(b) In considering whether to grant initial accreditation or preaccreditation status to an institution or program, taking into account actions by other recognized agencies which have denied accreditation or preaccreditation status to the institution or program, have placed the institution or program on public probationary status, or have revoked the accreditation or preaccreditation status of the institution or program.

(c) If another recognized agency places an institution or the principal program offered by an institution on public probationary status or revokes the accreditation of the institution or principal program within an institution, promptly reviewing the accreditation or preaccreditation status it has previously granted to that institution to determine if there is cause for it to withdraw or otherwise alter that status.

(Authority: 20 U.S.C. 1058 *et al.*)

Appendix H
United States Department of Justice
Excerpts from 56 Federal Register 35544
Regulations on The Americans With Disabilities Act

DEPARTMENT OF JUSTICE
Office of the Attorney General

28 CFR Part 36
[Order No. 1513–91]

Nondiscrimination on the Basis of Disability by Public Accommodations and in Commercial Facilities

AGENCY: Department of Justice.
ACTION: Final rule.

SUMMARY: This rule implements title III of the Americans with Disabilities Act, Public Law 101–336, which prohibits discrimination on the basis of disability by private entities in places of public accommodation, requires that all new places of public accommodation and commercial facilities be designed and constructed so as to be readily accessible to and usable by persons with disabilities, and requires that examinations or courses related to licensing or certification for professional and trade purposes be accessible to persons with disabilities.

EFFECTIVE DATE: January 26, 1992.

FOR FURTHER INFORMATION CONTACT:
Barbara S. Drake, Deputy Assistant Attorney General, Civil Rights Division; Stewart B. Oneglia, Chief, Coordination and Review Section, Civil Rights Division; and John Wodatch, Director, Office on the Americans with Disabilities Act, Civil Rights Division; all of the U.S. Department of Justice, Washington, DC 20530. They may be contacted through the Division's ADA Information Line at (202) 514-0301 (Voice), (202) 514-0381 (TDD), or (202) 514-0383 (TDD). These telephone numbers are not toll-free numbers.

Copies of this rule are available in the following alternate formats: large print, Braille, electronic file on computer disk, and audio-tape. Copies may be obtained from the Office on the Americans with Disabilities Act at (202) 514-0301 (Voice) or (202) 514-0381 (TDD). The rule is also available on electronic bulletin board at (202) 514-6193. These telephone numbers are not toll-free numbers.

SUPPLEMENTARY INFORMATION:

Background

The landmark Americans with Disabilities Act ("ADA" or "the Act"), enacted on July 26, 1990, provides comprehensive civil rights protections to individuals with disabilities in the areas of employment, public accommodations, State and local government services, and telecommunications.

The legislation was originally developed by the National Council on Disability, an independent Federal agency that reviews and makes recommendations concerning Federal laws, programs, and policies affecting individuals with disabilities. In its 1986 study, "Toward Independence," the National Council on Disability recognized the inadequacy of the existing, limited patchwork of protections for individuals with disabilities, and recommended the enactment of a comprehensive civil rights law requiring equal opportunity for individuals with disabilities throughout American life. Although the 100th Congress did not act on the legislation, which was first introduced in 1988, then-Vice-President George Bush endorsed the concept of comprehensive disability rights legislation during his presidential campaign and became a dedicated advocate of the ADA.

The ADA was reintroduced in modified form in May 1989 for consideration by the 101st Congress. In June 1989, Attorney General Dick Thornburgh, in testimony before the Senate Committee on Labor and Human Resources, reiterated the Bush Administration's support for the ADA and suggested changes in the proposed legislation. After extensive negotiations between Senate sponsors and the Administration, the Senate passed an amended version of the ADA on September 7, 1989, by a vote of 76-8.

In the House, jurisdiction over the ADA was divided among four committees, each of which conducted extensive hearings and issued detailed committee reports: the Committee on Education and Labor, the Committee on the Judiciary, the Committee on Public Works and transportation, and the Committee on Energy and Commerce. On October 12, 1989, the Attorney General testified in favor of the legislation before the Committee on the Judiciary. The Civil Rights Division, on February 22, 1990, provided testimony to the Committee on Small Business, which although technically without jurisdiction over the bill, conducted hearings on the legislation's impact on small business.

After extensive committee consideration and floor debate, the House of Representatives passed an amended version of the Senate bill on May 22, 1990, by a vote of 403–20. After resolving their differences in conference, the Senate and House took final action on the bill—the House passing it by a vote of 377–28 on July 12, 1990, and the Senate, a day later, by a vote of 91–6. The ADA was enacted into law with the President's signature at a White House ceremony on July 28, 1990.

Rulemaking History

On February 22, 1991, the Department of Justice published a notice of proposed rulemaking (NPRM) implementing title III of the ADA in the Federal Register (56 FR 7452). On February 28, 1991, the Department published a notice of proposed rulemaking implementing subtile A of title II of the ADA in the **Federal Register** (56 FR 8538). Each NPRM solicited comments on the definitions, standards, and procedures of the proposed rules. By the April 29, 1991, close of the comment period of the NPRM for title II, the Department had received 2,718 comments on the two proposed rules. Following the close of the comment period, the Department received an additional 222 comments.

In order to encourage public participation in the development of the Department's rules under the ADA, the Department held four public hearings. Hearings were held in Dallas, Texas on March 4–5, 1991; in Washington, DC on March 13–14–15, 1991; in San Francisco, California on March 18–19, 1991; and in Chicago, Illinois on March 27–28, 1991. At these hearings, 329 persons testified and 1,567 pages of testimony were compiled. Transcripts of the hearings were included in the Department's rulemaking docket.

The comments that the Department received occupy almost six feet of shelf space and contain over 10,000 pages. The Department received comments from individuals from all fifty States and the District of Columbia. Nearly 75% of the comments came from individuals and from organizations representing the interests of persons with disabilities. The Department received 292 comments from entities covered by the ADA and trade associations representing businesses in the private sector, and 67 from government units, such as mayors' offices, public school districts, and various State agencies working with individuals with disabilities.

The Department received one comment from a consortium of 511 organizations representing a broad spectrum of persons with disabilities. In addition, at least another 25 commenters endorsed the position expressed by this consortium or submitted identical comments on one or both proposed regulations.

An organization representing persons with hearing impairments submitted a large number of comments. This organization presented the Department with 479 individual comments, each providing in chart form a detailed representation of what type of auxiliary aid or service would be useful in the various categories of places of public accommodation.

The Department received a number of comments based on almost ten different form letters. For example, individuals who have a heightened sensitivity to a variety of chemical substances submitted 266 postcards detailing how exposure to various environmental conditions restricts their access to places of public accommodation and to commercial facilities. Another large group of form letters came from groups affiliated with independent living centers.

The vast majority of the comments addressed the Department's proposal implementing title III. Just over 100 comments addressed only issues presented in the proposed title II regulation.

The Department read and analyzed each comment that was submitted in a timely fashion. Transcripts of the four hearings were analyzed along with the written comments. The decisions that the Department has made in response to these comments, however, were not made on the basis of the number of commenters addressing any one point but on a thorough consideration of the merits of the points of view expressed in the comments. Copies of the written comments, including the transcripts of the four hearings, will remain available for public inspection in room 854 of the HOLC Building, 320 First Street, NW., Washington, DC from 10 a.m. to 5 p.m., Monday through Friday, except for legal holidays, until August 30, 1991.

The Americans with Disabilities Act gives to individuals with disabilities civil rights protections with respect to discrimination that are parallel to those provided to individuals on the basis of race, color, national origin, sex, and religion. It combines in its own unique formula elements drawn principally from two key civil rights statutes—the Civil Rights Act of 1964 and title V of the Rehabilitation Act of 1973. The ADA generally employs the framework of titles II (42 U.S.C. 2000a to 2000–6) and VII (42 U.S.C. 2000e to 2000e–16) of the Civil Rights Act of 1964 for coverage and enforcement and the terms and concepts of section 504 of the Rehabilitation Act of 1973 (29 U.S.C. 794) for what constitutes discrimination.

Other recently enacted legislation will facilitate compliance with the ADA. As amended in 1990, the Internal Revenue Code allows a deduction of up to $15,000 per year for expenses associated with the removal of qualified architectural and transportation barriers. The 1990 amendment also permits eligible small businesses to receive a tax credit for certain costs of compliance with the ADA. An eligible small business is one whose gross receipts do not exceed $1,000,000 or whose workforce does not consist of more than 30 full-time workers. Qualifying businesses may claim a credit of up to 50 percent of eligible access expenditures that exceed $250 but do not exceed $10,250. Examples of eligible access expenditures include the necessary and reasonable costs of removing barriers, providing auxiliary aids, and acquiring or modifying equipment or devices.

In addition, the Communications Act of 1934 has been amended by the Television Decoder Circuitry Act of 1990, Public Law 101–431, to require as of July 1, 1993, that all televisions with screens of 13 inches or wider have built-in decoder circuitry for displaying closed captions. This new law will eventually lessen dependence on the use of portable decoders in achieving compliance with the auxiliary aids and services requirements of the rule.

Overview of the Rule

The final rule establishes standards and procedures for the implementation of title III of the Act, which addresses discrimination by private entities in places of public accommodation, commercial facilities, and certain examinations and courses. The careful consideration Congress gave title III is reflected in the detailed statutory provisions and the expansive reports of the Senate Committee on Labor and Human Resources and the House Committees on the Judiciary, and Education and Labor. The final rule follows closely the language of the Act and supplements it, where appropriate, with interpretive material found in the committee reports.

The rule is organized into six subparts. Subpart A, "General," includes the purpose and application sections, describes the relationship of the Act to other laws, and defines key terms used in the regulation.

Subpart B, "General Requirements," contains material derived from what the statute calls the "General Rule," and the "General Prohibition," in sections 302(a) and 302(b)(1) respectively, of the Act. Topics addressed by this subpart include discriminatory denials of access or participation, landlord and tenant obligations, the provision of unequal benefits, indirect discrimination through contracting, the participation of individuals with disabilities in the most integrated setting appropriate to their needs, and discrimination based on association with individuals with disabilities. Subpart B also contains a number of "miscellaneous" provisions derived from title V of the Act that involve issues such as retaliation and coercion for asserting ADA rights, illegal drug use, insurance, and restrictions on smoking in places of public accommodation. Finally, subpart B contains additional general provisions regarding direct threats to health or safety, maintenance of accessible features of facilities and equipment, and the coverage of places of public accommodation located in private residences.

Subpart C, "Specific Requirements," addresses the "Specific Prohibitions" in section 302(b)(2) of the Act. Included in this subpart are topics such as discriminatory eligibility criteria; reasonable modifications in policies, practices or procedures; auxiliary aids and services; the readily achievable removal of barriers and alternatives to barrier removal; the extent to which inventories of accessible or special goods are required; seating in assembly areas; personal devices and services; and transportation provided by public accommodations. Subpart C also incorporates the requirements of section 309 of title III relating to examinations and courses.

Subpart D, "New Construction and Alterations," sets forth the requirements for new construction and alterations based on section 303 of the Act. It addresses such issues as what facilities are covered by the new construction requirements, what an alteration is, the application of the elevator exception, the path of travel obligations resulting from an alteration to a primary function area, requirements for commercial facilities located in private residences, and the application of alterations requirements to historic buildings and facilities.

Subpart E, "Enforcement," describes the Act's title III enforcement procedures, including private actions, as well as investigations and litigation conducted by the Attorney General. These provisions are based on sections 308 and 310(b) of the Act.

Subpart F, "Certification of State Laws or Local Building Codes," establishes procedures for the certification of State or local building accessibility ordinances that meet or exceed the new construction and alterations requirements of the ADA. These provisions are based on section 308(b)(1)(A)(ii) of the Act.

The section-by-section analysis of the rule explains in detail the provisions of each of these subparts.

The Department is also today publishing a final rule for the implementation and enforcement of subtitle A of title II of the Act. This rule prohibits discrimination on the basis of disability against qualified individuals with disabilities in all services, programs, or activities of State and local government.

Regulatory Process Matters

This final rule has been reviewed by the Office of Management and Budget (OMB) under Executive Order 12291. The Department is preparing a regulatory impact analysis (RIA) of this rule, and the Architectural and Transportation Barriers Compliance Board is preparing an RIA for its Americans with Disabilities Act Accessibility Guidelines for Buildings and Facilities (ADAAG) that are incorporated in Appendix A of the Department's final rule. Draft copies of both preliminary RIAs are available for comment; the Department will provide copies of these documents to the public upon request. Commenters are urged to provide additional information as to the costs and benefits associated with this rule. This will facilitate the development of a final RIA by January 1, 1992.

The Department's RIA will evaluate the economic impact of the final rule. Included among those title III provisions that are likely to result in significant economic impact are the requirements for auxiliary aids, barrier removal in existing facilities, and readily accessible new construction and alterations. An analysis of the costs of these provisions will be included in the RIA.

The preliminary RIA prepared for the notice of proposed rulemaking contained all of the available information that would have been included in a preliminary regulatory flexibility analysis, had one been prepared under the Regulatory Flexibility Act, concerning the rule's impact on small entities. The final RIA will contain all of the information that is required in a final regulatory flexibility analysis, and will serve as such an analysis. Moreover, the extensive notice and comment procedure followed by the Department in the promulgation of this rule, which included public hearings, dissemination of materials, and provision of speakers to affected groups, clearly provided any interested small entities with the notice and opportunity for comment provided for under the Regulatory Flexibility Act procedures.

This final rule will preempt State laws affected entities subject to the ADA only to the extent that those laws directly conflict with the statutory requirements of the ADA. Therefore, this rule is not subject to Executive Order 12612, and a Federalism Assessment is not required.

The reporting and recordkeeping requirements described in subpart F of the rule are considered to be information collection requirements as that term is defined by the Office of Management and Budget in 5 CFR part 1320. Accordingly, those information collection requirements have been submitted to OMB for review pursuant to the Paperwork Reduction Act.

Section-by-Section Analysis and Response to Comments

Subpart A—General

Section 36.101   Purpose

Section 36.101 states the purpose of the rule, which is to effectuate title III of the Americans with Disabilities Act of 1990. This title prohibits discrimination on the basis of disability by public accommodations, requires places of public accommodation and commercial facilities to be designed, constructed, and altered in compliance with the accessibility standards established by this part, and requires that examinations of courses related to licensing or certification for professional or trade purposes be accessible to persons with disabilities.

Section 36.102   Application

Section 36.102 specifies the range of entities and facilities that have obligations under the final rule. The rule applies to any public accommodation or commercial facility as those terms are defined in § 36.104. It also applies, in accordance with section 309 of the ADA, to private entities that offer examinations or courses related to applications, licensing, certification, or credentialing for secondary or postsecondary education, professional, or trade purposes. Except as provided in § 36.206, "Retaliation or coercion," this part does not apply to individuals other than public accommodations or to public entities. Coverage of private individuals and public entities is discussed in the preamble to § 36.206.

As defined in § 36.104, a public accommodation is a private entity that owns, leases or leases to, or operates a place of public accommodation. Section 36.102(b)(2) emphasizes that the general and specific public accommodations requirements of subparts B and C obligate a public accommodation only with respect to the operations of a place of public accommodation. This distinction is drawn in recognition of the fact that a private entity that meets the regulatory definition of public accommodation could also own, lease or lease to, or operate facilities that are not places of public accommodation. The rule would exceed the reach of the ADA if it were to apply the public accommodations requirements of subparts B and C to the operations of a private entity that do not involve a place of public accommodation. Similarly, § 36.102(b)(3) provides that the new construction and alterations requirements of subpart D obligate a public accommodation only with respect to facilities used as, or designed or constructed for use as, places of public accommodation or commercial facilities.

On the other hand, as mandated by the ADA and reflected in § 36.102(c), the new construction and alterations requirements of subpart D apply to a commercial facility whether or not the facility is a place of public accommodation, or is owned, leased, leased to, or operated by a public accommodation.

Section 36.102(e) states that the rule does not apply to any private club, religious entity, or public entity. Each of these terms is defined in § 36.104. The exclusion of private clubs and religious entities is derived from section 307 of the ADA; and the exclusion of public entities is based on the statutory definition of public accommodation in section 301(7) of the ADA, which excludes entities other than private entities from coverage under title III of the ADA.

Section 36.103   Relationship to Other Laws

Section 36.103 is derived from sections 501 (a) and (b) of the ADA. Paragraph (a) provides that, except as otherwise specifically provided by this part, the ADA is not intended to apply lesser standards than are required under title V of the Rehabilitation Act of 1973, as amended (29 U.S.C. 790–794), or the regulations implementing that title. The standards of title V of the Rehabilitation Act apply for purposes of the ADA to the extent that the ADA has not explicitly adopted a different standard from title V. Where the ADA explicitly provides a different standard from section 504, the ADA standard applies to the ADA, but not to section 504. For example, section 504 requires that all federally assisted programs and activities be readily accessible to and usable by individuals with handicaps, even if major structural alterations are necessary to make a program accessible. Title III of the ADA, in contrast, only reqires alterations to existing facilities if the modifications are "readily achievable," that is, able to be accomplished easily and without much difficulty or expense. A public accommodation that is covered under both section 504 and the ADA is still required to meet the "program accessibility" standard in order to comply with section 504, but would not be in violation of the ADA unless it failed to make "readily achievable" modifications. On the other hand, an entity covered by the ADA is required to make "readily achievable" modifications, even if the program can be made accessible without any architectural modifications. Thus, an entity covered by both section 504 and title III of the ADA must meet both the "program accessibility" requirement and the "readily achievable" requirement.

Paragraph (b) makes explicit that the rules does not affect the obligation of recipients of Federal financial assistance to comply with the requirements imposed under section 504 of the Rehabilitation Act of 1973.

Paragraph (c) makes clear that Congress did not intend to displace any of the rights or remedies provided by other Federal laws or other State or local laws (including State common law) that provide greater or equal protection to individuals with disabilities. A plaintiff may choose to pursue claims under a State law that does not confer greater substantive rights, or even confers fewer substantive rights, if the alleged violation is protected under the alternative law and the remedies are greater. For example, assume that a person with a physical disability seeks damages under a State law that allows compensatory and punitive damages for discrimination on the basis of physical disability, but does not allow them on the basis of mental disability. In that situation, the State law would provide narrower coverage, by excluding mental disabilities, but broader remedies, and an individual covered by both laws could choose to bring an action under both laws. Moreover, State tort claims confer greater remedies and are not preempted by the ADA. A plaintiff may join a State tort claim to a case brought under the ADA. In such a case, the plaintiff must, of course, prove all the elements of the State tort claim in order to prevail under that cause of action.

A commenter had concerns about privacy requirements for banking transactions using telephone relay services. Title IV of the Act provides adequate protections for ensuring the confidentiality of communications using the relay services. This issue is more appropriately addressed by the Federal Communications Commission in its regulation implementing title IV of the Act.

Section 36.104   Definitions

"Act." The word "Act" is used in the regulation to refer to the Americans with Disabilities Act of 1990, Pub. L. 101–336, which is also referred to as the "ADA."

"Commerce." The definition of "commerce" is identical to the statutory definition provided in section 301(l) of the ADA. It means travel, trade, traffic, commerce, transportation, or communication among the several States, between any foreign country or any territory or possession and any State, or between points in the same State but through another State or foreign country. Commerce is defined in the same manner as in title II of the Civil Rights Act of 1964, which prohibits racial discrimination in public accommodations.

The term "commerce" is used in the definition of "place of public accommodation." According to that definition, one of the criteria that an entity must meet before it can be considered a place of public accommodation is that its operations affect commerce. The term "commerce" is similary used in the definition of "commercial facility."

The use of the phrase "operations affect commerce" applies the full scope of coverage of the Commerce Clause of the Constitution in enforcing the ADA. The Constitution gives Congress broad authority to regulate interstate commerce, including the activities of local business enterprises (e.g., a physician's office, a neighborhood restaurant, a laundromat, or a bakery) that affect interstate commerce through the purchase or sale of products manufactured in other States, or by providing services to individuals from other States. Because of the integrated nature of the national economy, the ADA and this final rule will have extremely broad application.

"Commercial facilities" are those facilities that are intended for nonresidential use by a private entity and whose operations affect commerce. As explained under § 36.401, "New construction," the new construction and alteration requirements of subpart D of the rule apply to all commercial facilities, whether or not they are places of public accommodation. Those commercial facilities that are not places of public accommodation are not subject to the requirements of subparts B and C (e.g., those requirements concerning auxiliary aids and general nondiscrimination provisions).

Congress recognized that the employees within commercial facilities would generally be protected under title I (employment) of the Act. However, as the House Committee on Education and Labor pointed out, "[t]o the extent that new facilities are built in a manner that make[s] them accessible to all individuals, including potential employees, there will be less of a need for individual employers to engage in reasonable accommodations for particular employees." H.R. Rep. No. 485, 101st Cong., 2d Sess., pt. 2, at 117 (1990) [hereinafter "Education and Labor report"]. While employers of fewer than 15 employees are not covered by title I's employment discrimination provisions, there is no such limitation with respect to new construction covered under title III. Congress chose not to so limit the new construction provisions because of its desire for a uniform requirement of accessibility in new construction, because accessibility can be accomplished easily in the design and construction stage, and because future expansion of a business or sale or lease of the property to a larger employer or to a business that is a place of public accommodation is always a possibility.

The term "commercial facilities" is not intended to be defined by a dictionary or common industry definitions. Included in this category are factories, warehouses, office buildings, and other buildings in which employment may occur. The phrase, "whose operations affect commerce," is to be read broadly, to include all types of activities reached under the commerce clause of the Constitution.

Privately operated airports are also included in the category of commercial facilities. They are not, however, places of public accommodation because they are not terminals used for "specified public transportation." (Transportation by aircraft is specifically excluded from the statutory definition of "specified public transportation.") Thus, privately operated airports are subject to the new construction and alteration requirements of this rule (subpart D) but not to subparts B and C. (Airports operated by public entities are covered by title II of the Act.) Places of public accommodation located within airports, such as restaurants, shops, lounges, or conference centers, however, are covered by subparts B and C of this part.

The statute's definition of "commercial facilities" specifically includes only facilities "that are intended for nonresidential use" and specifically exempts those facilities that are covered or expressly exempted from coverage under the Fair Housing Act of 1968, as amended (42 U.S.C. 3601–3631). The interplay between the Fair Housing Act and the ADA with respect to those facilities that are "places of public accommodation" was the subject of many comments and is addressed in the preamble discussion of the definition of "place of public accommodation."

"Current illegal use of drugs." The phrase "current illegal use of drugs" is used in § 36.209. Its meaning is discussed in the preamble for that section.

"Disability." The definition of the term "disability" is comparable to the definition of the term "individual with handicaps" in section 7(8)(B) of the Rehabilitation Act and section 802(h) of the Fair Housing Act. The Education and Labor Committee report makes clear that the analysis of the term "individual with handicaps" by the Department of Health, Education, and Welfare in its regulations implementing section 504 (42 FR 22685 (May 4, 1977)) and the analysis by the Department of Housing and Urban Development in its regulation implementing the Fair Housing Amendments Act of 1988 (54 FR 3232 (Jan. 23, 1989)) should also apply fully to the term "disability" (Education and Labor report at 50).

The use of the term "disability" instead of "handicap" and the term "individual with a disability" instead of "individual with handicaps" represents an effort by the Congress to make use of up-to-date, currently accepted terminology. The terminology applied to individuals with disabilities is a very significant and sensitive issue. As with racial and ethnic terms, the choice of words to describe a person with a disability is overlaid with stereotypes, patronizing attitudes, and other emotional connotations. Many individuals with disabilities, and organizations representing such individuals, object to the use of such terms as "handicapped person" or "the handicapped." In other recent legislation, Congress also recognized this shift in terminology, e.g., by changing the name of the National Council on the Handicapped to the National Council on Disability (Pub. L. 100–630).

In enacting the Americans with Disabilities Act, Congress concluded that it was important for the current legislation to use terminology most in line with the sensibilities of most Americans with disabilities. No change in definition or substance is intended nor should be attributed to this change in phraseology.

The term "disability" means, with respect to an individual —

(A) A physical or mental impairment that substantially limits one or more of the major life activities of such individual;

(B) A record of such an impairment; or

(C) Being regarded as having such an impairment.

If an individual meets any one of these three tests, he or she is considered to be an individual with a disability for purposes of coverage under the Americans with Disabilities Act.

Congress adopted this same basic definition of "disability," first used in the Rehabilitation Act of 1973 and in the Fair Housing Amendments Act of 1988, for a number of reasons. It has worked well since it was adopted in 1974. There is a substantial body of administrative interpretation and judicial precedent on this definition. Finally, it would not be possible to guarantee comprehensiveness by providing a list of specific disabilities, especially because new disorders may be recognized in the future, as they have since the definition was first established in 1974.

Test A—A Physical or Mental Impairment That Substantially Limits One or More of the Major Life Activities of Such Individual

Physical or mental impairment. Under the first test, an individual must have a physical or mental impairment. As explained in paragraph (1)(i) of the definition, "impairment" means any physiological disorder or

condition, cosmetic disfigurement, or anatomical loss affecting one or more of the following body systems: Neurological, musculoskeletal; special sense organs (including speech organs that are not respiratory, such as vocal cords, soft palate, and tongue); respiratory, including speech organs; cardiovascular; reproductive; digestive; genitourinary; hemic and lymphatic; skin; and endocrine. It also means any mental or psychological disorder, such as mental retardation, organic brain syndrome, emotional or mental illness, and specific learning disabilities. This list closely tracks the one used in the regulations for section 504 of the Rehabilitation Act of 1973 (see, e.g., 45 CFR 84.3(j)(2)(i)).

Many commenters asked that "traumatic brain injury" be added to the list in paragraph (1)(i). Traumatic brain injury is already included because it is a physiological condition affecting one of the listed body systems, i.e., "neurological." Therefore, it was unnecessary for the Department to add the term to the regulation.

It is not possible to include a list of all the specific conditions, contagious and noncontagious diseases, or infections that would constitute physical or mental impairments because of the difficulty of ensuring the comprehensiveness of such a list, particularly in the light of the fact that other conditions or disorders may be identified in the future. However, the list of examples in paragraph (1)(iii) of the definition includes: Orthopedic, visual, speech and hearing impairments; cerebral palsy, epilepsy, muscular dystrophy, multiple sclerosis, cancer, heart disease, diabetes, mental retardation, emotional illness, specific learning disabilities, HIV disease (symptomatic or asymptomatic), tuberculosis, drug addiction, and alcoholism.

The examples of "physical or mental impairments" in paragraph (1)(iii) are the same as those contained in many section 504 regulations, except for the addition of the phrase "contagious and noncontagious" to describe the types of diseases and conditions included, and the addition of "HIV disease (symptomatic or asymptomatic)" and "tuberculosis" to the list of examples. These additions are based on the ADA committee reports, caselaw, and official legal opinions interpreting section 504. In *School Board of Nassau County* v. *Arline*, 480 U.S. 273 (1987), a case involving an individual with tuberculosis, the Supreme Court held that people with contagious diseases are entitled to the protections afforded by section 504. Following the *Arline* decision, this

Department's Office of Legal Counsel issued a legal opinion that concluded that symptomatic HIV disease is an impairment that substantially limits a major life activity; therefore it has been included in the definition of disability under this part. The opinion also concluded that asymptomatic HIV disease is an impairment that substantially limits a major life activity, either because of its actual effect on the individual with HIV disease or because the reactions of other people to individuals with HIV disease cause such individuals to be treated as though they are disabled. See Memorandum from Douglas W. Kmiec, Acting Assistant Attorney General, Office of Legal Counsel, Department of Justice, to Arthur B. Culvahouse, Jr., Counsel to the President (Sept. 27, 1988), *reprinted in* Hearings on S. 933, the Americans with Disabilities Act, Before the Subcomm. on the Handicapped of the Senate Comm. on Labor and Human Resources, 101st Cong., 1st Sess. 346 (1989). The phrase "symptomatic or asymptomatic" was inserted in the final rule after "HIV disease" in response to commenters who suggested that the clarification was necessary to give full meaning to the Department's opinion.

Paragraph (1)(iv) of the definition states that the phrase "physical or mental impairment" does not include homosexuality or bisexuality. These conditions were never considered impairments under other Federal disability laws. Section 511(a) of the statute makes clear that they are likewise not to be considered impairments under the Americans with Disabilities Act.

Physical or mental impairment does not include simple physical characteristics, such as blue eyes or black hair. Nor does it include environmental, cultural, economic, or other disadvantages, such as having a prison record, or being poor. Nor is age a disability. Similarly, the definition does not include common personality traits such as poor judgment or a quick temper where these are not symptoms of a mental or psychological disorder. However, a person who has these characteristics and also has a physical or mental impairment may be considered as having a disability for purposes of the Americans with Disabilities Act based on the impairment.

Substantial limitation of a major life activity. Under Test A, the impairment must be one that "substantially limits a major life activity." Major life activities include such things as caring for one's self, performing manual tasks, walking, seeing, hearing, speaking, breathing, learning, and working. For example, a person who is paraplegic is substantially limited in the major life activity of walking, a person who is blind is substantially limited in the major life activity of seeing, and a person who is mentally retarded is substantially limited in the major life activity of learning. A person with traumatic brain injury is substantially limited in the major life activities of caring for one's self, learning, and working because of memory deficit, confusion, contextual difficulties, and inability to reason appropriately.

A person is considered an individual with a disability for purposes of Test A, the first prong of the definition, when the individual's important life activities are restricted as to the conditions, manner, or duration under which they can be performed in comparison to most people. A person with a minor, trivial impairment, such as a simple infected finger, is not impaired in a major life activity. A person who can walk for 10 miles continuously is not substantially limited in walking merely because, on the eleventh mile, he or she begins to experience pain, because most people would not be able to walk eleven miles without experiencing some discomfort.

The Department received many comments on the proposed rule's inclusion of the word "temporary" in the definition of "disability." The preamble indicated that impairments are not necessarily excluded from the definition of "disability" simply because they are temporary, but that the duration, or expection duration, of an impairment is one factor that may properly be considered in determining whether the impairment substantially limits a major life activity. The preamble recognized, however, that temporary impairments, such as a broken leg, are not commonly regarded as disabilities, and only in rare circumstances would the degree of the limitation and its expected duration be substantial: Nevertheless, many commenters objected to inclusion of the word "temporary" both because it is not in the statute and because it is not contained in the definition of "disability" set forth in the title I regulations of the Equal Employment Opportunity Commission (EEOC). The word "temporary" has been deleted from the final rule to conform with the statutory language. The question of whether a temporary impairment is a disability must be resolved on a case-by-case basis, taking into consideration both the duration (or expected duration) of the impairment and the extent to which it actually limits a major life activity of the affected individual.

The question of whether a person has a disability should be assessed without regard to the availability of mitigating measures, such as reasonable modifications or auxiliary aids and services. For example, a person with hearing loss is substantially limited in the major life activity of hearing, even though the loss may be improved through the use of hearing aid. Likewise, persons with impairments, such as epilepsy or diabetes, that substantially limit a major life activity, are covered under the first prong of the definition of disability, even if the effects of the impairment are controlled by medication.

Many commenters asked that environmental illness (also known as multiple chemical sensitivity) as well as allergy to cigarette smoke be recognized as disabilities. The Department, however, declines to state categorically that these types of allergies or sensitivities are disabilities, because the determination as to whether an impairment is a disability depends on whether, given the particular circumstances at issue, the impairment substantially limits one or more major life activities (or has a history of, or is regarded as having such an effect).

Sometimes respiratory or neurological functioning is so severely affected that an individual will satisfy the requirements to be considered disabled under the regulation. Such an individual would be entitled to all of the protections afforded by the Act and this part. In other cases, individuals may be sensitive to environmental elements or to smoke but their sensitivity will not rise to the level needed to constitute a disability. For example, their major life activity of breathing may be somewhat, but not substantially, impaired. In such circumstances, the individuals are not disabled and are not entitled to the protections of the statute despite their sensitivity to environmental agents.

In sum, the determination as to whether allergies to cigarette smoke, or allergies or sensitivities characterized by the commenters as environmental illness are disabilities covered by the regulation must be made using the same case-by-case analysis that is applied to all other physical or mental impairments. Moreover, the addition of specific regulatory provisions relating to environmental illness in the final rule would be inappropriate at this time pending future consideration of the issue by the Architectural and Transportation Barriers Compli-

ance Board, the Environmental Protection Agency, and the Occupational Safety and Health Administration of the Department of Labor.

Test B—A Record of Such an Impairment

This test is intended to cover those who have a record of an impairment. As explained in paragraph (3) of the rule's definition of disability, this includes a person who has a history of an impairment that substantially limited a major life activity, such as someone who has recovered from an impairment. It also includes persons who have been misclassified as having an impairment.

This provision is included in the definition in part to protect individuals who have recovered from a physical or mental impairment that previously substantially limited them in a major life activity. Discrimination on the basis of such a past impairment is prohibited. Frequently occurring examples of the first group (those who have a history of an impairment) are persons with histories of mental or emotional illness, heart disease, or cancer; examples of the second group (those who have been misclassified as having an impairment) are persons who have been misclassified as having mental retardation or mental illness.

Test C—Being Regarded as Having Such an Impairment

This test, as contained in paragraph (4) of the definition, is intended to cover persons who are treated by a private entity or public accommodation as having a physical or mental impairment that substantially limits a major life activity. It applies when a person is treated as if he or she has an impairment that substantially limits a major life activity, regardless of whether that person has an impairment.

The Americans with Disabilities Act uses the same "regarded as" test set forth in the regulations implementing section 504 of the Rehabilitation Act. *See, e.g.*, 28 CFR 42.540(k)(2)(iv), which provides:

(iv) "Is regarded as having an impairment" means (A) Has a physical or mental impairment that does not substantially limit major life activities but that is treated by a recipient as constituting such a limitation; (B) Has a physical or mental impairment that substantially limits major life activities only as a result of the attitudes of others toward such impairment; or (C) Has none of the impairments defined in paragraph (k)(2)(i) of this section but is treated by a recipient as having such an impairment.

The perception of the private entity or public accommodation is a key element of this test. A person who perceives himself or herself to have an impairment, but does not have an impairment, and is not treated as if he or she has an impairment, is not protected under this test. A person would be covered under this test if a restaurant refused to serve that person because of a fear of "negative reactions" of others to that person. A person would also be covered if a public accommodation refused to serve a patron because it perceived that the patron had an impairment that limited his or her enjoyment of the goods or services being offered.

For example, persons with severe burns often encounter discrimination in community activities, resulting in substantial limitation of major life activities. These persons would be covered under this test based on the attitudes of others towards the impairment, even if they did not view themselves as "impaired."

The rationale for this third test, as used in the Rehabilitation Act of 1973, was articulated by the Supreme Court in *Arline*, 480 U.S. 273 (1987). The Court noted that, although an individual may have an impairment that does not in fact substantially limit a major life activity, the reaction of others may prove just as disabling. "Such an impairment might not diminish a person's physical or mental capabilities, but could nevertheless substantially limit that person's ability to work as a result of the negative reactions of others to the impairment." *Id*. at 283. The Court concluded that, by including this test in the Rehabilitation Act's definition, "Congress acknowledged that society's accumulated myths and fears about disability and disease are as handicapping as are the physical limitations that flow from actual impairment." *Id*. at 284.

Thus, a person who is not allowed into a public accommodation because of the myths, fears, and sterotypes associated with disabilities would be covered under this third test whether or not the person's physical or mental condition would be considered a disability under the first or second test in the definition.

If a person is refused admittance on the basis of an actual or perceived physical or mental condition, and the public accommodation can articulate no legitimate reason for the refusal (such as failure to meet eligibility criteria), a perceived concern about admitting persons with disabilities could be inferred and the individual would qualify for coverage under the "regarded as" test. A person who is covered because of being regarded as having an impairment is not required to show that the public accommodation's perception is inaccurate (e.g., that he will be accepted by others, or that insurance rates will not increase) in order to be admitted to the public accommodation.

Paragraph (5) of the definition lists certain conditions that are not included within the definition of "disability." The excluded conditions are: transvestism, transsexualism, pedophilia, exhibitionism, voyeurism, gender identity disorders not resulting from physical impairments, other sexual behavior disorders, compulsive gambling, kleptomania, pyromania, and psychoactive substance use disorders resulting from current illegal use of drugs. Unlike homosexuality and bisexuality, which are not considered impairments under either the Americans with Disabilities Act (see the definition of "disability," paragraph (1)(iv)) or section 504, the conditions listed in paragraph (5), except for transvestism, are not necessarily excluded as impairments under section 504. (Transvestism was excluded from the definition of disability for section 504 by the Fair Housing Amendments Act of 1988, Pub. L. 100–430, § 6(b).) The phrase "current illegal use of drugs" used in this definition is explained in the preamble to § 36.209.

"Drug." The definition of the term "drug" is taken from section 510(d)(2) of the ADA.

"Facility." "Facility" means all or any portion of buildings, structures, sites, complexes, equipment, rolling stock or other conveyances, roads, walks, passageways, parking lots, or other real or personal property, including the site where the building, property, structure, or equipment is located. Committee reports made clear that the definition of facility was drawn from the definition of facility in current Federal regulations (*see, e.g.*, Education and Labor report at 114). It includes both indoor and outdoor areas where human-constructed improvements, structures, equipment, or property have been added to the natural environment.

The term "rolling stock or other conveyances" was not included in the definition of facility in the proposed rule. However, commenters raised questions about the applicability of this part to places of public accommodation operated in mobile facilities (such as cruise ships, floating restaurants, or mobile health units). Those places of public accommodation are covered under this part, and would be included in the definition of "facility." Thus the requirements of subparts B and C would apply to those places of public accommodation. For example, a covered entity could not discriminate on the basis of disability in the full and equal enjoyment of the facilities (§ 36.201). Similarly, a cruise line could not apply eligibility criteria to potential passengers in a manner that would screen out individuals with disabilities, unless the criteria are "necessary," as provided in § 36.301.

However, standards for new construction and alterations of such facilities are not yet included in the Americans with Disabilities Act Accessibility Guidelines for Buildings and Facilities (ADAAG) adopted by § 36.406 and incorporated in Appendix A. The Department therefore will not interpret the new construction and alterations provisions of subpart D to apply to the types of facilities discussed here, pending further development of specific requirements.

Requirements pertaining to accessible transportation services provided by public accommodations are included in § 36.310 of this part; standards pertaining to accessible vehicles will be issued by the Secretary of Transportation pursuant to section 306 of the Act, and will be codified at 49 CFR part 37.

A public accommodation has obligations under this rule with respect to a cruise ship to the extent that its operations are subject to the laws of the United States.

The definition of "facility" only includes the site over which the private entity may exercise control or on which a place of public accommodation or a commercial facility is located. It does not include, for example, adjacent roads or walks controlled by a public entity that is not subject to this part. Public entities are subject to the requirements of title II of the Act. The Department's regulation implementing title II, which will be codified at 28 CFR part 35, addresses the obligations of public entities to ensure accessibility by providing curb ramps at pedestrian walkways.

"Illegal use of drugs." The definition of "illegal use of drugs" is taken from section 510(d)(1) of the Act and clarifies that the term includes the illegal use of one or more drugs.

"Individual with a disability" means a person who has a disability but does not include an individual who is currently illegally using drugs, when the public accommodation acts on the basis of such use. The phrase "current illegal use of drugs" is explained in the preamble to § 36.209.

"Place of public accommodation." The term "place of public accommodation" is an adaptation of the statutory definition of "public accommodation" in section 301(7) of the ADA and appears as an element of the regulatory definition of public accommodation. The final rule defines "place of public accommodation" as a facility, operated by a private entity, whose operations affect commerce and fall within at least one of 12 specified categories. The term "public accommodation," on the other hand, is reserved by the final rule for the private entity that owns, leases (or leases to), or operates a place of public accommodation. It is the public accommodation, and not the place of public accommodation, that is subject to the regulation's nondiscrimination requirements. Placing the obligation not to discriminate on the public accommodation, as defined in the rule, is consistent with section 302(a) of the ADA, which places the obligation not to discriminate on any person who owns, leases (or leases to), or operates a place of public accommodation.

Facilities operated by government agencies or other public entities as defined in this section do not qualify as places of public accommodation. The actions of public entities are governed by title II of the ADA and will be subject to regulations issued by the Department of Justice under that title. The receipt of government assistance by a private entity does not by itself preclude a facility from being considered as a place of public accommodation.

The definition of place of public accommodation incorporates the 12 categories of facilities represented in the statutory definition of public accommodation in section 301(7) of the ADA:

1. Places of lodging.
2. Establishments serving food or drink.
3. Places of exhibition or entertainment.
4. Places public gathering.
5. Sales or rental establishments.
6. Service establishments.
7. Stations used for specified public transportation.
8. Places of public display or collection.
9. Places of recreation.
10. Places of education.

11. Social service center establishments.

12. Places of exercise or recreation.

In order to be a place of public accommodation, a facility must be operated by a private entity, its operations must affect commerce, and it must fall within one of these 12 categories. While the list of categories is exhaustive, the representative examples of facilities within each category are not. Within each category only a few examples are given. The category of social service center establishments would include not only the types of establishments listed, day care centers, senior citizen centers, homeless shelters, food banks, adoption agencies, but also establishments such as substance abuse treatment centers, rape crisis centers, and halfway houses. As another example, the category of sales or rental establishments would include an innumerable array of facilities that would sweep far beyond the few examples given in the regulation. For example, other retail or wholesale establishments selling or renting items, such as bookstores, videotape rental stores, car rental establishment, pet stores, and jewelry stores would also be covered under this category, even though they are not specifically listed.

Several commenters requested clarification as to the coverage of wholesale establishments under the category of "sales or rental establishments." The Department intends for wholesale establishments to be covered under this category as places of public accommodation except in cases where they sell exclusively to other businesses and not to individuals. For example, a company that grows food produce and supplies its crops exclusively to food processing corporations on a wholesale basis does not become a public accommodation because of these transactions. If this company operates a road side stand where its crops are sold to the public, the road side stand would be a sales establishment covered by the ADA. Conversely, a sales establishment that markets its goods as "wholesale to the public" and sells to individuals would not be exempt from ADA coverage despite its use of the word "wholesale"as a marketing technique.

Of course, a company that operates a place of public accommodation is subject to this part only in the operation of that place of public accommodation. In the example given above, the wholesale produce company that operates a road side stand would be a public accommodation only for the purposes of the operation of that stand.

The company would be prohibited from discriminating on the basis of disability in the operation of the road side stand, and it would be required to remove barriers to physical access to the extent that it is readily achievable to do so (see § 36.304); however, in the event that it is not readily achievable to remove barriers, for example, by replacing a gravel surface or regrading the area around the stand to permit access by persons with mobility impairments, the company could meet its obligations through alternative methods of making its goods available, such as delivering produce to a customer in his or her car (see § 36.305). The concepts of readily achievable barrier removal and alternatives to barrier removal are discussed further in the preamble discussion of §§ 36.304 and 36.305.

Even if a facility does not fall within one of the 12 categories, and therefore does not qualify as a place of public accommodation, it still may be a commercial facility as defined in § 36.104 and be subject to the new construction and alterations requirements of subpart D.

A number of commenters questioned the treatment of residential hotels and other residential facilities in the Department's proposed rule. These commenters were essentially seeking resolution of the relationship between the Fair Housing Act and the ADA concerning facilities that are both residential in nature and engage in activities that would cause them to be classified as "places of public accommodation" under the ADA. The ADA's express exemption relating to the Fair Housing Act applies only to "commercial facilities" and not to "places of public accommodation."

A facility whose operations affect interstate commerce is a place of public accommodation for purposes of the ADA to the extent that its operations include those types of activities engaged in or services provided by the facilities contained on the list of 12 categories in section 301(7) of the ADA. Thus, a facility that provides social services would be considered a "social service center establishment." Similarly, the category "places of lodging" would exclude solely residential facilities because the nature of a place of lodging contemplates the use of the facility for short-term stays.

Many facilities, however, are mixed use facilities. For example, in a large hotel that has a separate residential apartment wing, the residential wing would not be covered by the ADA because of the nature of the occupancy of that part of the facility. This residential wing would, however, be covered by the Fair Housing Act. The separate nonresidential accommodations in the rest of the hotel would be a place of lodging, and thus a public accommodation subject to the requirements of this final rule. If a hotel allows both residential and short-term stays, but does not allocate space for these different uses in separate, discrete units, both the ADA and the Fair Housing Act may apply to the facility. Such determinations will need to be made on a case-by-case basis. Any place of lodging of the type described in paragraph (1) of the definition of place of public accommodation and that is an establishment located within a building that contains not more than five rooms for rent or hire and is actually occupied by the proprieter of the establishment as his or her residence is not covered by the ADA. (This exclusion from coverage does not apply to other categories of public accommodations, for example, professional officers or homeless shelters, that are located in a building that is also occupied as a private residence.)

A number of commenters noted that the term "residential hotel" may also apply to a type of hotel commonly known as a "single room occupancy hotel." Although such hotels or portions of such hotels may fall under the Fair Housing Act when operated or used as long-term residences, they are also considered "places of lodging" under the ADA when guests of such hotels are free to use them on a short-term basis. In addition, "single room occupancy hotels" may provide social services to their guests, often through the operation of Federal or State grant programs. In such a situation, the facility would be considered a "social service center establishment" and thus covered by the ADA as a place of public accommodation, regardless of the length of stay of the occupants.

A similar analysis would also be applied to other residential facilities that provide social services, including homeless shelters, shelters for people seeking refuge from domestic violence, nursing homes, residential care facilities, and other facilities where persons may reside for varying lengths of time. Such facilities should be analyzed under the Fair Housing Act to determine the application of that statute. The ADA, however, requires a separate and independent analysis. For example, if the facility, or a portion of the facility, is intended for or permits short-term stays, or if it can appropriately be categorized as a service establishment or as a social service establishment, then the facility or that portion of the facility used for the covered purpose is a place of public accommodation under the ADA. For example, a homeless shelter that is intended and used only for long-term residential stays and that does not provide social services to its residents would not be covered as a place of public accommodation. However, if this facility permitted short-term stays or provided social services to its residents, it would be covered under the ADA either as a "place of lodging" or as a "social service center establishment," or as both.

A private home, by itself, does not fall within any of the 12 categories. However, it can be covered as a place of public accommodation to the extent that it is used as a facility that would fall within one of the 12 categories. For example, if a professional office of a dentist, doctor, psychologist is located in a private home, the portion of the home dedicated to office use (including areas used both for the residence and the office, e.g., the entrance to the home that is also used as the entrance to the professional office) would be considered a place of public accommodation. Places of public accommodation located in residential facilities are specifically addressed in § 36.207.

If a tour of a commercial facility that is not otherwise a place of public accommodation, such as, for example, a factory or a movie studio production set, is open to the general public, the route followed by the tour is a place of public accommodation and the tour must be operated in accordance with the rule's requirements for public accommodations. The place of public accommodation defined by the tour does not include those portions of the commercial facility that are merely viewed from the tour route. Hence, the barrier removal requirements of § 36.304 only apply to the physical route followed by the tour participants and not to work stations or other areas that are merely adjacent to, or within view of, the tour route. If the tour is not open to the general public, but rather is conducted, for example, for selected business colleagues, partners, customers, or consultants, the tour route is not a place of public accommodation and the tour is not subject to the requirements for public accommodation.

Public accommodations that receive Federal financial assistance are subject to the requirements of section 504 of the Rehabilitation Act as well as the requirements of the ADA.

Private schools, including elementary

and secondary schools, are covered by the rule as places of public accommodation. The rule itself, however, does not require a private school to provide a free appropriate education or develop an individualized education program in accordance with regulations of the Department of Education implementing section 504 of the Rehabiliation Act of 1973, as amended (34 CFR part 104), and regulations implementing the Individuals with Disabilities Education Act (34 CFR part 300). The receipt of Federal assistance by a private school, however, would trigger application of the Department of Education's regulations to the extent mandated by the particular type of assistance received.

"Private club." The term "private club" is defined in accordance with section 307 of the ADA as a private club or establishment exempted from coverage under title II of the Civil Rights Act of 1964. Title II of the 1964 Act exempts any "private club or other establishment not in fact open to the public, except to the extent that the facilities of such establishment are made available to the customers or patrons of [a place of public accommodation as defined in title II]." The rule, therefore, as reflected in § 36.102(e) of the application section, limits the coverage of private clubs accordingly. The obligations of a private club that rents space to any other private entity for the operation of a place of public accommodation are discussed further in connection with § 36.201.

In determining whether a private entity qualifies as a private club under title II, courts have considered such factors as the degree of member control of club operations, the selectivity of the membership selection process, whether substantial membership fees are charged, whether the entity is operated on a nonprofit basis, the extent to which the facilities are open to the public, the degree of public funding, and whether the club was created specifically to avoid compliance with the Civil Rights Act. See *e.g., Tillman* v. *Wheaton Haven Recreation Ass'n,* 410 U.S. 431 (1973); *Daniel* v. *Paul,* 395 U.S. 298 (1969); *Olzman* v. *Lake Hills Swim Club, Inc.,* 495 F.2d 1333 (2d Cir. 1974); *Anderson* v. *Pass Christian Isles Golf Club, Inc.,* 488 F.2d 855 (5th Cir. 1974); *Smith* v. *YMCA,* 462 F.2d 634 (5th Cir. 1972); *Stout* v. *YMCA,* 404 F.2d 687 (5th Cir. 1968); *United States* v. *Richberg,* 398 F.2d 523 (5th Cir. 1968); *Nesmith* v. *YMCA,* 397 F.2d 96 (4th Cir. 1968); *United States* v. *Lansdowne Swim Club,* 713 F. Supp. 785 (E.D. Pa. 1989); *Durham*

v. *Red Lake Fishing and Hunting Club, Inc.,* 666 F. Supp. 954 (W.D. Tex. 1987); *New York* v. *Ocean Club, Inc.,* 602 F. Supp. 489 (E.D.N.Y. 1984); *Brown* v. *Loudoun Golf and Country Club, Inc.,* 573 F. Supp. 399 (E.D. Va. 1983); *United States* v. *Trustees of Fraternal Order of Eagles,* 472 F. Supp. 1174 (E.D. Wis. 1979); *Cornelius* v. *Benevolent Protective Order of Elks,* 382 F. Supp. 1182 (D. Conn. 1974).

"Private entity." The term "private entity" is defined as any individual or entity other than a public entity. It is used as part of the definition of "public accommodation" in this section.

The definition adds "individual" to the statutory definition of private entity (see section 301(6) of the ADA). This addition clarifies that an individual may be a private entity and, therefore, may be considered a public accommodation if he or she owns, leases (or leases to), or operates a place of public accommodation. The explicit inclusion of individuals under the definition of private entity is consistent with section 302(a) of the ADA, which broadly prohibits discrimination on the basis of disability by any person who owns, leases (or leases to), or operates a place of public accommodation.

"Public accommodation." The term "public accommodation" means a private entity that owns, leases (or leases to), or operates a place of public accommodation. The regulatory term, "public accommodation," corresponds to the statutory term, "person," in section 302(a) of the ADA. The ADA prohibits discrimination "by any person who owns, leases (or leases to), or operates a place of public accommodation." The text of the regulation consequently places the ADA's nondiscrimination obligations on "public accommodations" rather than on "persons" or on "places of public accommodation."

As stated in § 36.102(b)(2), the requirements of subparts B and C obligate a public accommodation only with respect to the operations of a place of public accommodation. A public accommodation must also meet the requirements of subpart D with respect to facilities used as, or designed or constructed for use as, places of public accommodation or commercial facilities.

"Public entity." The term "public entity" is defined in accordance with section 201(1) of the ADA as any State or local government; any department, agency, special purpose district, or other instrumentality of a State or States or local government; and the National Railroad Passenger

Corporation, and any commuter authority (as defined in section 103(8) of the Rail Passenger Service Act). It is used in the definition of "private entity" in § 36.104. Public entities are excluded from the definition of private entity and therefore cannot qualify as public accommodations under this regulation. However, the actions of public entities are covered by title II of the ADA and by the Department's title II regulations codified at 28 CFR part 35.

"Qualified interpreter." The Department received substantial comment regarding the lack of a definition of "qualified interpreter." The proposed rule defined auxiliary aids and services to include the statutory term, "qualified interpreters" (§ 36.303(b)), but did not define that term. Section 36.303 requires the use of a qualified interpreter where necessary to achieve effective communication, unless an undue burden or fundamental alteration would result. Commenters stated that a lack of guidance on what the term means would create confusion among those trying to secure interpreting services and often result in less than effective communication.

Many commenters were concerned that, without clear guidance on the issue of "qualified" interpreter, the rule would be interpreted to mean "available, rather than qualified" interpreters. Some claimed that few public accommodations would understand the difference between a qualified interpreter and a person who simply knows a few signs or how to fingerspell.

In order to clarify what is meant by "qualified interpreter" the Department has added a definition of the term to the final rule. A qualified interpreter means an interpreter who is able to interpret effectively, accurately, and impartially both receptively and expressively, using any necessary specialized vocabulary. This definition focuses on the actual ability of the interpreter in a particular interpreting context to facilitate effective communication between the public accommodation and the individual with disabilities.

Public comment also revealed that public accommodations have at times asked persons who are deaf to provide family members or friends to interpret. In certain circumstances, notwithstanding that the family member or friend is able to interpret or is a certified interpreter, the family member or friend may not be qualified to render the necessary interpretation because of factors such as emotional or personal involvement or considerations of confidentiality that may adversely affect the ability

to interpret "effectively, accurately, and impartially."

"Readily achievable." The definition of "readily achievable" follows the statutory definition of that term in section 301(9) of the ADA. Readily achievable means easily accomplishable and able to be carried out without much difficulty or expense. The term is used as a limitation on the obligation to remove barriers under §§ 36.304(a), 36.305(a), 36.308(a), and 36.310(b). Further discussions of the meaning and application of the term "readily achievable" may be found in the preamble section for § 36.304.

The definition lists factors to be considered in determining whether barrier removal is readily achievable in any particular circumstance. A significant number of commenters objected to § 36.306 of the proposed rule, which listed identical factors to be considered for determining "readily achievable" and "undue burden" together in one section. They asserted that providing a consolidated section blurred the distinction between the level of effort required by a public accommodation under the two standards. The readily achievable standard is a "lower" standard than the "undue burden" standard in terms of the level of effort required, but the factors used in determining whether an action is readily achievable or would result in an undue burden are identical (See Education and Labor report at 109). Although the preamble to the proposed rule clearly delineated the relationship between the two standards, to eliminate any confusion the Department has deleted § 36.306 of the proposed rule. That section, in any event, as other commenters noted, had merely repeated the lists of factors contained in the definitions of readily achievable and undue burden.

The list of factors included in the definition is derived from section 301(9) of the ADA. It reflects the congressional intention that a wide range of factors be considered in determining whether an action is readily achievable. It also takes into account that many local facilities are owned or operated by parent corporations or entities that conduct operations at many different sites. This section makes clear that, in some instances, resources beyond those of the local facility where the barrier must be removed may be relevant in determining whether an action is readily achievable. One must also evaluate the degree to which any parent entity has resources that may be allocated to the local facility.

The statutory list of factors in section 301(9) of the Act uses the term "covered entity" to refer to the larger entity of which a particular facility may be a part. "Covered entity" is not a defined term in the ADA and is not used consistently throughout the Act. The definition, therefore, substitutes the term "parent entity" in place of "covered entity" in paragraphs (3), (4), and (5) when referring to the larger private entity whose overall resources may be taken into account. This usage is consistent with the House Judiciary Committee's use of the term "parent company" to describe the larger entity of which the local facility is a part (H.R. Rep. No. 485, 101st Cong., 2d Sess., pt. 3, at 40–41, 54–55 (1990) (hereinafter "Judiciary report")).

A number of commenters asked for more specific guidance as to when and how the resources of a parent corporation or entity are to be taken into account in determining what is readily achievable. The Department believes that this complex issue is most appropriately resolved on a case-by-case basis. As the comments reflect, there is a wide variety of possible relationships between the site in question and any parent corporation or other entity. It would be unwise to posit legal ramifications under the ADA of even generic relationships (e.g., banks involved in foreclosures or insurance companies operating as trustees or in other similar fiduciary relationships), because any analysis will depend so completely on the detailed fact situations and the exact nature of the legal relationships involved. The final rule does, however, reorder the factors to be considered. This shift and the addition of the phrase "if applicable" make clear that the line of inquiry concerning factors will start at the site involved in the action itself. This change emphasizes that the overall resources, size, and operations of the parent corporation or entity should be considered to the extent appropriate in light of "the geographic separateness, and the administrative or fiscal relationship of the site or sites in question to any parent corporation or entity."

Although some commenters sought more specific numerical guidance on the definition of readily achievable, the Department has declined to establish in the final rule any kind of numerical formula for determining whether an action is readily achievable. It would be difficult to devise a specific ceiling on compliance costs that would take into account the vast diversity of enterprises covered by the ADA's public accommodations requirements and the economic situation that any particular entity would find itself in at any moment.

The final rule, therefore, implements the flexible case-by-case approach chosen by Congress.

A number of commenters requested that security considerations be explicitly recognized as a factor in determining whether a barrier removal action is readily achievable. The Department believes that legitimate safety requirements, including crime prevention measures, may be taken into account so long as they are based on actual risks and are necessary for safe operation of the public accommodation. This point has been included in the definition.

Some commenters urged the Department not to consider acts of barrier removal in complete isolation from each other in determining whether they are readily achievable. The Department believes that it is appropriate to consider the cost of other barrier removal actions as one factor in determining whether a measure is readily achievable.

"Religious entity." The term "religious entity" is defined in accordance with section 307 of the ADA as a religious organization or entity controlled by a religious organization, including a place of worship. Section 36.102(e) of the rule, states that the rule does not apply to any religious entity.

The ADA's exemption of religious organizations and religious entities controlled by religious organizations is very broad, encompassing a wide variety of situations. Religious organizations and entities controlled by religious organizations have no obligations under the ADA. Even when a religious organization carries out activities that would otherwise make it a public accommodation, the religious organization is exempt from ADA coverage. Thus, if a church itself operates a day care center, a nursing home, a private school, or a diocesan school system, the operations of the center, home, school, or schools would not be subject to the requirements of the ADA or this part. The religious entity would not lose its exemption merely because the services provided were open to the general public. The test is whether the church or other religious organization operates the public accommodation, not which individuals receive the public accommodation's services.

Religious entities that are controlled by religious organizations are also exempt from the ADA's requirements. Many religious organizations in the United States use lay boards and other secular or corporate mechanisms to operate schools and an array of social services. The use of a lay board or other mechanism does not itself remove the ADA's religious exemption. Thus, a parochial school, having religious doctrine in its curriculum and sponsored by a religious order, could be exempt either as a religious organization or as an entity controlled by a religious organization, even if it has a lay board. The test remains a factual one—whether the church or other religious organization controls the operations of the school or of the service or whether the school or service is itself a religious organization.

Although a religious organization or a religious entity that is controlled by a religious organization has no obligations under the rule, a public accommodation that is not itself a religious organization, but that operates a place of public accommodation in leased space on the property of a religious entity, which is not a place of worship, is subject to the rule's requirements if it is not under control of a religious organization. When a church rents meeting space, which is not a place of worship, to a local community group or to a private, independent day care center, the ADA applies to the activities of the local community group and day care center if a lease exists and consideration is paid.

"Service animal." The term "service animal" encompasses any guide dog, signal dog, or other animal individually trained to provide assistance to an individual with a disability. The term is used in § 36.302(c), which requires public accommodations generally to modify policies, practices, and procedures to accommodate the use of service animals in places of public accommodation.

"Specified public transportation." The definition of "specified public transportation" is identical to the statutory definition in section 301(10) of the ADA. The term means transportation by bus, rail, or any other conveyance (other than by aircraft) that provides the general public with general or special service (including charter service) on a regular and continuing basis. It is used in category (7) of the definition of "place of public accommodation," which includes stations used for specified public transportation.

The effect of this definition, which excludes transportation by aircraft, is that it excludes privately operated airports from coverage as places of public accommodation. However, places of public accommodation located within airports would be covered by this part. Airports that are operated by public entities are covered by title II of the ADA, and, if they are operated as part of a program receiving Federal financial assistance, by section 504 of the Rehabilitation Act. Privately operated airports are similarly covered by section 504 if they are operated as part of a program receiving Federal financial assistance. The operations of any portion of any airport that are under the control of an air carrier are covered by the Air Carrier Access Act. In addition, airports are covered as commercial facilities under this rule.

"State." The definition of "State" is identical to the statutory definition in section 3(3) of the ADA. The term is used in the definition of "commerce" and "public entity" in § 36.104.

"Undue burden." The definition of "undue burden" is analogous to the statutory definition of "undue hardship" in employment under section 101(10) of the ADA. The term undue burden means "significant difficulty or expense" and serves as a limitation on the obligation to provide auxiliary aids and services under § 36.303 and §§ 36.309(b)(3) and (c)(3). Further discussion of the meaning and application of the term undue burden may be found in the preamble discussion of § 36.303.

The definition lists factors considered in determining whether provision of an auxiliary aid or service in any particular circumstance would result in an undue burden. The factors to be considered in determining whether an action would result in an undue burden are identical to those to be considered in determining whether an action is readily achievable. However, "readily achievable" is a lower standard than "undue burden" in that it requires a lower level of effort on the part of the public accommodation (see Education and Labor report at 109).

Further analysis of the factors to be considered in determining undue burden may be found in the preamble discussion of the definition of the term "readily achievable."

Subpart B—General Requirements

Subpart B includes general prohibitions restricting a public accommodation from discriminating against people with disabilities by denying them the opportunity to benefit from goods or services, by giving them unequal goods or services, or by giving them indirect or separate goods or services. These general prohibitions are patterned after the basic, general prohibitions that exist in other civil rights laws that prohibit discrimination on the basis of race, sex, color, religion, or national origin.

Section 36.201   General

Section 36.201(a) contains the general rule that prohibits discrimination on the basis of disability in the full and equal enjoyment of goods, services, facilities, privileges, advantages, and accommodations of any place of public accommodation.

Full and equal enjoyment means the right to participate and to have an equal opportunity to obtain the same results as others to the extent possible with such accommodations as may be required by the Act and these regulations. It does not mean that an individual with a disability must achieve an identical result or level of achievement as persons without a disability. For example, an exercise class cannot exclude a person who uses a wheelchair because he or she cannot do all the exercises and derive the same result from the class as persons without a disability.

Section 302(a) of the ADA states that the prohibition against discrimination applies to "any person who owns, leases (or leases to), or operates a place of public accommodation," and this language is reflected in § 36.201(a). The coverage is quite extensive and would include sublessees, management companies, and any other entity that owns, leases, leases to, or operates a place of public accommodation, even if the operation is only for a short time.

The first sentence of paragraph (b) of § 36.201 reiterates the general principle that both the landlord that owns the building that houses the place of public accommodation, as well as the tenant that owns or operates the place of public accommodation, are public accommodations subject to the requirements of this part. Although the statutory language could be interpreted as placing equal responsibility on all private entities, whether lessor, lessee, or operator of a public accommodation, the committee reports suggest that liability may be allocated. Section 36.201(b) of that section of the proposed rule attempted to allocate liability in the regulation itself. Paragraph (b)(2) of that section made a specific allocation of liability for the obligation to take readily achievable measures to remove barriers, and paragraph (b)(3) made a specific allocation for the obligation to provide auxiliary aids.

Numerous commenters pointed out that these allocations would not apply in all situations. Some asserted that paragraph (b)(2)

of the proposed rule only addressed the situation when a lease gave the tenant the right to make alterations with permission of the landlord, but failed to address other types of leases, e.g., those that are silent on the right to make alterations, or those in which the landlord is not permitted to enter a tenant's premises to make alterations. Several commenters noted that many leases contain other clauses more relevant to the ADA than the alterations clause. For example, many leases contain a "compliance clause," a clause which allocates responsibility to a particular party for compliance with all relevant Federal, State, and local laws. Many commenters pointed out various types of relationships that were left unaddressed by the regulation, e.g., sale and leaseback arrangements where the landlord is a financial institution with no control or responsibility for the building; franchises; subleases; and management companies which, at least in the hotel industry, often have control over operations but are unable to make modifications to the premises.

Some commenters raised specific questions as to how the barrier removal allocation would work as a practical matter. Paragraph (b)(2) of the proposed rule provided that the burden of making readily achievable modifications within the tenant's place of public accommodation would shift to the landlord when the modifications were not readily achievable for the tenant or when the landlord denied a tenant's request for permission to make such modifications. Commenters noted that the rule did not specify exactly when the burden would actually shift from tenant to landlord and whether the landlord would have to accept a tenant's word that a particular action is not readily achievable. Others questioned if the tenant should be obligated to use alternative methods of barrier removal before the burden shifts. In light of the fact that readily achievable removal of barriers can include such actions as moving of racks and displays, some commenters doubted the appropriateness of requiring a landlord to become involved in day-to-day operations of its tenants' businesses.

The Department received widely differing comments in response to the preamble question asking whether landlord and tenant obligations should vary depending on the length of time remaining on an existing lease. Many suggested that tenants should have no responsibilities in "shorter leases," which commenters defined as ranging anywhere from 90 days to three years. Other commenters pointed out that the time remaining on the lease should not be a factor in the rule's allocation of responsibilities, but is relevant in determining what is readily achievable for the tenant. The Department agrees with this latter approach and will interpret the rule in that manner.

In recognition of the somewhat limited applicability of the allocation scheme contained in the proposed rule, paragraphs (b)(2) and (b)(3) have been deleted from the final rule. The Department has substituted instead a statement that allocation of responsibility as between the parties for taking readily achievable measures to remove barriers and to provide auxiliary aids and services both in common areas and within places of public accommodation may be determined by the lease or other contractual relationships between the parties. The ADA was not intended to change existing landlord/tenant responsibilities as set forth in the lease. By deleting specific provisions from the rule, the Department gives full recognition to this principle. As between the landlord and tenant, the extent of responsibility for particular obligations may be, and in many cases probably will be, determined by contract.

The suggested allocation of responsibilites contained in the proposed rule may be used if appropriate in a particular situation. Thus, the landlord would generally be held responsible for making readily achievable changes and providing auxiliary aids and services in common areas and for modifying policies, practices, or procedures applicable to all tenants, and the tenant would generally be responsible for readily achievable changes, provision of auxiliary aids, and modification of policies within its own place of public accommodation.

Many commenters objected to the proposed rule's allocation of responsibility for providing auxiliary aids and services solely to the tenant, pointing out that this exclusive allocation may not be appropriate in the case of larger public accommodations that operate their business by renting space out to smaller public accommodations. For example, large theaters often rent to smaller traveling companies and hospitals often rely on independent contractors to provide childbirth classes. Groups representing persons with disabilities objected to the proposed rule because, in their view, it permitted the large theater or hospital to evade ADA responsibilities by leasing to independent smaller entities. They suggested that these types of public accommodations are not really landlords because they are in the business of providing a service, rather than renting space, as in the case of a shopping center or office building landlord. These commenters believed that responsibility for providing auxiliary aids should shift to the landlord, if the landlord relies on a smaller public accommodation or independent contractor to provide services closely related to those of the larger public accommodation, and if the needed auxiliary aids prove to be an undue burden for the smaller public accommodation. The final rule no longer lists specific allocations to specific parties but, rather, leaves allocation of responsibilities to the lease negotiations. Parties are, therefore, free to allocate the responsibility for auxiliary aids.

Section 36.201(b)(4) of the proposed rule, which provided that alterations by a tenant on its own premises do not trigger a path of travel obligations on the landlord, has been moved to § 36.403(d) of the final rule.

An entity that is not in and of itself a public accommodation, such as a trade association or performing artist, may become a public accommodation when it leases space for a conference or performance at a hotel, convention center, or stadium. For an entity to become a public accommodation when it is the lessee of space, however, the Department believes that consideration in some form must be given. Thus, a Boy Scout troop that accepts donated space does not become a public accommodation because the troop has not "leased" space, as required by the ADA.

As a public accommodation, the trade association or performing artist will be responsible for compliance with this part. Specific responsibilities should be allocated by contract, but, generally, the lessee should be responsible for providing auxiliary aids and services (which could include interpreters, Braille programs, etc.) for the participants in its conference or performance as well as for assuring that displays are accessible to individuals with disabilities.

Some commenters suggested that the rule should allocate responsibilities for areas other than removal of barriers and auxiliary aids. The final rule leaves allocation of all areas to the lease negotiations. However, in general landlords should not be given responsibility for policies a tenant applies in operating its business, if such policies are solely those of the tenant. Thus, if a restaurant tenant discriminates by refusing to seat a patron, it would be the tenant, and not the landlord, who would be responsible, because the discriminatory policy is imposed solely by the tenant and not by the landlord. If, however, a tenant refuses to modify a "no pets" rule to allow service animals in its restaurant because the landlord mandates such a rule, then both the landlord and the tenant would be liable for violation of the ADA when a person with a service dog is refused entrance. The Department wishes to emphasize, however, that the parties are free to allocate responsibilities in any way they choose.

Private clubs are also exempt from the ADA. However, consistent with title II of the Civil Rights Act (42 U.S.C. 2000a(e), a private club is considered a public accommodation to the extent that "the facilities of such establishment are made available to the customers or patrons" of a place of public accommodation. Thus, if a private club runs a day care center that is open exclusively to its own members, the club, like the church in the example above, would have no responsibility for compliance with the ADA. Nor would the day care center have any responsibilities because it is part of the private club exempt from the ADA.

On the other hand, if the private club rents to a day care center that is open to the public, then the private club would have the same obligations as any other public accommodation that functions as a landlord with respect to compliance with title III within the day care center. In such a situation, both the private club that "leases to" a public accommodation and the public accommodation lessee (the day care center) would be subject to the ADA. This same principle would apply if the private club were to rent to, for example, a bar association, which is not generally a public accommodation but which, as explained above, becomes a public accommodation when it leases space for a conference.

Section 36.202   Activities

Section 36.202 sets out the general forms of discrimination prohibited by title III of the ADA. These general prohibitions are further refined by the specific prohibitions in subpart C. Section 36.213 makes clear that the limitations on the ADA's requirements contained in subpart C, such as "necessity" (§ 36.301(a)) and "safety" (§ 36.301(b)), are applicable to the prohibitions in § 36.202. Thus, it is unnecessary to add these limitations to § 36.202 as has

been requested by some commenters. In addition, the language of § 36.202 very closely tracks the language of section 302(b)(1)(A) of the Act, and that statutory provision does not expressly contain these limitations.

Deny participation—Section 36.202(a) provides that it is discriminatory to deny a person with a disability the right to participate in or benefit from the goods, services, facilities, privileges, advantages, or accommodations of a place of public accommodation.

A public accommodation may not exclude persons with disabilities on the basis of disability for reasons other than those specifically set forth in this part. For example, a public accommodation cannot refuse to serve a person with a disability because its insurance company conditions coverage or rates on the absence of persons with disabilities. This is a frequent basis of exclusion for a variety of community activities and is prohibited by this part.

Unequal benefit—Section 36.202(b) prohibits services or accommodations that are not equal to those provided others. For example, persons with disabilities must not be limited to certain performances at a theater.

Separate benefit—Section 36.202(c) permits different or separate benefits or services only when necessary to provide persons with disabilities opportunities as effective as those provided others. This paragraph permitting separate benefits "when necessary" should be read together with § 36.203(a), which requires integration in "the most integrated setting appropriate to the needs of the individual." The preamble to that section provides further guidance on separate programs. Thus, this section would not prohibit the designation of parking spaces for persons with disabilities.

Each of the three paragraphs (a)–(c) prohibits discrimination against an individual or class of individuals "either directly or through contractual, licensing, or other arrangements." The intent of the contractual prohibitions of these paragraphs is to prohibit a public accommodation from doing indirectly, through a contractual relationship, what it may not do directly. Thus, the "individual or class of individuals" referenced in the three paragraphs is intended to refer to the clients and customers of the public accommodation that entered into a contractual arrangement. It is not intended to encompass the clients or customers of other entities. A public accommodation, therefore, is not liable under this provision for discrimination that may be practiced by those with whom it has a contractual relationship, when that discrimination is not directed against its own clients or customers. For example, if an amusement park contracts with a food service company to operate its restaurants at the park, the amusement park is not responsible for other operations of the food service company that do not involve clients or customers of the amusement park. Section 36.202(d) makes this clear by providing that the term "individual or class of individuals" refers to the clients or customers of the public accommodation that enters into the contractual, licensing, or other arrangement.

Section 36.203   Integrated Settings

Section 36.203 addresses the integration of persons with disabilities. The ADA recognizes that the provision of goods and services in an integrated manner is a fundamental tenet of nondiscrimination on the basis of disability. Providing segregated accommodations and services relegates persons with disabilities to the status of second-class citizens. For example, it would be a violation of this provision to require persons with mental disabilities to eat in the back room of a restaurant or to refuse to allow a person with a disability the full use of a health spa because of stereotypes about the person's ability to participate. Section 36.203(a) states that a public accommodation shall afford goods, services, facilities, privileges, advantages, and accommodations to an individual with a disability in the most integrated setting appropriate to the needs of the individual. Section 36.203(b) specifies that, notwithstanding the existence of separate or different programs or activities provided in accordance with this section, an individual with a disability shall not be denied the opportunity to participate in such programs or activities that are not separate or different. Section 306.203(c), which is derived from section 501(d) of the Americans with Disabilities Act, states that nothing in this part shall be construed to require an individual with a disability to accept an accommodation, aid, service, opportunity, or benefit that he or she chooses not to accept.

Taken together, these provisions are intended to prohibit exclusion and segregation of individuals with disabilities and the denial of equal opportunities enjoyed by others, based on, among other things, presumptions, patronizing attitudes, fears, and stereotypes about individuals with disabilities. Consistent with these standards, public accommodations are required to make decisions based on facts applicable to individuals and not on the basis of presumptions as to what a class of individuals with disabilities can or cannot do.

Sections 36.203 (b) and (c) make clear that individuals with disabilities cannot be denied the opportunity to participate in programs that are not separate or different. This is an important and overarching principle of the Americans with Disabilities Act. Separate, special, or different programs that are designed to provide a benefit to persons with disabilities cannot be used to restrict the participation of persons with disabilities in general, integrated activities.

For example, a person who is blind may wish to decline participating in a special museum tour that allows persons to touch sculptures in an exhibit and instead tour the exhibit at his or her own pace with the museum's recorded tour. It is not the intent of this section to require the person who is blind to avail himself or herself of the special tour. Modified participation for persons with disabilities must be a choice, not a requirement.

Further, it would not be a violation of this section for an establishment to offer recreational programs specially designed for children with mobility impairments in those limited circumstances. However, it would be a violation of this section if the entity then excluded these children from other recreational services made available to nondisabled children, or required children with disabilities to attend only designated programs.

Many commenters asked that the Department clarify a public accommodation's obligations within the integrated program when it offers a separate program, but an individual with a disability chooses not to participate in the separate program. It is impossible to make a blanket statement as to what level of auxiliary aids or modifications are required in the integrated program. Rather, each situation must be assessed individually. Assuming the integrated program would be appropriate for a particular individual, the extent to which that individual must be provided with modifications will depend not only on what the individual needs but also on the limitations set forth in subpart C. For example, it may constitute an undue burden for a particular public accommodation, which provides a full-time interpreter in its special guided tour for individuals with hearing impairments, to hire an additional interpreter for those individuals who choose to attend the integrated program. The Department cannot identify categorically the level of assistance or aid required in the integrated program.

The preamble to the proposed rule contained a statement that some interpreted as encouraging the continuation of separate schools, sheltered workshops, special recreational programs, and other similar programs. It is important to emphasize that § 36.202(c) only calls for separate programs when such programs are "necessary" to provide as effective an opportunity to individuals with disabilities as to other individuals. Likewise, § 36.203(a) only permits separate programs when a more integrated setting would not be "appropriate." Separate programs are permitted, then, in only limited circumstances. The sentence at issue has been deleted from the preamble because it was too broadly stated and had been erroneously interpreted as Departmental encouragement of separate programs without qualification.

The proposed rule's reference in § 36.203(b) to separate programs or activities provided in accordance with "this section" has been changed to "this subpart" in recognition of the fact that separate programs or activities may, in some limited circumstances, be permitted not only by § 36.203(a) but also by § 36.202(c).

In addition, some commenters suggested that the individual with the disability is the only one who can decide whether a setting is "appropriate" and what the "needs" are. Others suggested that only the public accommodation can make these determinations. The regulation does not give exclusive responsibility to either party. Rather, the determinations are to be made based on an objective view, presumably one which would take into account views of both parties.

Some commenters expressed concern that § 36.203(c), which states that nothing in the rule requires an individual with a disability to accept special accommodations and services provided under the ADA, could be interpreted to allow guardians of infants or older people with disabilities to refuse medical treatment for their wards. Section 36.203(c) has been revised to make it clear that paragraph (c) is inapplicable to the concern of the commenters. A new paragraph (c)(2) has been added stating that nothing in the regulation authorizes the representative or guardian of an individual with a disability to decline food, water,

medical treatment, or medical services for that individual. New paragraph (c) clarifies that neither the ADA nor the regulation alters current Federal law ensuring the rights of incompetent individuals with disabilities to receive food, water, and medical treatment. See, *e.g.*, Child Abuse Amendments of 1984 (42 U.S.C. 5106a(b)(10), 5106g(10)); Rehabilitation Act of 1973, as amended (29 U.S.C. 794); Developmentally Disabled Assistance and Bill of Rights Act (42 U.S.C. 6042).

Sections 36.203(c) (1) and (2) are based on section 501(d) of the ADA. Section § 501(d) was designed to clarify that nothing in the ADA requires individuals with disabilities to accept special accommodations and services for individuals with disabilities that may segregate them:

The Committee added this section (501(d)) to clarify that nothing in the ADA is intended to permit discriminatory treatment on the basis of disability, even when such treatment is rendered under the guise of providing an accommodation, service, aid or benefit to the individual with disability. For example, a blind individual may choose not to avail himself or herself of the right to go to the front of a line, even if a particular public accommodation has chosen to offer such a modification of a policy for blind individuals. Or, a blind individual may choose to decline to participate in a special museum tour that allows persons to touch sculptures in an exhibit and instead tour the exhibit at his or her own pace with the museum's recorded tour.

(Judiciary report at 71–72.) The Act is not to be construed to mean that an individual with disabilities must accept special accommodations and services for individuals with disabilities when that individual chooses to participate in the regular services already offered. Because medical treatment, including treatment for particular conditions, is not a special accommodation or service for individuals with disabilities under section 501(d), neither the Act nor this part provides affirmative authority to suspend such treatment. Section 501(d) is intended to clarify that the Act is not designed to foster discrimination through mandatory acceptance of special services when other alternatives are provided; this concern does not reach to the provision of medical treatment for the disabling condition itself.

Section 36.213 makes clear that the limitations contained in subpart C are to be read into subpart B. Thus, the integration requirement is subject to the various defenses contained in subpart C, such as safety, if eligibility criteria are at issue (§ 36.301(b)), or fundamental alteration and undue burden, if the concern is provision of auxiliary aids (§ 36.303(a)).

Section 36.204   Administrative Methods

Section 36.204 specifies that an individual or entity shall not, directly, or through contractual or other arrangements, utilize standards or criteria or methods of administration that have the effect of discriminating on the basis of disability or that perpetuate the discrimination of others who are subject to common administrative control. The preamble discussion of § 36.301 addresses eligibility criteria in detail.

Section 36.204 is derived form section 302(b)(1)(D) of the Americans with Disabilities Act, and it uses the same language used in the employment section of the ADA (section 102(b)(3)). Both sections incorporate a disparate impact standard to ensure the effectiveness of the legislative mandate to end discrimination. This standard is consistent with the interpretation of section 504 by the U.S. Supreme Court in *Alexander* v. *Choate*, 469 U.S. 287 (1985). The Court in *Choate* explained that members of Congress made numerous statements during passage of section 504 regarding eliminating architectural barriers, providing access to transportation, and eliminating discriminatory effects of job qualfication procedures. The Court then noted: "These statements would ring hollow if the resulting legislation could not rectify the harms resulting from action that discrimianted by effect as well as by design." *Id* at 297 (footnote omitted).

Of course, § 36.204 is subject to the various limitations contained in subpart C including, for example, necessity (§ 36.301(a)), safety (§ 36.301(b)), fundamental alteration (§ 36.302(a)), readily achievable (§ 36.304(a)), and undue burden (§ 36.303(a)).

Section 36.205   Association

Section 36.205 implements section 302(b)(1)(E) of the Act, which provides that a public accommodation shall not exclude or otherwise deny equal goods, services, facilities, privileges, advantages, accommodations, or other opportunities to an individual or entity because of the known disability of an individual with whom the individual or entity is known to have a re-lationship or association. This section is unchanged from the proposed rule.

The individuals covered under this section include any individuals who are discriminated against because of their known association with an individual with a disability. For example, it would be a violation of this part for a day care center to refuse admission to a child because his or her brother has HIV disease.

This protection is not limited to those who have a familial relationship with the individual who has a disability. If a place of accommodation refuses admission to a person with cerebral palsy and his or her companions, the companions have an independent right of action under the ADA and this section.

During the legislative process, the term "entity" was added to section 302(b)(1)(E) to clarify that the scope of the provision is intended to encompass not only persons who have a known association with a person with a disability, but also entities that provide services to or are otherwise associated with such individuals. The provision was intended to ensure that entities such as health care providers, employees of social service agencies, and others who provide professional services to persons with disabilities are not subjected to discrimination because of their professional association with persons with disabilities. For example, it would be a violation of this section to terminate the lease of a entity operating an independent living center for persons with disabilities, or to seek to evict a health care provider because that individual or entity provides services to persons with mental impairments.

Section 36.206   Retaliation or Coercion

Section 36.206 implements section 503 of the ADA, which prohibits retaliation against any individual who exercises his or her rights under the Act. This section is unchanged from the proposed rule. Paragraph (a) of § 36.206 provides that no private entity or public entity shall discriminate against any individual because that individual has exercised his or her right to oppose any act or practice made unlawful by this part, or because that individual made a charge, testified, assisted, or participated in any manner in an investigation, proceeding, or hearing under the Act or this part.

Paragraph (b) provides that no private entity or public entity shall coerce, intimidate, threaten, or interfere with any individual in the exercise of his or her rights under this part or because that individual aided or encouraged any other individual in the exercise or enjoyment of any right granted or protected by the Act or this part.

Illustrations of practices prohibited by this section are contained in paragraph (c), which is modeled on a similar provision in the regulations issued by the Department of Housing and Urban Development to implement the Fair Housing Act (see 24 CFR 100.400(c)(1)). Prohibited actions may include:

(1) Coercing an individual to deny or limit the benefits, services, or advantages to which he or she is entitld under the Act or this part;

(2) Threatening, intimidating, or interfering with an individual who is seeking to obtain or use the goods, services, facilities, privileges, advantages, or accommodations of a public accommodation;

(3) Intimidating or threatening any person because that person is assisting or encouraging an individual or group entitled to claim the rights granted or protected by the Act or this part to exercise those rights; or

(4) Retaliating against any person because that person has participated in any investigation or action to enforce the Act or this part.

This section protects not only individuals who allege a violation of the Act or this part, but also any individuals who support or assist them. This section applies to all investigations or proceedings initiated under the Act or this part without regard to the ultimate resolution of the underlying allegations. Because this section prohibits any act of retaliation or coercion in response to an individual's effort to exercise rights established by the Act and this part (or to support the efforts of another individual), the section applies not only to public accomodations that are otherwise subject to this part, but also to individuals other than public accommodations or to public entities. For example, it would be a violation of the Act and this part for a private individual, e.g., a restaurant customer, to harass or intimidate an individual with a disability in an effort to prevent that individual from patronizing the restaurant. It would, likewise, be a violation of the Act and this part for a public entity to take adverse action against an employee who appeared as a witness on behalf of an individual who sought to enforce the Act.

Section 36.207   Places of Public Accommodation Located in Private Residences

A private home used exclusively as a residence is not covered by title III because it is neither a "commercial facility" nor a "place of public accommodation." In some situations, however, a private home is not used exclusively as a residence, but houses a place of public accommodation in all or part of a home (e.g., an accountant who meets with his or her clients at his or her residence). Section 36.207(a) provides that those portions of the private residence used in the operation of the place of public accommodation are covered by this part.

For instance, a home or a portion of a home may be used as a day care center during the day and a residence at night. If all parts of the house are used for the day care center, then the entire residence is a place of public accommodation because no part of the house is used exclusively as a residence. If an accountant uses one room in the house solely as his or her professional office, then a portion of the house is used exclusively as a place of public accommodation and a portion is used exclusively as a residence. Section 36.207 provides that when a portion of a residence is used exclusively as a residence, that portion is not covered by this part. Thus, the portions of the accountant's house, other than the professional office and areas and spaces leading to it, are not covered by this part. All of the requirements of this rule apply to the covered portions, including requirements to make reasonable modifications in policies, eliminate discriminatory eligibility criteria, take readily achievable measures to remove barriers or provide readily achievable alternatives (e.g., making house calls), provide auxiliary aids and services and undertake only accessible new construction and alterations.

Paragraph (b) was added in response to comments that sought clarification on the extent of coverage of the private residence used as the place of public accommodation. The final rule makes clear that the place of accommodation extends to all areas of the home used by clients and customers of the place of public accommodation. Thus, the ADA would apply to any door or entry way, hallways, a restroom, if used by customers and clients; and any other portion of the residence, interior or exteior, used by customers or clients of the public accommodation. This interpretation is simply an application of the general rule for all public accommodations, which extends statutory requirements to all portions of the facility used by customers and clients, including, if applicable, restrooms, hallways, and approaches to the public accommodation. As with other public accommodations, barriers at the entrance and on the sidewalk leading up to the public accommodation, if the sidewalk is under the control of the public accommodation, must be removed if doing so is readily achievable.

The Department recognizes that many businesses that operate out of personal residences are quite small, often employing only the homeowner and having limited total revenues. In these circumstances the effect of ADA coverage would likely be quite minimal. For example, because the obligation to remove existing architectural barriers is limited to those that are easily accomplishable without much difficulty or expense (*see* § 36.304), the range of required actions would be quite modest. It might not be readily achievable for such a place of public accommodation to remove any existing barriers. If it is not readily achievable to remove existing architectural barriers, a public accommodation located in a private residence may meet its obligations under the Act and this part by providing its goods or services to clients or customers with disabilities through the use of alternative measures, including delivery of goods or services in the home of the customer or client, to the extent that such alternative measures are readily achievable (*See* § 36.305).

Some commenters asked for clarification as to how the new construction and alteration standards of subpart D will apply to residences. The new construction standards only apply to the extent that the residence or portion of the residence was designed or intended for use as a public accommodation. Thus, for example, if a portion of a home is designed or constructed for use exclusively as a lawyer's office or for use both as a lawyer's office and for residential purposes, then it must be designed in accordance with the new construction standards in the appendix. Likewise, if a homeowner is undertaking alterations to convert all or part of his residence to a place of public accommodation, that work must be done in compliance with the alterations standards in the appendix.

The preamble to the proposed rule addressed the applicable requirements when a commercial facility is located in a private residence. That situation is now addressed in § 36.401(b) of subpart D.

Section 36.208   Direct Threat

Section 36.208(a) implements section 302(b)(3) of the Act by providing that this part does not require a public accommodation to permit an individual to participate in or benefit from the goods, services, facilities, privileges, advantages and accommodations of the public accommodation, if that individual poses a direct threat to the health or safety of others. This section is unchanged from the proposed rule.

The Department received a significant number of comments on this section. Commenters representing individuals with disabilities generally supported this provision, but suggested revisions to further limit its application. Commenters representing public accommodations generally endorsed modifications that would permit a public accommodation to exercise its own judgment in determining whether an individual poses a direct threat.

The inclusion of this provision is not intended to imply that persons with disabilities pose risks to others. It is intended to address concerns that may arise in this area. It establishes a strict standard that must be met before denying service to an individual with a disability or excluding that individual from participation.

Paragraph (b) of this section explains that a "direct threat" is a significant risk to the health or safety of others that cannot be eliminated by a modification of policies, practices, or procedures, or by the provision of auxiliary aids and services. This paragraph codifies the standard first applied by the Supreme Court in *School Board of Nassau County* v. *Arline*, 480 U.S. 273 (1987), in which the Court held that an individual with a contagious disease may be an "individual with handicaps" under section 504 of the Rehabilitation Act. In *Arline*, the Supreme Court recognized that there is a need to balance the interests of people with disabilities against legitimate concerns for public safety. Although persons with disabilities are generally entitled to the protection of this part, a person who poses a significant risk to others may be excluded if reasonable modifications to the public accommodation's policies, practices, or procedures will not eliminate that risk. The determination that a person poses a direct threat to the health or safety of others may not be based on generalizations or stereotypes about the effects of a particular disability; it must be based on an individual assessment that conforms to the requirements of paragraph (c) of this section.

Paragraph (c) establishes the test to use in determining whether an individual poses a direct threat to the health or safety of others. A public accommodation is required to make an individualized assessment, based on reasonable judgment that relies on current medical evidence or on the best available objective evidence, to determine: The nature, duration, and severity of the risk; the probability that the potential injury will actually occur, and whether reasonable modifications of policies, practices, or procedures will mitigate the risk. This is the test established by the Supreme Court in *Arline*. Such an inquiry is essential if the law is to achieve its goal of protecting disabled individuals from discrimination based on prejudice, stereotypes, or unfounded fear, while giving appropriate weight to legitimate concerns, such as the need to avoid exposing others to significant health and safety risks. Making this assessent will not usually require the services of a physician. Sources for medical knowledge include guidance from public health authorities, such as the U.S. Public Health Service, the Centers for Disease Control, and the National Institutes of Health, including the National Institute of Mental Health.

Many of the commenters sought clarification of the inquiry requirement. Some suggested that public accommodations should be prohibited from making any inquiries to determine if an individual with a disability would pose a direct threat to other persons. The Department believes that to preclude all such inquiries would be inappropriate. Under § 36.301 of this part, a public accommodation is permitted to establish eligibility criteria necessary for the safe operation of the place of public accommodation. Implicit in that right is the right to ask if an individual meets the criteria. However, any eligibility or safety standard establshed by a public accommodation must be based on actual risk, not on speculation or stereotypes; it must be applied to all clients or customers of the place of public accommodation; and inquiries must be limited to matters necessary to the application of the standard.

Some commenters suggested that the test established in the *Arline* decision, which was developed in the context of an employment case, is too stringent to apply in a public accommodations context where interaction between the public accommodation and its client or customer is often very brief. One suggested alternative was to permit public accommodations to exercise "good faith" judgment in determining whether an individual poses a direct threat, particulrly when a public accommodation is dealing with a client or customer engaged in disorderly or disruptive behavior.

The Department believes that the ADA clearly requires that any determination to exclude an individual from participation must be based on an objective standard. A public accommodation may establish neutral eligibility criteria as a condition of receiving its goods or services. As long as these criteria are necessary for the safe provision of the public accommodation's goods and services and applied neutrally to all clients or customers, regardless of whether they are individuals with disabilities, a person who is unable to meet the criteria may be excluded from participation without inquiry into the underlying reason for the inability to comply. In places of public accommodation such as restaurants, theaters, or hotels, where the contact between the public accommodation and its clients is transitory, the uniform application of an eligibility standard precluding violent or disruptive behavior by any client or customer should be sufficient to enable a public accommodation to conduct its business in an orderly manner.

Some other commenters asked for clarification of the application of this provision to persons, particularly children, who have short-term, contagious illnesses, such as fevers, influenza, or the common cold. It is common practice in schools and day care settings to exclude persons with such illnesses until the symptoms subside. The Department believes that these commenters misunderstand the scope of this rule. The ADA only prohibits discrimination against an individual with a disability. Under the ADA and this part, a "disability" is defined as a physical or mental impairment that substantially limits one or more major life activities. Common, short-term illnesses that predictably resolve themselves within a matter of days do not "substantially limit" a major life activity; therefore, it is not a violation of this part to exclude an individual from receiving the services of a public accommodation because of such transitory illness. However, this part does apply to persons who have long-term illnesses. Any determination with respect to a person who has a chronic or long-term illness must be made in compliance with the requirements of this section.

Section 36.209   Illegal Use of Drugs

Section 36.209 effectuates section 510 of the ADA, which clarifies the Act's application to people who use drugs illegally. Paragraph (a) provides that this part does not prohibit discrimination based on an individual's current illegal use of drugs.

The Act and the regulation distinguish between illegal use of drugs and the legal use of substances, whether or not those substances are "controlled substances," as defined in the Controlled Substances Act (21 U.S.C. 812). Some controlled substances are prescription drugs that have legitimate medical uses. Section 36.209 does not affect use of controlled substances pursuant to a valid prescription, under supervision by a licensed health care professional, or other use that is authorized by the Controlled Substances Act or any other provision of Federal law. It does apply to illegal use of those substances, as well as to illegal use of controlled substances that are not prescription drugs. The key question is whether the individual's use of the substance is illegal, not whether the substance has recognized legal uses. Alcohol is not a controlled substance, so use of alcohol is not addressed by § 36.209. Alcoholics are individuals with disabilities, subject to the protections of the statute.

A distinction is also made between the use of a substance and the status of being addicted to that substance. Addiction is a disability, and addicts are individuals with disabilities protected by the Act. The protection, however, does not extend to actions based on the illegal use of the substance. In other words, an addict cannot use the fact of his or her addiction as a defense to an action based on illegal use of drugs. This distinction is not artificial. Congress intended to deny protection to people who engage in the illegal use of drugs, whether or not they are addicted, but to provide protection to addicts so long as they are not currently using drugs.

A third distinction is the difficult one between current use and former use. The definition of "current illegal use of drugs" in § 36.104, which is based on the report of the Conference Committee, H.R. Conf. Rep. No. 596, 101st Cong., 2d Sess. 64 (1990), is "illegal use of drugs that occurred recently enough to justify a reasonable belief that a person's drug use is current or that continuing use is a real and ongoing problem."

Paragraph (a)(2)(i) specifies that an individual who has successfully completed a supervised drug rehabilitation program or has otherwise been rehabilitated successfully and who is not engaging in current illegal use of drugs is protected. Paragraph (a)(2)(ii) clarifies that an individual who is currently participating in a supervised rehabilitation program and is not engaging in current illegal use of drugs is protected. Paragraph (a)(2)(iii) provides that a person who is erroneously regarded as engaging in current illegal use of drugs, but who is not engaging in such use, is protected.

Paragraph (b) provides a limited exception to the exclusion of current illegal users of drugs from the protections of the Act. It prohibits denial of health services, or services provided in connection with drug rehabilitation, to an individual on the basis of current illegal use of drugs, if the individual is otherwise entitled to such services. As explained further in the discussion of § 36.302, a health care facility that specializes in a particular type of treatment, such as care of burn victims, is not required to provide drug rehabilitation services, but it cannot refuse to treat an individual's burns on the grounds that the individual is illegally using drugs.

A commenter argued that health care providers should be permitted to use their medical judgment to postpone discretionary medical treatment of individuals under the influence of alcohol or drugs. The regulation permits a medical practitioner to take into account an individual's use of drugs in determining appropriate medical treatment. Section 36.209 provides that the prohibitions on discrimination in this part do not apply when the public accommodation acts on the basis of current illegal use of drugs. Although those prohibitions do apply under paragraph (b), the limitations established under this part also apply. Thus, under § 36.208, a health care provider or other public accommodation covered under § 36.209(b) may exclude an individual whose current illegal use of drugs poses a direct threat to the health or safety of others, and, under § 36.301, a public accommodation may impose or apply eligibility criteria that are necessary for the provision of the services being offered, and may impose legitimate safety requirements that are necessary for safe operation. These same limitations also apply to individuals with disabilities who use alcohol or prescriptions drugs. The Department believes that these provisions address this commenter's concerns.

Other commenters pointed out that abstention from the use of drugs is an essential condition for participation in some drug rehabilitation programs, and may be a necessary requirement in inpatient or residential settings. The Department believes that this comment is well-founded. Congress clearly did not intend to exclude from drug treatment programs the very individuals who need such programs because of their use of drugs. In such a situation, however, once an individual has been admitted to a program, abstention may be a necessary and appropriate condition to continued participation. The final rule therefore provides that a drug rehabilitation or treatment program may deny participation to individuals who use drugs while they are in the program.

Paragraph (c) expresses Congress's intention that the Act be neutral with respect to testing for illegal use of drugs. This paragraph implements the provision in section 510(b) of the Act that allows entities "to adopt or administer reasonable policies or procedures, including but not limited to drug testing," that ensure an individual who is participating in a supervised rehabilitation program, or who has completed such a program or otherwise been rehabilitated successfully, is no longer engaging in the illegal use of drugs. Paragraph (c) is not to be construed to encourage, prohibit, restrict, or authorize the conducting of testing for the illegal use of drugs.

Paragraph (c) of § 36.209 clarifies that it is not a violation of this part to adopt or administer reasonable policies or procedures to ensure that an individual who formerly engaged in the illegal use of drugs is not currently engaging in illegal use of drugs. Any such policies or procedures must, of course, be reasonable, and must be designed to identify accurately the illegal use of drugs. This paragraph does not authorize inquiries, tests, or other procedures that would disclose use of substances that are not controlled substances or are taken under supervision by a licensed health care professional, or other uses authorized by the Controlled Substances Act or other provisions of Federal law, because such uses are not included in the definition of "illegal use of drugs."

One commenter argued that the rule should permit testing for lawful use of prescription drugs, but most favored the explanation that tests must be limited to *unlawful* use in order to avoid revealing the use of prescription medicine used to treat disabilities. Tests revealing legal use of prescription drugs might violate the prohibition in § 36.301 of attempts to unnecessarily identify the existence of a disability.

Section 36.210   Smoking

Section 36.210 restates the clarification in section 501(b) of the Act that the Act does not preclude the prohibition of, or imposition of restrictions on, smoking. Some commenters argued that § 36.210 does not go far enough, and that the regulation should prohibit smoking in all places of public accommodation. The reference to smoking in section 501 merely clarifies that the Act does not require public accommodations to accommodate smokers by permitting their smoke in places of public accommodations.

Section 36.211   Maintenance of Accessible Features

Section 36.211 provides that a public accommodation shall maintain in operable working condition those features of facilities and equipment that are required to be readily accessible to and usable by persons with disabilities by the Act or this part. The Act requires that, to the maximum extent feasible, facilities must be accessible to, *and usable by*, individuals with disabilities. This section recognizes that it is not sufficient to provide features such as accessible routes, elevators, or ramps, if those features are not maintained in a manner that enables individuals with disabilities to use them. Inoperable elevators, locked accessible doors, or "accessible" routes that are obstructed by furniture, filing cabinets, or potted plants are neither "accessible to" nor "usable by" individuals with disabilities.

Some commenters objected that this section appeared to establish an absolute requirement and suggested that language from the preamble be included in the text of the regulation. It is, of course, impossible to guarantee that mechanical devices will never fail to operate. Paragraph (b) of the final regulation provides that this section does not prohibit isolated or temporary interruptions in service or access due to maintenance or repairs. This paragraph is intended to clarify that temporary obstructions or isolated instances of mechanical failure would not be considered violations of the Act or this part. However, allowing obstructions or "out of service" equipment to persist beyond a reasonable period of time would violate this part, as would repeated mechanical failures due to improper or inadequate maintenance. Failure of the public accommodation to ensure that accessible routes are properly maintained and free of obstructions, or failure to arrange prompt repair of inoperable elevators or other equipment intended to provide access, would also violate this part.

Other commenters requested that this section be expanded to include specific requirements for inspection and maintenance of equipment, for training staff in the proper operation of equipment, and for maintenance of specific items. The Department believes that this section properly establishes the general requirement for maintaining access and that further, more detailed requirements are not necessary.

Section 36.212   Insurance

The Department received numerous comments on proposed § 36.212. Most supported the proposed regulation but felt that it did not go far enough in protecting individuals with disabilities and persons associated with them from discrimination. Many commenters argued that language from the preamble to the proposed regulation should be included in the text of the final regulation. Other commenters argued that even that language was not strong enough, and that more stringent standards should be established. Only a few commenters argued that the Act does not apply to insurance underwriting practices or the terms of insurance contracts. These commenters cited language from the Senate committee report (S. Rep. No. 116, 101st Cong., 1st Sess., at 84-86 (1989) (hereinafter "Senate report")), indicating that Congress did not intend to affect existing insurance practices.

The Department has decided to adopt the language of the proposed rule without change. Sections 36.212 (a) and (b) restate section 501(c) of the Act, which provides that the Act shall not be construed to restrict certain insurance practices on the part of insurance companies and employers, as long as such practices are not used to evade the purposes of the Act. Section 36.212(c) is a specific application of § 36.202(a), which prohibits denial of participation on the basis disability. It provides that a public accommodation may not refuse to serve an individual with a disability because of limitations on coverage or rates in its insurance policies (see Judiciary report at 56).

Many commenters supported the requirements of § 36.212(c) in the proposed rule because it addressed an important reason for denial of services by public accommodations. One commenter argued that services could be denied if the insurance coverage required exclusion of people whose disabilities were reasonably related to the risks involved in that particular place of public accommodation. Sections 36.208 and 36.301 establish criteria for denial of participation on the basis of legitimate safety concerns. This paragraph does not prohibit consideration of such concerns in insurance policies, but provides that any exclusion on the basis of disability must be based on the permissible criteria, rather than on the terms of the insurance contract.

Language in the committee reports indicates that Congress intended to reach insurance practices by prohibiting differential treatment of individuals with disabilities in insurance offered by public accommodations unless the differences are justified. "Under the ADA, a person with a disability cannot be denied insurance or be subject to different terms or conditions of insurance based on disability alone, if the disability does not pose increased risks." (Senate report at 84; Education and Labor report at 136). Section 501(c) (1) of the Act was intended to emphasize that "insurers may continue to sell to and underwrite individuals applying for life, health, or other insurance on an individually underwritten basis, or to service such insurance products, *so long as the standards used are based on sound actuarial data and not on speculation*" (Judiciary report at 70 (emphasis added); see also Senate report at 85; Education and Labor report at 137).

The committee reports indicate that underwriting and classification of risks must be "based on sound actuarial principles or be related to actual or reasonably anticipated experience" (see, *e.g.*, Judiciary report at 71). Moreover, "while a plan which limits certain kinds of coverage based on classification of risk would be allowed ***, the plan may not refuse to insure, or refuse to continue to insure, or limit the amount, extent, or kind of coverage available to an individual, or charge a different rate for the same coverge solely because of a physical or mental impairment, except where the refusal, limitation, or rate differential is based on sound actuarial principles or is related to actual or reasonably anticipated experience" (Senate report at 85; Education and Labor report at 136–37; Judiciary report at 71). The ADA, therefore, does not prohibit use of legitimate actuarial considerations to justify differential treatment of individuals with disabilities in insurance.

The committee reports provide some

guidance on how nondiscrimination principles in the disability rights area relate to insurance practices. For example, a person who is blind may not be denied coverage based on blindness independent of actuarial risk classification. With respect to group health insurance coverage, an individual with a pre-existing condition may be denied coverage for that condition for the period specified in the policy, but cannot be denied coverage for illness or injuries unrelated to the pre-existing condition. Also, a public accommodation may offer insurance policies that limit coverage for certain procedures or treatments, but may not entirely deny coverage to a person with a disability.

The Department requested comment on the extent to which data that would establish statistically sound correlations are available. Numerous commenters cited pervasive problems in the availability and cost of insurance for individuals with disabilities and parents of children with disabilities. No commenters cited specific data, or sources of data, to support specific exclusionary practices. Several commenters reported that, even when statistics are available, they are often outdated and do not reflect current medical techology and treatment methods. Concern was expressed that adequate efforts are not made to distinguish those individuals who are high users of health care from individuals in the same diagnostic groups who may be low users of health care. One insurer reported that "hard data and actuarial statistics are not available to provide precise numerical justifications for every underwriting determination," but argued that decisions may be based on "logical principles generally accepted by actuarial science and fully consistent with state insurance laws." The commenter urged that the Department recognize the validity of information other than statistical data as a basis for insurance determinations.

The most frequent comment was a recommendation that the final regulation should require the insurance company to provide a copy of the actuarial data on which its actions are based when requested by the applicant. Such a requirement would be beyond anything contemplated by the Act or by Congress and has therefore not been included in the Department's final rule. Because the legislative history of the ADA clarifies that different treatment of individuals with disabilities in insurance may be justified by sound actuarial data, such actuarial data will be critical to any potential litigation on this issue. This information would presumably be obtainable in a court proceeding where the insurer's actuarial data was the basis for different treatment of persons with disabilities. In addition, under some State regulatory schemes, insurers may have to file such actuarial information with the State regulatory agency and this information may be obtainable at the State level.

A few commenters representing the insurance industry conceded that underwriting practices in life and health insurance are clearly covered, but argued that property and casualty insurance are not covered. The Department sees no reason for this distinction. Although life and health insurance are the areas where the regulation will have its greatest application, the Act applies equally to unjustified discrimination in all types of insurance provided by public accommodations. A number of commenters, for example, reported difficuties in obtaining automobile insurance because of their disabilities, despite their having good driving records.

Section 36.213   Relationship of Subpart 8 to Subparts C and D

This section explains that subpart B sets forth general principles of nondiscrimination applicable to all entities subject to this regulation, while subparts C and D provide guidance on the application of this part to specific situations. The specific provisions in subparts C and D, including the limitations on those provisions, control over the general provisions in circumstances where both specific and general provisions apply. Resort to the general provisions of subpart B is only appropriate where there are no applicable specific rules of guidance in subparts C or D. This interaction between the specific requirements and the general requirements operates with regard to contractual obligations as well.

One illustration of this principle is its application to the obligation of a public accommodation to provide access to services by removal of architectural barriers or by alternatives to barrier removal. The general requirement, established in subpart B by § 36.203, is that a public accommodation must provide its services to individuals with disabilities in the most integrated setting appropriate. This general requirement would appear to categorically prohibit "segregated" seating for persons in wheelchairs. Section 36.304, however, only requires removal of architectural barriers to the extent that removal is "readily achievable." If providing access to all areas of a restaurant, for example, would not be "readily achievable," a public accommodation may provide access to selected areas only. Also § 36.305 provides that, where barrier removal is not readily achievable, a public accommodation may use alternative, readily achievable methods of making services available, such as curbside service or home delivery. Thus in this manner, the specific requirements of §§ 36.304 and 36.305 control over the general requirement of § 36.203.

Subpart C—Specific Requirements

In general, subpart C implements the "specific prohibitions" that comprise section 302(b)(2) of the ADA. It also addresses the requirements of section 309 of the ADA regarding examinations and courses.

Section 36.301   Eligibility Criteria

Section 36.301 of the rule prohibits the imposition or application of eligibility criteria that screen out or tend to screen out an individual with a disability or any class of individuals with disabilities from fully and equally enjoying any goods, services, facilities, privileges, advantages, and accommodations, unless such criteria can be shown to be necessary for the provision of the goods, services, facilities, privileges, advantages, or accommodations being offered. This prohibition is based on section 302(b)(2)(A)(i) of the ADA.

It would violate this section to establish exclusive or segregative eligibility criteria that would bar, for example, all persons who are deaf from playing on a golf course or all individuals with cerebral palsy from attending a movie theatre, or limit the seating of individuals with Down's syndrome to only particular areas of a restaurant. The wishes, tastes, or preferences of other customers may not be asserted to justify criteria that would exclude or segregate individuals with disabilities.

Section 36.301 also prohibits attempts by a public accommodation to unnecessarily identify the existence of a disability; for example, it would be a violation of this section for a retail store to require an individual to state on a credit application whether the applicant has epilepsy, mental illness, or any other disability, or to inquire unnecessarily whether an individual has HIV disease.

Section 36.301 also prohibits policies that unnecessarily impose requirements or burdens on individuals with disabilities that are not placed on others. For example, public accommodations may not require that an individual with a disability be accompanied by an attendant. As provided by § 36.306, however, a public accommodation is not required to provide services of a personal nature including assistance in toileting, eating, or dressing.

Paragraph (c) of § 36.301 provides that public accommodations may not place a surcharge on a particular individual with a disability or any group of individuals with disabilities to cover the costs of measures, such as the provision of auxiliary aids and services, barrier removal, alternatives to barrier removal, and reasonable modifications in policies, practices, and procedures, that are required to provide that individual or group with the nondiscriminatory treatment required by the Act or this part.

A number of commenters inquired as to whether deposits required for the use of auxiliary aids, such as assistive listening devices, are prohibited surcharges. It is the Department's view that reasonable, completely refundable, deposits are not to be considered surcharges prohibited by this section. Requiring deposits is an important means of ensuring the availability of equipment necessary to ensure compliance with the ADA.

Other commenters sought clarification as to whether § 36.301(c) prohibits professionals from charging for the additional time that it may take in certain cases to provide services to an individual with disabilities. The Department does not intend § 36.301(c) to prohibit professionals who bill on the basis of time from charging individuals with disabilities on that basis. However, fees may not be charged for the provision of auxiliary aids and services, barrier removal, alternatives to barrier removal, reasonable modifications in policies, practices, and procedures, or any other measures necessary to ensure compliance with the ADA.

Other commenters inquired as to whether day care centers may charge for extra services provided to individuals with disabilities. As stated above, § 36.302(c) is intended only to prohibit charges for measures necessary to achieve compliance with the ADA.

Another commenter asserted that charges may be assessed for home delivery provided as an alternative to barrier removal under § 36.305, when home delivery is provided to all customers for a fee. Charges for home delivery are permissible if home delivery is not considered an alternative to barrier removal. If the public accommodation offers an alternative, such as curb, carry-out, or sidewalk service for which no surcharge is assessed, then it may charge for home delivery in accordance with its standard pricing for home delivery.

In addition, § 36.301 prohibits the imposition of criteria that "tend to screen out an individual with a disability. This concept, which is derived from current regulations under section 504 (see *e.g.*, 45 CFR 84.13), makes it discriminatory to impose policies or criteria that, while not creating a direct bar to individuals with disabilities, indirectly prevent or limit their ability to participate. For example, requiring presentation of a driver's license as the sole means of identification for purposes of paying by check would violate this section in situations where, for example, individuals with severe vision impairments or developmental disabilities or epilepsy are ineligible to receive a driver's license and the use of an alternative means of identification, such as another photo I.D. or credit card, is feasible.

A public accommodation may, however, impose neutral rules and criteria that screen out, or tend to screen out, individuals with disabilities, if the criteria are necessary for the safe operation of the public accommodation. Examples of safety qualifications that would be justifiable in appropriate circumstances would include height requirements for certain amusement park rides or a requirement that all participants in a recreational rafting expedition be able to meet a necessary level of swimming proficiency. Safety requirements must be based on actual risks and not on speculation, stereotypes, or generalizations about individuals with disabilities.

Section 36.302   Modifications in Policies, Practices, or Procedures

Section 36.302 of the rule prohibits the failure to make reasonable modifications in policies, practices, and procedures when such modifications may be necessary to afford any goods, services, facilities, privileges, advantages, or accommodations, unless the entity can demonstrate that making such modifications would fundamentally alter the nature of such goods, services, facilities, privileges, advantages, or accommodations. This prohibition is based on section 302(b)(2)(A)(ii) of the ADA.

For example, a parking facility would be required to modify a rule barring all vans or all vans with raised roofs, if an individual who uses a wheelchair-accessible van wishes to park in that facility, and if overhead structures are high enough to accommodate the height of the van. A department store may need to modify a policy of only permitting one person at a time in a dressing room, if an individual with mental retardation needs and requests assistance in dressing from a companion. Public accommodations may need to revise operational policies to ensure that services are available to individuals with disabilities. For instance, a hotel may need to adopt a policy of keeping an accessible room unoccupied until an individual with a disability arrives at the hotel, assuming the individual has properly reserved the room.

One example of application of this principle is specifically included in a new § 36.302(d) on check-out aisles. That paragraph provides that a store with check-out aisles must ensure that an adequate number of accessible check-out aisles is kept open during store hours, or must otherwise modify its policies and practices, in order to ensure that an equivalent level of convenient service is provided to individuals with disabilities as is provided to others. For example, if only one check-out aisle is accessible, and it is generally used for express service, one way of providing equivalent service is to allow persons with mobility impairments to make all of their purchases at that aisle. This principle also applies with respect to other accessible elements and services. For example, a particular bank may be in compliance with the accessibility guidelines for new construction incorporated in appendix A with respect to automated teller machines (ATM) at a new branch office by providing one accessible walk-up machine at that location, even though an adjacent walk-up ATM is not accessible and the drive-up ATM is not accessible. However, the bank would be in violation of this section if the accessible ATM was located in a lobby that was locked during evening hours while the drive-up ATM was available to customers without disabilities during those same hours. The bank would need to ensure that the accessible ATM was available to customers during the hours that any of the other ATM's was available.

A number of commenters inquired as to the relationship between this section and § 36.307, "Accessible or special goods." Under § 36.307, a public accommodation is not required to alter its inventory to include accessible or special goods that are designed for, or facilitate use by, individuls with disabilities. The rule enunciated in § 36.307 is consistent with the "fundamental alteration" defense to the reasonable modifications requirement of § 36.302. Therefore, § 36.302 would not require the inventory of goods provided by a public accom-

modation to be altered to include goods with accessibility features. For example, § 36.302 would not require a bookstore to stock Brailled books or order Brailled books, if it does not do so in the normal course of its business.

The rule does not require modifications to the legitimate areas of specialization of service providers. Section 36.302(b) provides that a public accommodation may refer an individual with a disability to another public accommodation, if that individual is seeking, or requires, treatment or services outside of the referring public accommodation's area of specialization, and if, in the normal course of its operations, the referring public accommodation would make a similar referral for an individual without a disability who seeks or requires the same treatment or services.

For example, it would not be discriminatory for a physician who specializes only in burn treatment to refer an individual who is deaf to another physician for treatment of an injury other than a burn injury. To require a physician to accept patients outside of his or her specialty would fundamentally alter the nature of the medical practice and, therefore, not be required by this section.

A clinic specializing exclusively in drug rehabilitation could similarly refuse to treat a person who is not a drug addict, but could not refuse to treat a person who is a drug addict simply because the patient tests positive for HIV. Conversely, a clinic that specializes in the treatment of individuals with HIV could refuse to treat an individual that does not have HIV, but could not refuse to treat a person for HIV infection simply because that person is also a drug addict.

Some commenters requested clarification as to how this provision would apply to situations where manifestations of the disability in question, itself, would raise complications requiring the expertise of a different practitioner. It is not the Department's intention in § 36.302(b) to prohibit a physician from referring an individual with a disability to another physician, if the disability itself creates specialized complications for the patient's health that the physician lacks the experience or knowledge

to address (see Education and Labor report at 106).

Section 36.302(c)(1) requires that a public accommodation modify its policies, practices, or procedures to permit the use of a service animal by an individual with a disability in any area open to the general public. The term "service animal" is defined in § 36.104 to include guide dog, signal dogs, or any other animal individually trained to provide assistance to an individual with a disability.

A number of commenters pointed to the difficulty of making the distinction required by the proposed rule between areas open to the general public and those that are not. The ambiguity and uncertainty surrounding these provisions has led the Department to adopt a single standard for all public accommodations.

Section 36.302(c)(1) of the final rule now provides that "[g]enerally, a public accommodation shall modify policies, practices, and procedures to permit the use of a service animal by an individual with a disability." This formulation reflects the general intent of Congress that public accommodations take the necessary steps to accommodate service animals and to ensure that individuals with disabililties are not separated from their service animals. It is intended that the broadest feasible access be provided to service animals in all places of public accommodation, including movie theaters, restaurants, hotels, retail stores, hospitals, and nursing homes (see Education and Labor report at 106; Judiciary report at 59). The section also acknowledges, however, that, in rare circumstances, accommodation of service animals may not be required because a fundamental alteration would result in the nature of the goods, services, facilities, privileges, or accommodations offered or provided, or the safe operation of the public accommodation would be jeopardized.

As specified in § 36.302(c)(2), the rule does not require a public accommodation to supervise or care for any service animal. If a service animal must be separated from an individual with a disability in order to avoid a fundamental alteration or a threat to safety, it is the responsibility of the individual with the disability to arrange for the care and supervision of the animal during the period of separation.

A museum would not be required by § 36.302 to modify a policy barring the touching of delicate works of art in order to enhance the participation of individuals who are blind, if the touching threatened the integrity of the work. Damage to a museum piece would clearly be a fundamental alteration that is not required by this section.

Section 36.303   Auxiliary Aids and Services

Section 36.303 of the final rule requires a public accommodation to take such steps as may be necessary to ensure that no individual with a disability is excluded, denied services, segregated or otherwise treated differently than other individuals because of the absence of auxiliary aids and services, unless the public accommodation can demonstrate that taking such steps would fundamentally alter the nature of the goods, services, facilities, advantages, or accommodations being offered or would result in an undue burden. This requirement is based on section 302(b) (2)(A)(iii) of the ADA.

Implicit in this duty to provide auxiliary aids and services is the underlying obligation of a public accommodation to communicate effectively with its customers, clients, patients, or participants who have disabilities affecting hearing, vision, or speech. To give emphasis to this underlying obligation, § 36.303(c) of the rule incorporates language derived from section 504 regulations for federally conducted programs (see *e.g.*, 28 CFR 39.160(a)) that requires that appropriate auxiliary aids and services be furnished to ensure that communication with persons with disabilities is as effective as communication with others.

Auxiliary aids and services include a wide range of services and devices for ensuring effective communication. Use of the most advanced technology is not required so long as effective communication is ensured. The Department's proposed § 36.303(b) provided a list of examples of auxiliary aids and services that was taken from the definition of auxiliary aids and services in section 3(1) of the ADA and was supplemented by examples from regulations implementing section 504 in federally conducted programs (see *e.g.*, 28 CFR 39.103). A substantial number of commenters suggested that additional examples be added to this list. The Department has added several items to this list but wishes to clarify that the list is not an all-inclusive or exhaustive catalogue of possible or available auxiliary aids or services. It is not possible to provide an exhaustive list, and such an attempt would omit new devices that will become available with emerging technology.

The Department has added videotext displays, computer-aided transcription services, and open and closed captioning to the list of examples. Videotext displays have become an important means of accessing auditory communications through a public address system. Transcription services are used to relay aurally delivered material almost simultaneously in written form to persons who are deaf or hard of hearing. This technology is often used at conferences, conventions, and hearings. While the proposed rule expressly included television decoder equipment as an auxiliary aid or service, it did not mention captioning itself. The final rule rectifies this omission by mentioning both closed and open captioning.

In this section, the Department has changed the proposed rule's phrase "orally delivered materials," to the phrase, "aurally delivered materials." This new phrase tracks the language in the definition of "auxiliary aids and services" in section 3 of the ADA and is meant to include nonverbal sounds and alarms and computer-generated speech.

Several persons and organizations requested that the Department replace the term "telecommunications devices for deaf persons" or "TDD's" with the term "text telephone." The Department has declined to do so. The Department is aware that the Architectural and Transportation Barriers Compliance Board has used the phrase "text telephone" in lieu of the statutory term "TDD" in its final accessibility guidelines. Title IV of the ADA, however, uses the term "Telecommunications Device for the Deaf," and the Department believes it would be inappropriate to abandon this statutory term at this time.

Paragraph (b)(2) lists examples of aids and services for making visually delivered materials accessible to persons with visual impairments. Many commenters proposed additional examples such as signage or mapping audio description services, secondary auditory programs (SAP), telebraillers, and reading machines. While the Department declines to add these items to the list in the regulation, they may be considered appropriate auxiliary aids and services.

Paragraph (b)(3) refers to the acquisition or modification of equipment or devices. For example, tape players used for an audio-guided tour of a museum exhibit may require the addition of Brailled adhesive labels to the buttons on a reasonable number of the tape players to facilitate their use by individuals who are blind. Similarly, permanent or portable assistive listening systems for persons with hearing impairments may be required at a hotel conference center.

Several commenters suggested the addition of current technological innovations in microelectronics and computerized control systems (e.g., voice recognition systems, automatic dialing telephones, and infrared elevator and light control systems) to the list of auxiliary aids and services. The Department interprets auxiliary aids and services as those aids and services designed to provide effective communications, i.e., making aurally and visually delivered information available to persons with hearing, speech, and vision impairments. Methods of making services, programs, or activities accessible to, or usable by, individuals with mobility or manual dexterity impairments are addressed by other sections of this part, including the requirements for modifications in policies, practices, or procedures (§ 36.302), the elimination of existing architectural barriers (§ 36.304), and the provision of alternatives to barriers removal (§ 36.305).

Paragraph (b)(4) refers to other similar services and actions. Several commenters asked for clarification that "similar services and actions" include retrieving items from shelves, assistance in reaching a marginally accessible seat, pushing a barrier aside in order to provide an accessible route, or assistance in removing a sweater or coat. While retrieving an item from a shelf might be an "auxiliary aid or service" for a blind person who could not locate the item without assistance, it might be a readily achievable alternative to barrier removal for a person using a wheelchair who could not reach the shelf, or a reasonable modification to a self-service policy for an individual who lacked the ability the grasp the item. (Of course, a store would not be required to provide a personal shopper.) As explained above, auxiliary aids and services are those aids and services required to provide effective communications. Other forms of assistance are more appropriately addressed by other provisions of the final rule.

The auxiliary aid requirement is a flexible one. A public accommodation can choose among various alternatives as long as the result is effective communication. For example, a restaurant would not be required to provide menus in Braille for patrons who are blind if the waiters in the restaurant are made available to read the menu. Similarly, a clothing boutique would not be required to have Brailled price tags

if sales personnel provide price information orally upon request; and a bookstore would not be required to make available a sign language interpreter, because effective communication can be conducted by notepad.

A critical determination is what constitutes an effective auxiliary aid or service. The Department's proposed rule recommended that, in determining what auxiliary aid to use, the public accommodation consult with an individual before providing him or her with a particular auxiliary aid or service. This suggestion sparked a significant volume of public comment. Many persons with disabilities, particularly persons who are deaf or hard of hearing, recommended that the rule should require that public accommodations give "primary consideration" to the "expressed choice" of an individual with a disability. These commenters asserted that the proposed rule was inconsistent with congressional intent of the ADA, with the Department's proposed rule implementing title II of the ADA, and with longstanding interpretations of section 504 of the Rehabilitation Act.

Based upon a careful review of the ADA legislative history, the Department believes that Congress did not intend under title III to impose upon a public accommodation the requirement that it give primary consideration to the request of the individual with a disability. To the contrary, the legislative history demonstrates congressional intent to strongly encourage consulting with persons with disabilities. In its analysis of the ADA's auxiliary aids requirements for public accommodations, the House Education and Labor Committee stated that it "expects" that "public accommodation(s) will consult with the individual with a disability before providing a particular auxiliary aid or service" (Education and Labor report at 107). Some commenters also cited a different committee statement that used mandatory language as evidence of legislative intent to require primary consideration. However, this statement was made in the context of reasonable accommodations required by title I with respect to employment (Education and Labor report at 67). Thus, the Department finds that strongly encouraging consultation with persons with disabilities, in lieu of mandating primary consideration of their expressed choice, is consistent with congressional intent.

The Department wishes to emphasize that public accommodations must take steps necessary to ensure that an individual with a disability will not be excluded, denied services, segregated or otherwise treated differently from other individuals because of the use of inappropriate or ineffective auxiliary aids. In those situations requiring an interpreter, the public accommodations must secure the services of a qualified interpreter, unless an undue burden would result.

In the analysis of § 36.303(c) in the proposed rule, the Department gave as an example the situation where a note pad and written materials were insufficient to permit effective communication in a doctor's office when the matter to be decided was whether major surgery was necessary. Many commenters objected to this statement, asserting that it gave the impression that only decisions about major surgery would merit the provision of a sign language interpreter. The statement would, as the commenters also claimed, convey the impression to other public accommodations that written communications would meet the regulatory requirements in all but the most extreme situations. The Department, when using the example of major surgery, did not intend to limit the provision of interpreter services to the most extreme situations.

Other situations may also require the use of interpreters to ensure effective communication depending on the facts of the particular case. It is not difficult to imagine a wide range of communications involving areas such as health, legal matters, and finances that would be sufficiently lengthy or complex to require an interpreter for effective communication. In some situations, an effective alternative to use of a notepad or an interpreter may be the use of a computer terminal upon which the representative of the public accommodation and the customer or client can exchange typewritten messages.

Section 36.303(d) specifically addresses requirements for TDD's. Partly because of the availability of telecommunications relay services to be established under title IV of the ADA, § 36.303(d)(2) provides that a public accommodation is not required to use a telecommunication device for the deaf (TDD) in receiving or making telephone calls incident to its operations. Several commenters were concerned that relay services would not be sufficient to provide effective access in a number of situations. Commenters argued that relay systems (1) do not provide effective access to the automated systems that require the caller to respond by pushing a button on a touch tone phone, (2)

cannot operate fast enough to convey messages on answering machines, or to permit a TDD user to leave a recorded message, and (3) are not appropriate for calling crisis lines relating to such matters as rape, domestic violence, child abuse, and drugs where confidentiality is a concern. The Department believes that it is more appropriate for the Federal Communications Commission to address these issues in its rulemaking under title IV.

A public accommodation is, however, required to make a TDD available to an individual with impaired hearing or speech, if it customarily offers telephone service to its customers, clients, patients, or participants on more than an incidental convenience basis. Where entry to a place of public accommodation requires use of a security entrance telephone, a TDD or other effective means of communication must be provided for use by an individual with impaired hearing or speech.

In other words, individual retail stores, doctors' offices, restaurants, or similar establishments are not required by this section to have TDD's, because TDD users will be able to make inquiries, appointments, or reservations with such establishments through the relay system established under title IV of the ADA. The public accommodation will likewise to be able to contact TDD users through the relay system. On the other hand, hotels, hospitals, and other similar establishments that offer nondisabled individuals the opportunity to make outgoing telephone calls on more than an incidental convenience basis must provide a TDD on request.

Section 36.303(e) requires places of lodging that provide televisions in five or more guest rooms and hospitals to provide, upon request, a means for decoding closed captions for use by an individual with impaired hearing. Hotels should also provide a TDD or similar device at the front desk in order to take calls from guests who use TDD's in their rooms. In his way guests with hearing impairments can avail themselves of such hotel services as making inquiries of the front desk and ordering room service. The term "hospital" is used in its general sense and should be interpreted broadly.

Movie theaters are not required by § 36.303 to present open-captioned films. However, other public accommodations that impart verbal information through soundtracks on films, video tapes, or slide shows are required to make such information accessible to persons with hearing impairments. Captioning is one means to make the information accessible to individuals with disabilities.

The rule specifies that auxiliary aids and services include the acquisition or modification of equipment or devices. For example, tape players used for an audio-guided tour of a museum exhibit may require the addition of Brailled adhesive labels to the buttons on a reasonable number of the tape players to facilitate their use by individuals who are blind. Similarly, a hotel conference center may need to provide permanent or portable assistive listening systems for persons with hearing impairments.

As provided in § 36.303(f), a public accommodation is not required to provide any particular aid or service that would result either in a fundamental alteration in the nature of the goods, services, facilities, privileges, advantages, or accommodations offered or in an undue burden. Both of these statutory limitations are derived from existing regulations and caselaw under section 504 and are to be applied on a case-by-case basis (see, e.g., 28 CFR 39.160(d) and *Southeastern Community College* v. *Davis*, 442 U.S. 397 (1979)). Congress intended that "undue burden" under § 36.303 and "undue hardship," which is used in the employment provisions of title I of the ADA, should be determined on a case-by-case basis under the same standards and in light of the same factors (Judiciary report at 59). The rule, therefore, in accordance with the definition of undue hardship in section 101(10) of the ADA, defines undue burden as "significant difficulty or expense" (see §§ 36.104 and 36.303(a)) and requires that undue burden be determined in light of the factors listed in the definition in 36.104.

Consistent with regulations implementing section 504 in federally conducted programs (see, e.g., 28 CFR 39.160(d)), § 36.303(f) provides that the fact that the provision of a particular auxiliary aid or service would result in an undue burden does not relieve a public accommodation from the duty to furnish an alternative auxiliary aid or service, if available, that would not result in such a burden.

Section 36.303(g) of the proposed rule has been deleted from this section and included in a new § 36.306. That new section continues to make clear that the auxiliary aids requirement does not mandate the provision of individually prescribed devices, such as prescription eyeglasses or hearing aids.

The costs of compliance with the requirements of this section may not be financed by surcharges limited to particular individuals with disabilities or any group of individuals with disabilities (§ 36.301(c)).

Section 36.309   Examinations and Courses

Section 36.309(a) sets forth the general rule that any private entity that offers examinations or courses related to applications, licensing, certification, or credentialing for secondary or postsecondary education, professional, or trade purposes shall offer such examinations or courses in a place and manner accessible to persons with disabilities or offer alternative accessible arrangements for such individuals.

Paragraph (a) restates section 309 of the Americans with Disabilities Act. Section 309 is intended to fill the gap that is created when licensing, certification, and other testing authorities are not covered by section 504 of the Rehabilitation Act or title II of the ADA. Any such authority that is covered by section 504, because of the receipt of Federal money, or by title II, because it is a function of a State or local government, must make all of its programs accessible to persons with disabilities, which includes physical access as well as modifications in the way the test is administered, e.g., extended time, written instructions, or assistance of a reader.

Many licensing, certification, and testing authorities are not covered by section 504, because no Federal money is received; nor are they covered by title II of the ADA because they are not State or local agencies. However, States often require the licenses provided by such authorities in order for an individual to practice a particular profession or trade. Thus, the provision was included in the ADA in order to assure that persons with disabilities are not foreclosed from educational, professional, or trade opportunities because an examination or course is conducted in an inaccessible site or without needed modifications.

As indicated in the Application section of this part (§ 36.102), § 36.309 applies to any private entity that offers the specified types of examinations or courses. This is consistent with section 309 of the Americans with Disabilities Act, which states that the requirements apply to "any person" offering examinations or courses.

The Department received a large number of comments on this section, reflecting the importance of ensuring that the key gateways to education and employment are open to individuals with disabilities. The most frequent comments were objections to the fundamental alteration and undue burden provisions in §§ 36.309(b)(3) and (c)(3) and to allowing courses and examinations to be provided through alternative accessible arrangements, rather than in an integrated setting.

Although section 309 of the Act does not refer to a fundamental alteration or undue burden limitation, those limitations do appear in section 302(b)(2)(A)(iii) of the Act, which establishes the obligation of public accommodations to provide auxiliary aids and services. The Department, therefore, included it in the paragraphs of § 36.309 requiring the provision of auxiliary aids. One commenter argued that similar limitations should apply to all of the requirements of § 36.309, but the Department did not consider this extension appropriate.

Commenters who objected to permitting "alternative accessible arrangements" argued that such arrangements allow segregation and should not be permitted, unless they are the least restrictive available alternative, for example, for someone who cannot leave home. Some commenters made a distinction between courses, where interaction is an important part of the educational experience, and examinations, where it may be less important. Because the statute specifically authorizes alternative accessible arrangements as a method of meeting the requirements of section 309, the Department has not adopted this suggestion. The Department notes, however, that, while examinations of the type covered by § 36.309 may not be covered elsewhere in the regulation, courses will generally be offered in a "place of education," which is included in the definition of "place of public accommodation" in § 36.104, and, therefore, will be subject to the integrated setting requirement of § 36.203.

Section 36.309(b) sets forth specific requirements for examinations. Examinations covered by this section would include a bar exam or the Scholastic Aptitude Test prepared by the Educational Testing Service. Paragraph (b)(1) is adopted from the Department of Education's section 504 regulation on admission tests to postsecondary educational programs (34 CFR 104.42(b)(3)). Paragraph (b)(1)(i) requires that a private entity offering an examination covered by the section must assure that the examination is selected and administered so as to best ensure that the examination accurately reflects an individual's aptitude or achievement level or other factor the examination purports to meas-

ure, rather than reflecting the individual's impaired sensory, manual, or speaking skills (except where those skills are the factors that the examination purports to measure).

Paragraph (b)(1)(ii) requires that any examination specially designed for individuals with disabilities be offered as often and in as timely a manner as other examinations. Some commenters noted that persons with disabilities may be required to travel long distances when the locations for examinations for individuals with disabilities are limited, for example, to only one city in a State instead of a variety of cities. The Department has therefore revised this paragraph to add a requirement that such examinations be offered at locations that are as convenient as the location of other examinations.

Commenters representing organizations that administer tests wanted to be able to require individuals with disabilities to provide advance notice and appropriate documentation, at the applicants' expense, of their disabilities and of any modifications or aids that would be required. The Department agrees that such requirements are permissible, provided that they are not unreasonable and that the deadline for such notice is no earlier than the deadline for others applying to take the examination. Requiring individuals with disabilities to file earlier applications would violate the requirement that examinations designed for individuals with disabilities be offered in as timely a manner as other examinations.

Examiners may require evidence that an applicant is entitled to modifications or aids as required by this section, but requests for documentation must be reasonable and must be limited to the need for the modification or aid requested. Appropriate documentation might include a letter from a physician or other professional, or evidence of a prior diagnosis or accommodation, such as eligibility for a special education program. The applicant may be required to bear the cost of providing such documentation, but the entity administering the examination cannot charge the applicant for the cost of any modifications or auxiliary aids, such as interpreters, provided for the examination.

Paragraph (b)(1)(iii) requires that examinations be administered in facilities that are accessible to individuals with disabilities or alternative accessible arrangements are made.

Paragraph (b)(2) gives examples of modifications to examinations that may be necessary in order to comply with this section. These may include providing more time for completion of the examination or a change in the manner of giving the examination, e.g., reading the examination to the individual.

Paragraph (b)(3) requires the provision of auxiliary aids and services, unless the private entity offering the examination can demonstrate that offering a particular auxiliary aid would fundamentally alter the examination or result in an undue burden. Examples of auxiliary aids include taped examinations, interpreters or other effective methods of making aurally delivered materials available to individuals with hearing impairments, readers for individuals with visual impairments or learning disabilities, and other similar services and actions. The suggestion that individuals with learning disabilities may need readers is included, although it does not appear in the Department of Education regulation, because, in fact, some individuals with learning disabilities have visual perception problems and would benefit from a reader.

Many commenters pointed out the importance of ensuring that modifications provide the individual with a disability an equal opportunity to demonstrate his or her knowledge or ability. For example, a reader who is unskilled or lacks knowledge of specific terminology used in the examination may be unable to convey the information in the questions or to follow the applicant's instructions effectively. Commenters pointed out that, for persons with visual impairments who read Braille, Braille provides the closest functional equivalent to a printed test. The Department has, therefore, added Brailled examinations to the examples of auxiliary aids and services that may be required. For similar reasons, the Department also added to the list of examples of auxiliary aids and services large print examinations and answer sheets; "qualified" readers and transcribers to write answers.

A commenter suggested that the phrase "fundamentally alter the examination" in this paragraph of the proposed rule be revised to more accurately reflect the function affected. In the final rule the Department has substituted the phrase "fundamentally alter the measurement of the skills or knowledge the examination is intended to test."

Paragraph (b)(4) gives examples of alternative accessible arrangements. For instance, the private entity might be required to provide the examination at an individual's home with a proctor. Alternative arrangements must provide conditions for individuals with disabilities that are comparable to the conditions under which other individuals take the examinations. In other words, an examination cannot be offered to an individual with a disability in a cold, poorly lit basement, if other individuals are given the examination in a warm, well lit classroom.

Some commenters who provide examinations for licensing or certification for particular occupations or professions urged that they be permitted to refuse to provide modifications or aids for persons seeking to take the examinations if those individuals, because of their disabilities, would be unable to perform the essential functions of the profession or occupation for which the examination is given, or unless the disability is reasonably determined in advance as not being an obstacle to certification. The Department has not changed its rule based on this comment. An examination is one stage of a licensing or certification process. An individual should not be barred from attempting to pass that stage of the process merely because he or she might be unable to meet other requirements of the process. If the examination is not the first stage of the qualification process, an applicant may be required to complete the earlier stages prior to being admitted to the examination. On the other hand, the applicant may not be denied admission to the examination on the basis of doubts about his or her abilities to meet requirements that the examination is not designed to test.

Paragraph (c) sets forth specific requirements for courses. Paragraph (c)(1) contains the general rule that any course covered by this section must be modified to ensure that the place and manner in which the course is given is accessible. Paragraph (c)(2) gives examples of possible modifications that might be required, including extending the time permitted for completion of the course, permitting oral rather than written delivery of an assignment by a person with a visual impairment, or adapting the manner in which the course is conducted (i.e., providing cassettes of class handouts to an individual with a visual impairment). In response to comments, the Department has added to the examples in paragraph (c)(2) specific reference to distribution of course materials. If course materials are published and available from other sources, the entity offering the course may give advance notice of what materials will be used so as to allow an individual to obtain them in Braille or on tape but materials provided by the course offerer must be made available in alternative formats for individuals with disabilities.

In language similar to that of paragraph (b), paragraph (c)(3) requires auxiliary aids and services, unless a fundamental alteration or undue burden would result, and paragraph (c)(4) requires that courses be administered in accessible facilities. Paragraph (c)(5) gives examples of alternative accessible arrangements. These may include provision of the course through videotape, cassettes, or prepared notes. Alternative arrangements must provide comparable conditions to those provided to others, including similar lighting, room temperature, and the like. An entity offering a variety of courses, to fulfill continuing education requirements for a profession, for example, may not limit the selection or choice of courses available to individuals with disabilities.

PART 36—NONDISCRIMINATION ON THE BASIS OF DISABILITY BY PUBLIC ACCOMMODATIONS AND IN COMMERCIAL FACILITIES

Subpart A—General

Subpart B—General Requirements

Subpart C—Specific Requirements

Subpart D—New Construction and Alterations

Subpart E—Enforcement

Subpart F—Certification of State Laws or Local Building Codes

Appendix A to Part 36—Standards for Accessible Design

Appendix B to Part 36—Preamble to Regulation on Nondiscrimination on the Basis of Disability by Public Accommodations and in Commercial Facilities (Published July 26, 1991)

Authority: 5 U.S.C. 301; 28 U.S.C. 509, 510; Pub. L. 101–336, 42 U.S.C. 12186.

Subpart A—General

§ 36.101   Purpose.

The purpose of this part is to implement title III of the Americans with Disabilities Act of 1990 (42 U.S.C. 12181), which prohibits discrimination on the basis of disability by public accommodations and requires places of public accommodation and commercial facilities to be designed, constructed, and altered in compliance with the accessibility standards established by this part.

§ 36.102   Application

(a) *General.* This part applies to any—
(1) Public accommodation;
(2) Commercial facility; or
(3) Private entity that offers examinations or courses related to applications, licensing, certification, or credentialing for secondary or postsecondary education, professional, or trade purposes.

(b) *Public accommodations.*
(1) The requirements of this part applicable to public accommodations are set forth in subparts B, C, and D of this part.
(2) The requirements of subparts B and C of this part obligate a public accommodation only with respect to the operations of a place of public accommodation.
(3) The requirements of subpart D of this part obligate a public accommodation only with respect to—
(i) A facility used as, or designed or constructed for use as, a place of public accommodation; or
(ii) A facility used as, or designed and constructed for use as, a commercial facility.

(c) *Commercial facilities.* The requirements of this part applicable to commercial facilities are set forth in subpart D of this part.

(d) *Examinations and courses.* The requirements of this part applicable to private entities that offer examinations or courses as specified in paragraph (a) of this section are set forth in § 36.309.

(e) *Exemptions and exclusions.* This part does not apply to any private club (except to the extent that the facilities of the private club are made available to customers or patrons of a place of public accommodation), or to any religious entity or public entity.

§ 36.103   Relationship to other laws.

(a) *Rule of interpretation.* Except as otherwise provided in this part, this part shall not be construed to apply a lesser standard than the standards applied under title V of the Rehabilitation Act of 1973 (29 U.S.C. 791) or the regulations issued by Federal agencies pursuant to that title.

(b) *Section 504.* This part does not affect the obligations of a recipient of Federal financial assistance to comply with the requirements of section 504 of the Rehabilitation Act of 1973 (29 U.S.C. 794) and regulations issued by Federal agencies implementing section 504.

(c) *Other laws.* This part does not invalidate or limit the remedies, rights, and procedures of any other Federal laws, or State or local laws (including State common law) that provide greater or equal protection for the rights of individuals with disabilities or individuals associated with them.

§ 36.104   Definitions.

For purposes of this part, the term—
Act means the Americans with Disabilities Act of 1990 (Pub. L. 101–336, 104, Stat. 327, 42 U.S.C. 12101–12213 and 47 U.S.C. 225 and 611).
Commerce means travel, trade, traffic, commerce, transportation, or communication—
(1) Among the several States;
(2) Between any foreign country or any territory or possession and any State; or
(3) Between points in the same State but through another State or foreign country.
Commercial facilities means facilities—
(1) Whose operations will affect commerce;
(2) That are intended for nonresidential use by a private entity; and
(3) That are not—
(i) Facilities that are covered or expressly exempted from coverage under the Fair Housing Act of 1968, as amended (42 U.S.C. 3601–3631);
(ii) Aircraft; or
(iii) Railroad locomotives, railroad freight cars, railroad cabooses, commuter or intercity passenger rail cars (including coaches, dining cars, sleeping cars, lounge cars, and food service cars), any other railroad cars described in section 242 of the Act or covered under title II of the

Act, or railroad rights-of-way. For purposes of this definition, "rail" and "railroad" have the meaning given the term "railroad" in section 202(e) of the Federal Railroad Safety Act of 1970 (45 U.S.C. 431(e)).

Current illegal use of drugs means illegal use of drugs that occurred recently enough to justify a reasonable belief that a person's drug use is current or that continuing use is a real and ongoing problem.

Disability means, with respect to an individual, a physical or mental impairment that substantially limits one or more of the major life activities of such individual; a record of such an impairment; or being regarded as having such an impairment.

(1) The phrase *physical or mental impairment* means—

(i) Any physiological disorder or condition, cosmetic disfigurement, or anatomical loss affecting one or more of the following body systems: neurological; musculoskeletal; special sense organs; respiratory, including speech organs; cardiovascular; reproductive; digestive; genitourinary; hemic and lymphatic; skin; and endocrine;

(ii) Any mental or psychological disorder such as mental retardation, organic brain syndrome, emotional or mental illness, and specific learning disabilities;

(iii) The phrase physical or mental impairment includes, but is not limited to, such contagious and noncontagious diseases and conditions as orthopedic, visual, speech, and hearing impairments, cerebral palsy, epilepsy, muscular dystrophy, multiple sclerosis, cancer, heart disease, diabetes, mental retardation, emotional illness, specific learning disabilities, HIV disease (whether symptomatic or asymptomatic), tuberculosis, drug addiction, and alcoholism;

(iv) The phrase *physical or mental impairment* does not include homosexuality or bisexuality.

(2) The phrase *major life activities* means functions such as caring for one's self, performing manual tasks, walking, seeing, hearing, speaking, breathing, learning, and working.

(3) The phrase *has a record of such an impairment* means has a history of, or has been misclassified as having, a mental or physical impairment that substantially limits one or more major life activities.

(4) The phrase *is regarded as having an impairment* means—

(i) Has a physical or mental impairment that does not substantially limit major life activities but that is treated by a private entity as constituting such a limitation;

(ii) Has a physical or mental impairment that substantially limits major life activities only as a result of the attitudes of others toward such impairment; or

(iii) Has none of the impairments defined in paragraph (1) of this definition but is treated by a private entity as having such an impairment.

(5) The term *disability* does not include—

(i) Transvestism, transsexualism, pedophilia, exhibitionism, voyeurism, gender identity disorders not resulting from physical impairments, or other sexual behavior disorders;

(ii) Compulsive gambling klepto-mania, or pyromania; or

(iii) Psychoactive substance use disorders resulting from current illegal use of drugs.

Drug means a controlled substance, as defined in schedules I through V of section 202 of the Controlled Substances Act (21 U.S.C. 812).

Facility means all or any portion of buildings, structures, sites, complexes, equipment, rolling stock or other conveyances, roads, walks, passageways, parking lots, or other real or personal property, including the site where the building, property, structure, or equipment is located.

Illegal use of drugs means the use of one or more drugs, the possession or distribution of which is unlawful under the Controlled Substances Act (21 U.S.C. 812). The term "illegal use of drugs" does not include the use of a drug taken under supervision by a licensed health care professional, or other uses authorized by the Controlled Substances Act or other provisions of Federal law.

Individual with a disability means a person who has a disability. The term "individual with a disability" does not include an individual who is currently engaging in the illegal use of drugs, when the private entity acts on the basis of such use.

Place of public accommodation means a facility, operated by a private entity, whose operations affect commerce and fall within at least one of the following categories—

(1) An inn, hotel, motel, or other place of lodging, except for an establishment located within a building that contains not more than five rooms for rent or hire and that is actually occupied by the proprietor of the establishment as the residence of the proprietor;

(2) A restaurant, bar, or other establishment serving food or drink;

(3) A motion picture house, theater, concert hall, stadium, or other place of exhibition or entertainment;

(4) An auditorium, convention center, lecture hall, or other place of public gathering;

(5) A bakery, grocery store, clothing store, hardware store, shopping center, or other sales or rental establishment,

(6) A laundromat, dry-cleaner, bank, barber shop, beauty shop, travel service, shoe repair service, funeral parlor, gas station, office of an accountant or lawyer, pharmacy, insurance office, professional office of a health care provider, hospital, or other service establishment;

(7) A terminal, depot, or other station used for specified public transportation;

(8) A museum, library, gallery, or other place of public display or collection;

(9) A park, zoo, amusement park, or other place of recreation;

(10) A nursery, elementary, secondary, undergraduate, or postgraduate private school, or other place of education;

(11) A day care center, senior citizen center, homeless shelter, food bank, adoption agency, or other social service center establishment; and

(12) A gymnasium, health spa, bowling alley, golf course, or other place of exercise or recreation.

Private club means a private club or establishment exempted from coverage under title II of the Civil Rights Act of 1964 (42 U.S.C. 2000a(e)).

Private entity means a person or entity other than a public entity.

Public accommodation means a private entity that owns, leases (or leases to), or operates a place of public accommodation.

Public entity means—

(1) Any State or local government;

(2) Any department, agency, special purpose district, or other instrumentality of a State or States or local government; and

(3) The National Railroad Passenger Corporation, and any commuter authority (as defined in section 103(8) of the Rail Passenger Service Act). (45 U.S.C. 541)

Qualified interpreter means an interpreter who is able to interpret effectively, accurately and impartially both receptively and expressively, using any necessary specialized vocabulary.

Readily achievable means easily accomplishable and able to be carried out without much difficulty or expense. In determining whether an action is readily achievable factors to be considered include—

(1) The nature and cost of the action needed under this part;

(2) The overall financial resources of the site or sites involved in the action; the number of persons employed at the site; the effect on expenses and resources; legitimate safety requirements that are necessary for safe operation, including crime prevention measures; or the impact otherwise of the action upon the operation of the site;

(3) The geographic separateness, and the administrative or fiscal relationship of the site or sites in question to any parent corporation or entity;

(4) If applicable, the overall financial resources of any parent corporation or entity; the overall size of the parent corporation or entity with respect to the number of its employees; the number, type, and location of its facilities; and

(5) If applicable, the type of operation or operations of any parent corporation or entity, including the composition, structure, and functions of the workforce of the parent corporation or entity.

Religious entity means a religious organization, including a place of worship.

Service animal means any guide dog, signal dog, or other animal individually trained to do work or perform tasks for the benefit of an individual with a disability, including, but not limited to, guiding individuals with impaired vision, alerting individuals with impaired hearing to intruders or sounds, providing minimal protection or rescue work, pulling a wheelchair, or fetching dropped items.

Specified public transportation means transportation by bus, rail, or any other conveyance (other than by aircraft) that provides the general public with general or special service (including charter service) on a regular and continuing basis.

State means each of the several States, the District of Columbia, the Commonwealth of Puerto Rico, Guam, American Samoa, the Virgin Islands, the Trust Territory of the Pacific Islands, and the Commonwealth of the Northern Mariana Islands.

Undue burden means significant difficulty or expense. In determining whether an action would result in an undue burden, factors to be considered include—

(1) The nature and cost of the action needed under this part;

(2) The overall financial resources of the site or sites involved in the action; the number of persons employed at the site; the effect on expenses and resources; legitimate safety requirements that are necessary for safe operation, including crime prevention measures; or the impact otherwise of the action upon the operation of the site;

(3) The geographic separateness, and the administrative or fiscal relationship of the site or sites in question to any parent corporation or entity;

(4) If applicable, the overall financial resources of any parent corporation or entity; the overall size of the parent corporation or entity with respect to the number of its employees; the number, type, and location of its facilities; and

(5) If applicable, the type of operation or operations of any parent corporation or entity, including the composition, structure, and functions of the workforce of the parent corporation or entity.

§§ 36.105–36.200 [Reserved].

Subpart B—General Requirements

§ 36.201 General

(a) *Prohibition of discrimination.* No individual shall be discriminated against on the basis of disability in the full and equal enjoyment of the goods, services, facilities, privileges, advantages, or accommodations of any place of public accommodation by any private entity who owns, leases (or leases to), or operates a place of public accommodation.

(b) *Landlord and tenant responsibilities.* Both the landlord who owns the building that houses a place of public accommodation and the tenant who owns or operates the place of public accommodation are public accommodations subject to the requirements of this part. As between the parties, allocation of responsibility for complying with the obligations of this part may be determined by lease or other contract.

§ 36.202 Activities.

(a) *Denial of participation.* A public accommodation shall not subject an individual or class of individuals on the basis of a disability or disabilities of such individual or class, directly, or through con-

tractual, licensing, or other arrangements, to a denial of the opportunity of the individual or class to participate in or benefit from the goods, services, facilities, privileges, advantages, or accommodations of a place of public accommodation.

(b) *Participation in unequal benefit.* A public accommodation shall not afford an individual or class of individuals, on the basis of a disability or disabilities of such individual or class, directly, or through contractual, licensing, or other arrangements, with the opportunity to participate in or benefit from a good, service, facility, privilege, advantage, or accommodation that is not equal to that afforded to other individuals.

(c) *Separate benefit.* A public accommodation shall not provide an individual or class of individuals, on the basis of a disability or disabilities of such individual or class, directly, or through contractual, licensing, or other arrangements with a good, service, facility, privilege, advantage, or accommodation that is different or separate from that provided to other individuals, unless such action is necessary to provide the individual or class of individuals with a good, service, facility, privilege, advantage, or accommodation, or other opportunity that is as effective as that provided to others.

(d) *Individual or class of individuals.* For purposes of paragraphs (a) through (c) of this section, the term "individual or class of individuals" refers to the clients or customers of the public accommodation that enters into the contractual licensing, or other arrangement.

§ 36.203 Integrated settings.

(a) *General.* A public accommodation shall afford goods, services, facilities, privileges, advantages, and accommodations to an individual with a disability in the most integrated setting appropriate to the needs of the individual.

(b) *Opportunity to participate.* Notwithstanding the existence of separate or different programs or activities provided in accordance with this subpart, a public accommodation shall not deny an individual with a disability an opportunity to participate in such programs or activities that are not separate or different.

(c) *Accommodations and services.*

(1) Nothing in this part shall be construed to require an individual with a disability to accept an accommodation, aid, service, opportunity, or benefit available

under this part that such individual chooses not to accept.

(2) Nothing in the Act or this part authorizes the representative or guardian of an individual with a disability to decline food, water, medical treatment, or medical services for that individual.

§36.204   Administrative methods.

A public accommodation shall not, directly or through contractual or other arrangements, utilize standards or criteria or methods of administration that have the effect of discriminating on the basis of disability, or that perpetuate the discrimination of others who are subject to common administrative control.

§ 36.205   Association.

A public accommodation shall not exclude or otherwise deny equal goods, services, facilities, privileges, advantages, accommodations, or other opportunities to an individual or entity because of the known disability of an individual with whom the individual or entity is known to have a relationship or association.

§36.206   Retaliation or coercion.

(a) No private or public entity shall discriminate against any individual because that individual has opposed any act or practice made unlawful by this part, or because that individual made a charge, testified, assisted, or participated in any manner in an investigation, proceeding, or hearing under the Act or this part.

(b) No private or public entity shall coerce, intimidate, threaten, or interfere with any individual in the exercise or enjoyment of, or on account of his or her having exercised or enjoyed, or on account of his or her having aided or encouraged any other individual in the exercise or enjoyment of, any right granted or protected by the Act or this part.

(c) Illustrations of conduct prohibited by this section include, but are not limited to:

(1) Coercing an individual to deny or limit the benefits, services, or advantages to which he or she is entitled under the Act or this part;

(2) Threatening, intimidating, or interfering with an individual with a disability who is seeking to obtain or use the goods, services, facilities, privileges, advantages, or accommodations of a public accommodation;

(3) Intimidating or threatening any person because that person is assisting or encouraging an individual or group entitled to claim the rights granted or protected by the Act or this part to exercise those rights; or

(4) Retaliating against any person because that person has participated in any investigation or action to enforce the Act or this part.

§36.207   Places of public accommodation located in private residences.

(a) When a place of public accommodation is located in a private residence, the portion of the residence used exclusively as a residence is not covered by this part, but that portion used exclusively in the operation of the place of public accommodation or that portion used both for the place of public accommodation and for residential purposes is covered by this part.

(b) The portion of the residence covered under paragraph (a) of this section extends to those elements used to enter the place of public accommodation, including the homeowner's front sidewalk, if any, the door or entryway, and hallways; and those portions of the residence, interior or exterior, available to or used by customers or clients, including restrooms.

§ 36.208   Direct threat.

(a) This part does not require a public accommodation to permit an individual to participate in or benefit from the goods, services, facilities, privileges, advantages and accommodations of that public accommodation when that individual poses a direct threat to the health or safety of others.

(b) *Direct threat* means a significant risk to the health or safety of others that cannot be eliminated by a modification of policies, practices, or procedures, or by the provision of auxiliary aids or services.

(c) In determining whether an individual poses a direct threat to the health or safety of others, a public accommodation must make an individualized assessment, based on reasonable judgment that relies on current medical knowledge or on the best available objective evidence, to ascertain; the nature, duration, and severity of the risk; the probability that the potential injury will actually occur, and whether reasonable modifications of policies, practices, or procedures will mitigate the risk.

§ 36.209   Illegal use of drugs.

(a) *General.*

(1) Except as provided in paragraph (b) of this section, this part does not prohibit discrimination against an individual based on that individual's current illegal use of drugs.

(2) A public accommodation shall not discriminate on the basis of illegal use of drugs against an individual who is not engaging in current illegal use of drugs and who—

(i) Has successfully completed a supervised drug rehabilitation program or has otherwise been rehabilitated successfully;

(ii) Is participating in a supervised rehabilitation program; or

(iii) Is erroneously regarded as engaging in such use.

(b) *Health and drug rehabilitation services.*

(1) A public accommodation shall not deny health services, or services provided in connection with drug rehabilitation, to an individual on the basis of that individual's current illegal use of drugs, if the individual is otherwise entitled to such services.

(2) A drug rehabilitation or treatment program may deny participation to individuals who engage in illegal use of drugs while they are in the program.

(c) *Drug testing.*

(1) This part does not prohibit a public accommodation from adopting or administering reasonable policies or procedures, including but not limited to drug testing, designed to ensure that an individual who formerly engaged in the illegal use of drugs is not now engaging in current illegal use of drugs.

(2) Nothing in this paragraph (c) shall be construed to encourage, prohibit, restrict, or authorize the conducting of testing for the illegal use of drugs.

§ 36.210   Smoking.

This part does not include the prohibition of, or the imposition of restrictions on, smoking in places of public accommodation.

§ 36.211   Maintenance of accessible features.

(a) A public accommodation shall maintain in operable working condition those features of facilities and equipment that are required to be readily accessible to and usable by persons with disabilities by the Act or this part.

(b) This section does not prohibit isolated or temporary interruptions in service or access due to maintenance or repairs.

§ 36.212   Insurance.

(a) This part shall not be construed to prohibit or restrict—

(1) Any insurer, hospital or medical service company, health maintenance organization, or any agent, or entity that administers benefit plans, or similar organizations from underwriting risks, classifying risks, or administering such risks that are based on or not inconsistent with State law; or

(2) A person or organization covered by this part from establishing, sponsoring, observing or administering the terms of a bona fide benefit plan that are based on underwriting risks, classifying risks, or administering such risks that are based on or not inconsistent with State law; or

(3) A person or organization covered by this part from establishing, sponsoring, observing or administering the terms of a bona fide benefit plan that is not subject to State laws that regulate insurance.

(b) Paragraphs (a) (1), (2), and (3) of this section shall not be used as a subterfuge to evade the purposes of the Act or this part.

(c) A public accommodation shall not refuse to serve an individual with a disability because its insurance company conditions coverage or rates on the absence of individuals with disabilities.

§ 36.213   Relationship of subpart B to subparts C and D of this part.

Subpart B of this part sets forth the general principles of nondiscrimination applicable to all entities subject to this part. Subparts C and D of this part provide guidance on the application of the statute to specific situations. The specific provisions, including limitations on those provisions, control over the general provisions in circumstances where both specific and general provisions apply.

§§ 36.214–36.300   [Reserved]

Subpart C—Specific Requirements

§ 36.301   Eligibility criteria.

(a) *General.* A public accommodation shall not impose or apply eligibility criteria that screen out or tend to screen out an individual with a disability or any class of individuals with disabilities from fully and equally enjoying any goods, services, facilities, privileges, advantages, or accommodations, unless such criteria can be shown to be necessary for the provision of the goods, services, facilities, privileges, advantages, or accommodations being offered.

(b) *Safety.* A public accommodation may impose legitimate safety requirements that are necessary for safe operation. Safety requirements must be based on actual risks and not on mere speculation, stereotypes, or generalizations about individuals with disabilities.

(c) *Charges.* A public accommodation may not impose a surcharge on a particular individual with a disability or any group of individuals with disabilities to cover the costs of measures, such as the provision of auxiliary aids, barrier removal, alternatives to barrier removal, and reasonable modifications in policies, practices, or procedures, that are required to provide that individual or group with the nondiscriminatory treatment required by the Act or this part.

§ 36.302 Modifications in policies, practices, or procedures.

(a) *General.* A public accommodation shall make reasonable modifications in policies, practices, or procedures, when the modifications are necessary to afford goods, services, facilities, privileges, advantages, or accommodations to individuals with disabilities, unless the public accommodation can demonstrate that making the modifications would fundamentally alter the nature of the goods, services, facilities, privileges, advantages, or accommodations.

(b) *Specialties*—

(1) *General.* A public accommodation may refer an individual with a disability to another public accommodation, if that individual is seeking, or requires, treatment or services outside of the referring public accommodation's area of specialization, and if, in the normal course of its operations, the referring public accommodation would make a similar referral for an individual without a disability who seeks or requires the same treatment or services.

(2) *Illustration—medical specialties.* A health care provider may refer an individual with a disability to another provider, if that individual is seeking, or re-

quires, treatment or services outside of the referring provider's area of specialization, and if the referring provider would make a similar referral for an individual without a disability who seeks or requires the same treatment or services. A physician who specializes in treating only a particular condition cannot refuse to treat an individual with a disability for that condition, but is not required to treat the individual for a different condition.

(c) *Service animals*—

(1) *General.* Generally, a public accommodation shall modify policies, practices, or procedures to permit the use of a service animal by an individual with a disability.

(2) *Care or supervision of service animals.* Nothing in this part requires a public accommodation to supervise or care for a service animal.

(d) *Check-out aisles.* A store with check-out aisles shall ensure that an adequate number of accessible check-out aisles are kept open during store hours, or shall otherwise modify its policies and practices, in order to ensure that an equivalent level of convenient service is provided to individuals with disabilities as is provided to others. If only one check-out aisle is accessible, and it is generally used for express service, one way of providing equivalent service is to allow persons with mobility impairments to make all their purchases at that aisle.

§ 36.303 Auxiliary aids and services.

(a) *General.* A public accommodation shall take those steps that may be necessary to ensure that no individual with a disability is excluded, denied services, seggregated or otherwise treated differently than other individuals because of the absence of auxiliary aids and services, unless the public accommodation can demonstrate that taking those steps would fundamentally alter the nature of the goods, services, facilities, privileges, advantages, or accommodations being offered or would result in an undue burden, i.e., significant difficulty or expense.

(b) *Examples.* The term "auxiliary aids and services" includes—

(1) Qualified interpreters, notetakers, computer-aided transcription services, written materials, telephone handset amplifiers, assistive listening devices, assistive listening systems, telephones compatible with hearing aids, closed caption decoders, open and closed captioning, tele-

communications devices for deaf persons (TTD's), videotext displays, or other effective methods of making aurally delivered materials available to individuals with hearing impairments;

(2) Qualified readers, taped texts, audio recordings, Brailled materials, large print materials, or other effective methods of making visually delivered materials available to individuals with visual impairments;

(3) Acquisition or modification of equipment or devices; and

(4) Other similar services and actions.

(c) *Effective communication.* A public accommodation shall furnish appropriate auxiliary aids and services where necessary to ensure effective communication with individuals with disabilities.

(d) *Telecommunication devices for the deaf (TDDs).*

(1) A public accommodation that offers a customer, client, patient, or participant the opportunity to make outgoing telephone calls on more than an incidental convenience basis shall make available, upon request, a TDD for the use of an individual who has impaired hearing or a communication disorder.

(2) This part does not require a public accommodation to use a TDD for receiving or making telephone calls incident to its operations.

(e) *Closed caption decoders.* Places of lodging that provide television in five or more guest rooms and hospitals that provide televisions for patient use shall provide, upon request, a means for decoding captions for use by an individual with impaired hearing.

(f) *Alternatives.* If provision of a particular auxiliary aid or service by a public accommodation would result in a fundamental alteration in the nature of the goods, services, facilities, privileges, advantages, or accommodations being offered or in an undue burden, i.e., significant difficulty or expense, the public accommodation shall provide an alternative auxiliary aid or service, if one exists, that would not result in an alteration or such burden but would nevertheless ensure that, to the maximum extent possible, individuals with disabilities receive the goods, services, facilities, privileges, advantages, or accommodations offered by the public accommodation.

§ 36.309 Examinations and courses.

(a) *General.* Any private entity that offers examinations or courses related to applications, licensing, certification, or credentialing for secondary or postsecondary education, professional, or trade purposes shall offer such examinations or courses in a place and manner accessible to persons with disabilities or offer alternative accessible arrangements for such individuals.

(b) *Examinations.*

(1) Any private entity offering an examination covered by this section must assure that—

(i) The examination is selected and administered so as to best ensure that, when the examination is administered to an individual with a disability that impairs sensory, manual, or speaking skills, the examination results accurately reflect the individual's aptitude or achievement level or whatever other factor the examination purports to measure, rather than reflecting the individual's impaired sensory, manual, or speaking skills (except where those skills are the factors that the examination purports to measure);

(ii) An examination that is designed for individuals with impaired sensory, manual, or speaking skills is offered at equally convenient locations, as often, and in as timely a manner as are other examinations; and

(iii) The examination is administered in facilities that are accessible to individuals with disabilities or alternative accessible arrangements are made.

(2) Required modifications to an examination may include changes in the length of time permitted for completion of the examination and adaptation of the manner in which the examination is given.

(3) A private entity offering an examination covered by this section shall provide appropriate auxiliary aids for persons with impaired sensory, manual, or speaking skills, unless that private entity can demonstrate that offering a particular auxiliary aid would fundamentally alter the measurement of the skills or knowledge the examination is intended to test or would result in an undue burden. Auxiliary aids and services required by this section may include taped examinations, interpreters or other effective methods of making orally delivered materials available to individuals with hearing impairments, Brailled or large print examinations and answer sheets or qualified readers for individuals with visual impairments or learning disabilities, transcribers for individuals with manual im-

pairments, and other similar services and actions.

(4) Alternative accessible arrangements may include, for example, provision of an examination at an individual's home with a proctor if accessible facilities or equipment are unavailable. Alternative arrangements must provide comparable conditions to those provided for nondisabled individuals.

(c) *Courses.*

(1) Any private entity that offers a course covered by this section must make such modifications to that course as are necessary to ensure that the place and manner in which the course is given are accessible to individuals with disabilities.

(2) Required modifications may include changes in the length of time permitted for the completion of the course, substitution of specific requirements, or adaptation of the manner in which the course is conducted or course materials are distributed.

(3) A private entity that offers a course covered by this section shall provide appropriate auxiliary aids and services for persons with impaired sensory, manual, or speaking skills, unless the private entity can demonstrate that offering a particular auxiliary aid or service would fundamentally alter the course or would result in an undue burden. Auxiliary aids and services required by this section may include taped texts, interpreters or other effective methods of making orally delivered materials available to individuals with hearing impairments, Brailled or large print texts or qualified readers for individuals with visual impairments and learning disabilities, classroom equipment adapted for use by individuals with manual impairments, and other similar services, and actions.

(4) Courses must be administered in facilities that are accessible to individuals with disabilities or alternative accessible arrangements must be made.

(5) Alternative accessible arrangements may include, for example provision of the course through videotape, cassettes, or prepared notes. Alternative arrangements must provide comparable conditions to those provided for nondisabled individuals.

Index